ICEBOUND

The *Jeannette* Expedition's
Quest for the North Pole

Leonard F. Guttridge

BERKLEY BOOKS, NEW YORK

A Berkley Book
Published by The Berkley Publishing Group
A division of Penguin Putnam Inc.
375 Hudson Street
New York, New York 10014

Copyright © 1986 by the United States Naval Institute Annapolis, Maryland
Book design by Tiffany Kukec
Cover design by Steven Ferlauto
Cover photograph by PNI

PRINTING HISTORY
Naval Institute Press hardcover edition published in 1986
Berkley trade paperback edition / December 2001

Visit our website at
www.penguinputnam.com

Library of Congress Cataloging-in-Publication Data

Guttridge, Leonard F.
Icebound : the Jeannette Expedition's quest for the North Pole / by Leonard F. Guttridge.
p. cm.
Originally published: Annapolis, Md. : Naval Institute Press, ©1986.
Includes bibliographical references (p.   ).
ISBN 0-425-18178-2
1. Jeannette Expedition (1879–1881)   2. Jeannette (Ship)   3. Arctic regions—Discovery and exploration—American.   4. North Pole.   I. Title.

G630.A5G87   2001
910'.091632—dc21
00-065195

Praise for *Icebound*

"This is a dramatic story and Guttridge tells it well. He has uncovered some intriguing new information, including the reason the expedition's full story was never revealed." —*The Cleveland Plain Dealer*

"Uncommonly stirring . . . the kind of book about exploration that we feared had been banished by space travel." —*John Barkham Reviews*

"Guttridge unfolds a gripping story of suspense and adventure. He has ferreted out the facts about the *Jeannette* and the ship's company, and the colorful characters abound." —*Publishers Weekly*

"Guttridge does a fine job of re-creating the drama of the *Jeannette*. He is particularly adept at portraying the deteriorating relationships of men driven almost mad from frustration and disappointment." —*Sea History*

"An unforgettable story illustrating that in exploring the extremes of our environment we discover much about the extremes within ourselves." —Arlene Blum, Ph.D.

"Reads with the flair of an intriguing novel." —*Concise Book Reviews*

"The author has done an excellent job of analyzing relationships between the members of the *Jeannette*'s crew." —George Van B. Cochran, M.D., The Explorers Club

"Entertaining, informative, and suspenseful." —Lisle A. Rose, author of *Assault on Eternity*

continued...

Praise for *Ghosts of Cape Sabine*

"*Ghosts of Cape Sabine* shares elements of the bestsellers *Into Thin Air* and *The Perfect Storm*. But this one trumps them both with its tales of not just death, but execution, suicide and . . . cannibalism. Author Leonard F. Guttridge chillingly re-creates it all through recently uncovered journals, letters and diaries."
　　　　　　　　　　　　　　　　　　　　　　　　　　　　—*P.O.V.*

"Cannibalism, near mutiny, bureaucratic wrangling, and the execution by firing squad of a private caught stealing from the ship's stores. The horrors of an Arctic nightmare receive detailed . . . treatment."
　　　　　　　　　　　　　　　　　　　　　　　　　—*The Boston Globe*

"Making the most of his material, Guttridge narrates fluidly and pointedly and will easily net the aficionados of adventure and disaster tales."
　　　　　　　　　　　　　　　　　　　　　　　　　　　—*Booklist*

"Guttridge's pursuit of records, letters, and diaries has enabled him to reconstruct the whole story, and it is as fascinating and exciting as any adventure novel."
　　　　　　　　　　　　　　　　　　　　—*The Atlantic Monthly*

"Guttridge's account—vivid in its whiteness and raw in its themes—is a thriller. There's adventure aplenty here, not to mention execution, mutiny, starvation, suicide, and cannibalism. [*Ghosts of Cape Sabine*] deserves an honored place."
　　　　　　　　　　　　　　　　　　　　　　　　　—Salon.com

For Vivien and Bruce

CONTENTS

CONTENTS

ACKNOWLEDGMENTS

Many kind persons as well as organizations assisted in the preparation of this book. A complete listing cannot be undertaken but I would be remiss in failing to mention those whose aid or inspiration proved especially useful. Mr. Thomas De Long was most generous in granting access to George and Emma DeLong's personal papers, and his published genealogy of the De Long family pointed the way to additional sources. For prompt and courteous help I am also indebted to the research staffs of the Virginia Historical Society, Richmond, Va; the Franklin D. Roosevelt Memorial Library, Hyde Park, NY; The Mariners' Museum, Newport News, Va; The California Academy of Sciences, San Francisco, CA; National Archives Cartography Division, Alexandria, Va; and in Washington DC the National Archives, Old Navy and Army Branch; Smithsonian Institution Archives; the Smithsonian Institution's Division of Naval History (Doctor Harold Langley); the Library of Congress, particularly its Manuscript Division and its Geography and Map Division. A special note of thanks is due Alison Wilson of the National Archives Scientific, Economic and Natural Resources Division; Doctor Dean C. Allard, Jr., and his staff at the Operational Archives, Naval Historical Center, Washington DC; Jan K. Herman, Historian and Editor, Naval Medical Command, Washington DC; and the courteous staff at one of two fond haunts of mine, the Navy Department Library, Naval Historical Center,

Washington DC. The other favorite haunt is the U.S. Naval Academy Museum, Annapolis, Md., to whose curator, James W. Cheevers, I am indebted for his ready guidance and cooperation.

And also in Annapolis, the U.S. Naval Institute's officials and staff were unstinting in not only routine assistance but what is surely as valuable—their zeal and encouragement.

None of the foregoing, nor anyone else except myself, is responsible for the views expressed in this book or any errors that may have occurred. On this latter point, it should be noted that the names of certain characters were variously spelled in contemporary publications and even in official documentation. All effort has been made to establish the correct form. Regarding placenames, Siberian in particular, I have opted for the spelling as shown on today's maps, except in those cases where the original name (and some of the actual villages or settlements themselves) has ceased to exist. Such instances are few and minor, and in each I have chosen the form that seems to me to be the most reliable.

INTRODUCTION

Ninety years and one week before the Apollo spacecraft left its Florida launchpad to carry men to the moon for the first time, the USS *Jeannette* steamed out of San Francisco Harbor and, once beyond the Golden Gate, turned her reinforced bow due north. The *Jeannette* expedition also had a maiden objective: to place man for the first time at the top of his own world.

To compare these two endeavors further is to invite irony. At the time of the *Jeannette*, the moon, while distant and unapproachable, was nonetheless a familiar object, one that had brightened the night sky since earthbound creatures first gazed upwards; but man had yet to behold the crown of his own planet. The moon could be studied in comfort through high-powered telescopes; but earth's northernmost reaches could only be explored at the cost of hardship and lives. There were maps of the lunar face, even passably detailed charts of more remote Mars for armchair scientists and professional astronomers to dream and ponder upon; but the terrestrial regions above the seventieth parallel were the stuff of myth and speculation.

In the mid and late nineteenth century, secrets of geography were in the process of being resolved. Since the most recent African journeys of Henry Morton Stanley, even "The Dark Continent" had become more a romantic catchphrase than an epithet reflecting the state of European knowledge about that enormous landmass. But what technical and popular journals alike called "The Arctic Question" continued to obsess imaginations in every modern land. Men had set forth repeatedly in search of answers, many to perish in the quest. The lure persisted, and one expedition followed another, each determined to unlock what had come to be considered as the supreme riddle, earth's last great secret. Repeatedly the northern latitudes defied exploration. Finally, in 1909, only sixty years before Neil Armstrong was to stand on the moon, Robert Peary reached the North Pole.

Each attempt to grasp the polar prize had foundered on or retreated before a complex barrier, of which ice mass and storm were the most spectacular components. But no less a striking feature of the frigid latitudes was their apparent power to excite latent feelings, to bring baneful elements to the surface. Thus with each dogged mile gained toward their goal, the would-be conquerers were apt to find themselves progressively hobbled by their own passions, oftentimes fatal impedimenta they had unwittingly borne within them on the long voyage out from civilization.

To cross into the polar domain in the late nineteenth century and early twentieth was to plunge into ineffable isolation. The world of cities and farms fell far astern. The glacial environment that replaced it overwhelmed and dominated, gripping all the senses and consuming most thought. The explorers' mobility was restricted to floe and shipboard, and communication limited to that with shipmates. Parties icebound above the Arctic Circle were cut off with a totality unimaginable today. In 1969 the world saw via television the first step ever taken on the surface of the moon. We have all grown accustomed to seeing pictures of astronauts floating gravity-free in the void of space or in the corridors of their spacecraft and to overhearing their chit-chat with Mission Control. And their planetary base is never out of sight or hearing of our space travelers. How different it was for early Arctic explorers, who would disappear into the frozen north for years and sometimes forever.

The first Americans to invade the northern polar zones in the second half of the nineteenth century had gone out as rescue parties in search of survivors from the mammoth British expedition that Sir John Franklin had led to catastrophe while seeking a Northwest Passage. (No survivors of Franklin's party were ever found.) One such pioneer was Elisha Kane, whose Arctic ventures appear in retrospect as periodic attempts to escape domestic problems and perhaps the notoriety of his love affair with a young spiritualist. In 1856 Kane forced a passage through the ice-choked Smith Sound, only to be turned back by the massive Humboldt Glacier.

Isaac Hayes had followed in 1860, convinced that "the sea about the North Pole must lie within the ice belt known to invest it." Hayes's assumption of ice-free waters at the Pole typified a prevalent naivete among explorers, an eagerness to swallow theories founded upon no reliable evidence. Hayes, in any case, had small chance of reaching that dreamed-of tepid polar pool. His financing for a subsequent attempt depended on Henry Grinnell, a wealthy New York merchant, who was undergoing a change of heart. Grinnell's hopes for commercial exploitation of the Arctic had inspired him to finance one expedition after another, but he was beginning to question the competence if not sanity of some of the adventurers looking to him for funds. As a result of tightened purse strings, Hayes was obliged to go north in a ship scarcely more able to penetrate ice belts than an angler's cockleshell.

So keen was the public fascination with attempts to solve the Arctic Question that circulation wars among newspapers appeared sometimes to depend on outdoing others in the amount of column space devoted to this or that dash for the Pole. "Dash" was a word hardly befitting enterprises that took so long to prepare and to carry into action. But the most widely read journalists managed to employ a prose style that did convey some spirit of vigor and speed. Because of the fierce competition for readers, the reporters' cabled dispatches and countless "exclusive interviews" with returning voyagers became more and more tinctured with the bizarre. And this further quickened the appetites of newspaper audiences for any story that purported to detail suffering and pluck in remote icefields.

To these vicarious thrill-hunters, the reports of the Hall expedition filtering piecemeal across front pages in the early 1870s amounted to an eagerly digested feast. Conceived as a U.S. federal project for planting Old Glory at the top of the world, the expedition was manned entirely by civilians, mostly German, whose brooding American "captain," Charles Francis Hall, most of them had mistrusted from the start. Hall had sailed in the schooner *Polaris* in late 1871, and in due course penetrated deeper into the polar domain than had any previous expedition, reaching the icebound gateway to what he religiously believed to be a large open sea. This frozen channel, the northernmost passage between Greenland and Ellsmere Island, was as far as Hall got. Having narrowly escaped entrapment in the ice and taken refuge in an inlet he christened Thank God Harbor, he sledded inland to nearby hills for a panoramic view of the northern desolation he intended to cross the following spring. But shortly after his descent back to Thank God Harbor he was stricken ill and died. The party's chief scientist, attending Hall as physician, recorded the cause of death as apoplexy.

The berg to which the *Polaris* had anchored split, ice beset the vessel, and not until October 1872 did a storm shake her free. She had swung away into the blackness leaving nineteen men stranded on a floe. After a further six months drifting through Baffin Bay and Davis Strait, and constantly on guard against one another in case of cannibalism, survivors were picked up off Labrador by a coastal steamer and soon returned to Washington. Their shipmates, on board the *Polaris* when the storm liberated her from the berg, were marooned when the ship broke up but were eventually discovered by a whaler and taken to that vessel's home port of Dundee, Scotland, from where they too were soon on their way back to America.

On their arrival in the United States both *Polaris* parties were officially told to say nothing about their experiences until a proper investigation. Ugly rumors had circulated. The Navy Department soon issued a report on Hall's expedition, stressing its accomplishments and scientific gains while at the same time perpetuating the myth of warm water at the top of the world. Nothing was said about the allegations that Captain Hall had died of arsenic deliberately administered until a naval board of inquiry dismissed them as "wicked untruths," whereupon the furor over the *Polaris* expedition subsided.*

---

*Hall's remains were exhumed in 1968. Close study revealed an intake of fatal doses of arsenic. See *Weird and Tragic Shores* by Chauncey Loomis, New York, 1971.

"A mum affair." This was how a chief clerk at the Navy Department alluded to officialdom's abrupt halt to further inquiry into the faraway death of Charles Francis Hall and the collapse of his expedition. It is a strange coincidence that the clerk wrote those words to George Washington De Long. For Lieutenant De Long was right then planning an expedition fated to stir so many charges and countercharges that "a mum affair" is practically an understatement if used to label tactics deemed necessary to prevent the world from learning the truth about the *Jeannette*'s last voyage.

Much was at stake. Regard for Victorian sensibilities might alone have determined that some information be suppressed. But more than that, the appearance of certain facts in public print would have wrecked promising careers, blemished reputations, endangered fortunes, and, above all, might have dimmed contemporary dreams of America's destiny. As the 1900s dawned, the United States had plans to become a naval power the rest of the world would have to reckon with.

Today, with these visions of the United States as an international power fulfilled, it requires more than a little effort to appreciate the alarm with which leaders earnestly drafting a program for America's twentieth-century naval strength viewed any potential for scandal. That their patriotic concern for the nation's future was not always unsullied by immediate political or even monetary considerations made their fears all the more acute. And it was such an assortment of motives that bred a compulsion to cover up the mysteries left in the *Jeannette*'s wake. Thus there formed a veritable skein of deception and concealment, in the process of which documents were destroyed or suppressed, witnesses suborned, and compacts of silence entered into without compunction.

Contemporary readers who liked their accounts of polar endeavor spiced with intrigue and human conflict were indeed denied a banquet. Had the full story of the *Jeannette* unfolded at the time, it would surely have read as a tale of the Arctic with a decided flavor of the fashionable gothic.

It is a tale now possible to tell. We can detect why a veteran criminal lawyer who had fearlessly sworn to dredge the bottom of the *Jeannette* affair instead choked back his questions before a congressional panel. We know why, for the first time in a brilliant career, the lawyer confessed defeat. Now might be discerned the motives that drove one of the two most conspicuous survivors to commit his wife to a madhouse in the midst of his homecoming festivity. And we learn at last the true nature of the other's unspeakable burden.

Nothing of what can be disclosed detracts in the least from the courage and determination that journalists of the day truthfully reported. There were no cowards on the *Jeannette*. For sheer grit this expedition is notable. Equally so for the optimism with which it put to sea in the first place. All had the highest of hopes, even those who left shore privately torn by misgivings. They would festoon the Arctic wastes with miles of humming telephone lines, would illuminate the North Pole with Edison's Electric Light. As urged by scientists who had taken a keen interest in their preparations, they would conduct a variety of experiments, meticulously recording each observation. The ship's surgeon would monitor the human body's reaction to Arctic stress by taking regular urine samples as methodically and conscientiously as would the naturalist mount and preserve his downed rare birds and the navigator study the aurora. Shelfloads of ledgers would fill with scientific notes. So much was to be discovered, so much to be taken back to civilization for proud display before the world's learned councils. Few parties sailing under U.S. naval colors set forth with more exciting dreams.

Few met with more frustration.

After a harrowing ordeal, the survivors of the *Jeannette* expedition returned home leaving the Arctic Question unanswered. The polar secret seemed as inviolable as ever. But in their frozen no man's land the men of the *Jeannette* had unlocked secrets of another sort, unrelated to external phenomena. From within themselves came resources of imagination and endurance. But other traits also surfaced, traits that a more merciful fate would never have called forth.

To do justice to the *Jeannette*'s diverse but uniformly gallant company demands a frank and unvarnished recounting of all these manifestations. Only through this approach can we come anywhere near to sharing their strange and dramatic story, which is the purpose of this book.

George W. De Long, Lieutenant, U.S. Navy, commanding

Charles W. Chipp, Lieutenant, U.S. Navy, executive officer

John W. Danenhower, Master, U.S. Navy, navigation officer

George W. Melville, Passed Assistant Engineer, U.S. Navy

James M. Ambler, Passed Assistant Surgeon, U.S. Navy

William M. Dunbar, Seaman, for special duty as ice pilot

Jerome J. Collins, entered as seaman, for special service as meteorologist

Raymond L. Newcomb, entered as seaman, for special service as naturalist

John Cole, Boatswain

Walter Lee, Machinist

James H. Bartlett, First-class fireman

George W. Boyd, Second-class fireman

Alfred Sweetman, Carpenter

The following seamen:

    William F. C. Nindemann

    Louis P. Noros

    Herbert W. Leach

    Henry Wilson

    Carl A. Görtz

    Peter E. Johnson

    Edward Starr

Henry D. Warren
Heinrich H. Kaak
Albert G. Kuehne
Frank E. Mansen
Hans H. Erikson
Adolph Dressler
Nelsk Iverson
Walter Sharvell
George Lauterbach

Cook and Steward:
    Ah Sam
    Charles Tang Sing

Hunters (joined ship at St. Michaels, Alaska):
    Alexey
    Aniguin

CHAPTER ONE

A Curious Departure

*Man will not be content with a mystery unexplored, will not rest with
a perpetual interrogation point at the end of the earth's axis, whose
query he cannot answer.*

New York Times *editorial, 26 July 1879*

AN OVERNIGHT DRIZZLE following a dust-laden gale had muddied the sidewalks. Citizens who donned their summer finery in anticipation of the day's excitement stepped forth with apprehension, but toward noon warm sunlight broke up the overcast. By horsedrawn carriage, tram, cable car, and foot, thousands flocked to the waterfront, many heading for the dilapidated piers along the Embarcadero. Old Meigs Wharf at the foot of Market Street threatened to collapse under the weight of the crowd, and a police squad had to draw its nightsticks to prevent more people from swarming in. The crowd was so thick on Telegraph Hill that a local newspaperman thought its crest resembled "the bristling back of a porcupine." Offshore, the bay swarmed with yachts, steam launches, tugs, and assorted fishing boats. All San Francisco, it appeared, had turned out to bid farewell to the USS *Jeannette*.

The object of this attention was not herself a particularly grand sight. The 420-ton barque-rigged coal burner was not, in fact, even comely. From her iron-belted bow to her narrowly rounded stern, she looked weatherbeaten and mud stained. Her appearance might have been redeemed by the snowy white of her new sails, but the canvas remained furled. Since coming down from Mare Island Navy Yard two weeks ago, the vessel had lain at anchor halfway between the Alameida Ferry landing and Yerba Buena Island. Her decks were piled to above the bulwarks with stores taken on at the last minute and awaiting stowage below, if space could be found. The crew sauntered listlessly fore and aft or draped themselves over the side, staring back at the people across the harbor.

No, what attracted the crowds that blustery Tuesday, 8 July 1879, was not so much the *Jeannette* herself as the purpose for which they knew her to be officially ordained—to reach the North Pole via the Bering Strait. The gala atmosphere that enveloped the crowd by midday owed much to a feeling among the spectators that they shared in the prelude to an unprecedented gamble. As the 1 July *Science News* of New York noted, "The important question is, what are the chances of reaching the Pole by the route through Bering Strait? Very little is known of the region north of those waters."

In contrast, a great deal was known about the expedition's plans and goals, as they had been widely debated in daily newspapers and scientific journals alike, notwithstanding the commander's fierce wish to limit expectations. Arctic ventures in themselves held inherent fascination, but none within the memory of those assembled had been attended by such a wealth of interest and expectation as the *Jeannette* expedition.

What would be the rewards of piercing the veil of ignorance? The expedition's potential accomplishments would be breathtaking indeed. "It may determine laws of meteorology, hydrography, astronomy and gravitation, reveal ocean currents, develop new fisheries, discover lands and peoples hitherto unknown, and by extending the world's knowledge of such fundamental principles of earth-life as magnetism and electricity, and the various collateral branches of atmospheric science, solve great problems important to humanity." As stated in the *New York Commercial Advertiser*, "Should success crown the efforts of the gallant commander, it will be one of the most brilliant geographical adventures ever won by man. The solution of the Northern mystery would be the event of the nineteenth century."

The event of the century. It was a phrase typical of the new journalistic flamboyance espoused and largely created by James Gordon Bennett, the playboy eccentric who had inherited ownership of the *New York Herald* and almost immediately had doubled its circulation. Without Bennett's drive, political influence and financial commitment, the *Jeannette* expedition would never have matured.

Laudatory comments upon this latest Bennett enterprise, many of them culled from envious rival organs, had reappeared in his *Herald* interspersed with its own lavish encomiums and were regularly telegraphed to the Pacific coast for local newspapers to copy. During the *Jeannette*'s fitting out at the Mare Island yard the *New York Herald* had sent westward a veritable drumfire of lively features on polar exploration, and by the departure date few San Franciscans doubted that the ship to which their city had played host for half a year was destined, if all went according to plan, for a place in the American annals of the sea alongside the *Mayflower*, the *Bonhomme Richard*, and the *Constitution*.

Generous faith was placed in both the *Jeannette* and her people. "The vessel goes thoroughly equipped," reported the *Commercial Advertiser*, and "is manned by an enthusiastic company and under the command of an officer of the navy." None of them regular blue-jackets, the crew would nevertheless be subject to naval rules and regulations, a wise precaution, it was believed, that would reduce the likelihood of such conflicts of authority and discipline as had jeopardized former American penetrations of the Far North. The popular press frequently emphasized that this was in fact a U.S. naval enterprise, "a national work [that] will extend the geographical survey and topographical knowledge of the northern boundary in the interests of commerce and navigation."

The hopes and presumptions were not uniformly intoxicating. Many Americans were utterly oblivious to the Arctic Question. Some politicians viewed efforts to solve it as only instances of lives needlessly imperiled and dollars wasted. But in the post–Civil War era, a national spirit of challenge and modernity was gaining ascendancy. The ignorant or skeptical on matters of science and exploration wielded declining influence. This was particularly manifest in the great metropolitan centers, San Francisco among them, where important decisions increasingly tipped in favor of scientific advancement and mercantile expansion.

The people of San Francisco had turned out not only to gaze at the vessel they hoped would bring home a bounty of scientific knowledge and kudos for the American spirit of adventure. They were anxious to catch a glimpse of the commander and his beautiful wife. Those thronging Market Street had the best view, but all had a long wait. The *Jeannette* was publicly scheduled to sail at two P.M. It was three before the couple emerged from their suite at the Palace Hotel and joined friends in a waiting carriage for the ride down to the dockside. At the Alameida landing, police cleared an area for the vehicle's arrival and a cluster of dignitaries was on hand to greet it. Onlookers might have noticed that throughout the handshakes, embraces, and final words on the wharf, the commander of the expedition appeared tense and abstracted. His wife had the most to say.

The party disappeared on board the *Jeannette*, and another thirty minutes passed. Finally, the ship hoisted anchor. Her specially augmented six-blade propeller threshed. Members of the crew scrambled high up in the port rigging where they waved strenuously and hurrahed. The crowds onshore cried back, voices swelling into a roar as the ship began her passage seaward with yards squared, ensigns set, and all signal flags aflutter. It was at this moment that the *Jeannette*, bathed in brilliant sunshine and escorted by four municipal steam-tugs and all fifteen rainbow-hued craft of the San Francisco Yacht Club, took on a sudden and remarkable lustre. One of the spectators at the foot of Clay Street afterwards recalled that the ship seemed for a brief interval to muster full pride and seize while she could her fair measure of glory.

Standing on the bridge in full-dress uniform, Lieutenant George Washington De Long cut a stalwart figure. On closer inspection he appeared a man of average stature and graceful motion, with narrow blue eyes behind pince-nez spectacles, a broad nose, and a neatly brushed arrowhead mustache that only partly obscured an unexpectedly truculent mouth. No one just then, not even his adored Emma beside him, could have precisely gauged De Long's emotions as he and the *Jeannette* got under way at last. Manning and fitting out for the expedition had been an ordeal beyond anything he had anticipated. Possessed of a mild streak of humor and not insensitive to irony, De Long might have reflected that the fitting-out phase of his grand adventure had been so difficult that the actual search for the North Pole must prove, by comparison, smooth sailing.

As the *Jeannette* and her colorful escorts moved slowly through San Francisco Bay, bearing west to pass Alcatraz Island, the lieutenant realized that a humiliating toll was to be exacted from him before his ship could clear the Golden Gate. Earlier that day the U.S. naval tug *Monterey* had brought the commandant of Mare Island down to the city on a business trip. The tug, leaving its wharf for the return to the navy yard only minutes after the *Jeannette* hove anchor, crossed her wake without a single hail or farewell blast on the whistle. And the *Monterey*'s manifest slight was of a piece with the studied absence of anything remotely resembling a salute from the *Alaska*, the *Alert*, and the *Tuscarora*, three U.S. warships anchored close enough to have participated in the *Jeannette*'s send-off. Of the many scores of vessels that bade the *Jeannette* godspeed and good luck with whistles, sirens, and a vivid display of masthead colors and signal flags, not a single craft flew the ensign of the service in which George De Long had held commissioned rank for twelve years and whose civilian director, the secretary of the navy, had personally advised him that "when you sail I intend you to have the same power that is conferred upon admirals commanding fleets."

De Long was chagrined, certainly, but far from puzzled by the manifest decision of fellow naval officers in the vicinity to ignore the *Jeannette*'s leave-taking. Their discourtesy reflected a last-minute coolness on the part of the Navy Department in Washington. And this official high-level indifference De Long in turn perceived as the result of an unexpected display of unconcern on the part of the expedition's own promoter, to whom the naval establishment was politically indebted. In a final rebuff which not merely hurt De Long's pride but might well endanger the enterprise, the Secretary of the Navy had even refused the *Jeannette* an escort vessel to carry some of her excessive load part way north. It was with this "recollection . . . fresh in my mind" that the extraordinary show of bad manners in San Francisco Bay "made me think that the Government had shaken us adrift from the highest to the lowest and left us to paddle along by ourselves."

The floating procession rounded North Point and should have been picking up headway by this time. But the *Jeannette* moved sluggishly, and to the watchers on Telegraph Hill her consort of tugs and yachts seemed to hold themselves in check to avoid an embarrassing surge ahead of the honored ship. It was close to six when the *Jeannette* labored abreast of Fort Point. Eleven guns thundered from the ramparts of the Presidio, to which the *Jeannette*'s crew responded with a chorus of cheers, double strength, as if in grateful acknowledgment of the army's atonement for the navy's snub.

Between the North and South Heads half a dozen yachts waited like sentinels, white sails and crimson bunting bright and sharp against the fogbank spreading across a sun-reddened horizon. "It was a mortification to me," De Long wrote later, "not to see a Navy boat of any kind." At twelve minutes past six the *Jeannette* and her entourage of sail and smoking funnels had cleared the Heads. A bell clanged below deck and the *Jeannette* hove to for the last goodbyes. Guests on board as far as the Golden Gate had received a tour of the ship, with dinner then served in the officers' wardroom. One of the guests, William Bradford, a New England artist who specialized in polar scenes, described the final farewell between De Long and his wife as especially affecting because "she could not share his trials in the heroic endeavor . . . in which her heart was as much bound up as his."

The yachts turned prows homeward for San Francisco, all save the Yacht Club's flagship *Frolic*, which was to return with the party from the *Jeannette*. De Long sat with his wife in the *Jeannette*'s whaleboat for the transfer to the *Frolic*, a short trip during which, Bradford wrote, "the silence was oppressive, the only sound being the thump of the oars in the rowlocks and the swash of water. When we reached the side of the yacht Lieutenant De Long pressed his wife's hand and simply said 'Goodbye.' " Once on board the yacht Emma De Long "bent upon her husband a look in which there was expressed the most poignant feeling. . . . For an instant he seemed to hesitate, as if un-nerved by her attitude and expression." De Long then ordered his oarsmen to pull away for the *Jeannette*.

As he later wrote to Emma from northern waters, he remembered that when she had stepped on board the *Frolic* "the full force of what my going away meant struck home at once. . . . It seemed so natural to see you about me that I could not realize it would not always be so. Even while we were steaming out from the city with you on board, it seemed so regular and natural that you should be there that I could not understand a separation. When we both got into the boat, that seemed all right too for we had frequently gotten into boats together, but when you threw your arms around my neck and kissed me goodbye . . . I felt stunned." From the poopdeck of the *Jeannette* he glimpsed Emma's white face as the *Frolic* passed astern, "then in a minute you seemed to be miles away."

On the yacht, Emma De Long's understanding friends had gone below at her request. De Long on the *Jeannette*, for the last mute exchange with his wife, was as discreetly abandoned by his officers. They were two lone figures on vessels steadily receding from each other at a combined six or seven knots. At that moment it seemed to Emma as if she and her husband were the last two mortals left alive. The lieutenant felt similarly. "I could see your hand-kerchief and answered it by waving my cap as long as I could make out anything at all." The *Frolic* vanished into the east.

In no mood to complete the unfinished dinner in the wardroom De Long adjourned to his private room in the spar deck cabin and when night fell he was busy at his journal. "The ship is now beginning her voyage to that unknown part of the world lying north of Bering Strait. May God's blessing attend us all."

CHAPTER TWO

GEORGE AND EMMA

Impulsive? Yes and I am glad of it. I owe my success in life to that very fact. As for being hard on men, I can only say . . . I never allow any argument. It is my office to command and theirs to obey. I never ask a man to do anything I would not do myself.

Lieutenant De Long to Emma Wotton, 6 June 1869

THE FIRST AND last captain of the *Jeannette* was born in New York City on 22 August 1844, to working-class parents of Huguenot stock. The young George Francis led a severely sheltered childhood and was forbidden to mingle with other boys. During this formative period he never learned to sail, skate, or swim. If he had a playmate of any permanence it was a slightly younger cousin, whom his parents had adopted and reared as their daughter. He became something of a neighborhood oddity, the lonely lad forever on the sidelines watching others play.

Returning home from school one wintry afternoon, he was pelted with snowballs by other boys who took him for a snob or a sissy. Frozen fragments lodged in his ear and caused infection, and for three months he was in a doctor's care fighting deafness. (A minor augury this, De Long's first encounter with hostile ice.)

After his ear healed, he worked briefly as the doctor's assistant. De Long's mother, who his future wife concluded must have been a "morbidly solici- tous" woman where George was concerned, wanted him to enter a "safe" profession such as that of a doctor or perhaps a priest or lawyer. In an early display of persuasive rhetoric that he would often employ in adulthood, De Long reminded his mother that physicians ran the risk of catching their patients' diseases, priests were often assigned dangerous jungle missions, and lawyers were not all that immune to peril, having sometimes to consort with felons.

A pressure built within De Long to wrench clear of the parental strait- jacket, and in his imagination he came to identify escape with the far oceans. He was apprenticed to a Brooklyn attorney, but whenever possible he fled to the local library, there to devour Marryat's sea stories. He daydreamed of critical situations on the high seas where only his valor, quick thinking, and unfailing powers of oratory saved the day. These he knew to be indisputable qualities of leadership, and by age sixteen George De Long had changed his middle name from Francis to Washington.

The lawyer for whom he worked pulled political strings and secured his entrance into the U.S. Naval Academy. De Long's mother was distressed at this, and his father's health had begun to decline, but their son may have consoled them both with a quotation from one of his letters of application to the Academy. "I am a poor boy seeking and trying to do well, and anxious to repay my parents for their care, and at the same time lead a life I may not be ashamed of."

In 1865 George De Long graduated tenth in his class. His maiden berth was as a midshipman on the seven-gun sloop of war *Canandaigua*, preparing for sea at the Brooklyn Navy Yard whose commandant he promptly incensed by demanding additional bunks in the vessel's steerage quarters. This was not the last time De Long would start out on the wrong foot. He was to cultivate almost a penchant for doing so, one that the woman he married found most endearing and proof of his dauntlessness in the face of authority.

The *Canandaigua* was in European waters in 1867 when De Long's father died. Family friends and the lawyer who had employed him, concerned for his widowed mother, tried to have the Navy Department grant his discharge or at least an extended furlough. But they were now of the wrong political complexion to exert much weight, and, in any case, the *Canandaigua* had recently run aground in the Adriatic. De Long could not be spared while the ship was disabled, and he was still aboard in June 1868 when she put into Havre on the French coast to undergo repairs.

It was at Havre that he met Emma Jane Wotton, the seventeen-year-old daughter of a veteran mariner who had commanded his own ocean packet at the age of twenty-one and had since grown rich as a senior stockholder in the New York and Havre Steamship Company. The Wottons rented a mansion on Le Côte, the wealthy residential eminence overlooking the harbor, and regularly entertained the officers of American ships in port. At a *soiree dansant* they staged for the *Canandaigua*'s crew, Ensign De Long, confessing himself hopelessly smitten, monopolized Emma's every moment.

In a romantic memoir composed near the close of her life, Emma De Long recalled him as an ardent wooer, breathlessly talkative. On her part, she refused to be rushed. For one thing, after countless Atlantic crossings with her father, she was belatedly completing her formal education on dry land by attending one of Havre's most exclusive lycées. Also, she had convinced herself that a young consumptive Frenchman, who she knew adored her, clung to life only because of her regular visits. De Long, when she told him of this obligation, thought her solicitude for the wilting youth all very praiseworthy but asked, "Can you not feel some pity for me too? I cannot lose you without a struggle. For you I will dare anything."

He wrote those words in one of several impassioned letters to Emma after the *Canandaigua* had sailed. When she replied telling him that the French youth's death had released her from the sad duty to which she had sworn herself, she framed her words carefully lest they give the impression that nothing now stood in the path of a betrothal. It had not escaped her notice that George De Long was of the sort to jump rashly to conclusions.

As so apparent later on, De Long did not give up easily. When the *Canandaigua* put into New York in the spring of 1869 he buttonholed

Emma's father, himself just in from a voyage, and announced his intention of securing leave and sailing posthaste for Havre. De Long probably impressed Captain James Avery Wotton as a young man far too sure of always getting what he wanted. In any case, "Captain Jimmy," as he was known in seafaring circles, wished to save his daughter from the lot of a naval officer's wife. He could not object to a betrothal on grounds of her age, having himself eloped with a sixteen-year-old to begin a union undeniably fruitful: Emma was the fifth of ten children. But he advised De Long to stay clear of Havre until the Wottons were reunited and had talked the matter over.

What Emma's family eventually decided on was a cold-blooded plan based on De Long's imminent promotion to lieutenant followed as a matter of course by an extended sea duty. This would serve as a "test period" during which the two were forbidden to communicate. If at the end of that time they wished to marry, Emma's parents would willingly give their blessing. The proposed arrangement staggered De Long but Emma concurred in it, and more than two years went by before they resumed contact. By then, De Long was a lieutenant on the sloop of war *Lancaster*, stationed with the South Atlantic Fleet. Emma wrote him, hoping that "the severe and long test has not injured you permanently"; within forty-eight hours of the letter's arrival De Long had his trunks packed and had applied for a lengthy furlough.

The American ships had begun maneuvers off the Brazilian coast. It was not the moment to seek leave but when De Long got no satisfactory response from the fleet admiral he wrote the secretary of the navy in Washington that it was "imperative and necessary" for him to return home. He even volunteered to sail at his own expense, but more convenient means were found. De Long was detailed to take a rating who had been court-martialed and ordered dismissed from the navy back to America. The two shared a cabin on a British steamer, De Long with his pistol handy and the prisoner in double irons, after two escape attempts the British crew had aided.

As soon as he had delivered the prisoner in New York, De Long secured three months leave and sailed for Europe. He found the Wottons, like the rest of Havre society, maintaining a graceful way of life, notwithstanding the Franco-Prussian War. The USS *Shenandoah* was in harbor to protect American nationals and interests, and Emma's parents had opened their doors to the warship's officers. Parties and balls were frequent, with Emma an alluring target for, it seemed to De Long, a dismaying number of rival Americans. Again he had his work cut out. But he prevailed until Emma had said yes and a wedding date was set.

Emma's father made a last-ditch effort to stop the proceedings by arguing that under French law neither the U.S. consul nor the American priest summoned to perform the rites at the Wottons' home held the authority to do so. The couple could be legally wed only on American territory, the closest of which was the U.S. legation in Paris, a city only just emerging from Prussian siege. But Captain Jimmy's triumph was fleeting. The American consul at Havre (who later married Emma's sister) reminded everybody that the *Shenandoah*'s decks were American territory. Off rushed one of the ship's lieutenants to make preparations. The *Shenandoah* was swiftly transformed into a fairyland of flags and Chinese lanterns, and that same night, 1 March 1871, the two were married on board. Many years later, paying tribute to George De Long's tenacity, Emma gave him full credit for having from the beginning "foreseen that we were really suited to each other."

They settled in New York. Eight weeks after the birth of a daughter, christened Sylvie after Emma's sister, De Long was made second in command of the *Nantucket*, bound for the West Indies. He wrote home lightly fretful letters. "I am blue as the devil and as mad as a hornet. The life that calls a man to stay in a country where it takes him three months to hear from his wife and child is barbarous and ought to be abolished." But something more troubling took place during his service on the *Nantucket* of which he supplied Emma only hints. The *Nantucket*'s people, who were understrength and thus overworked, drank a great deal. De Long found them "insubordinate . . . a hard set . . . I have always some man in irons or on bread and water." He brooded over the scars that his disciplinary efforts might leave upon his own character. "Ship's life is a hard thing on the temper." Not only fostering a man's acknowledged bad traits, it "brought out new ones that he did not suppose himself mean enough for." The occasion suggests the self-analytical mood apt to descend on him when faced with dilemmas of discipline.

De Long was next assigned to a U.S. naval vessel permanently moored in New York harbor as the city's ceremonial flagship. He arranged things so that Emma could occupy the admiral's cabin, no doubt reinforcing the opinion some now held of him as a too breezily self-assured young officer whose attractive wife, moreover, defied tradition herself by refusing to remain quietly in the background. He courted more disfavor in certain naval circles through his readiness to criticize superiors, aware that what he wrote of them in private correspondence almost invariably found its way to the highest levels of the Navy Department.

Those few who applauded De Long's outspokenness as contributing to the betterment of the service included Commander Daniel L. Braine of the war-scarred sloop *Juniata*. Complimenting the lieutenant on his pluck, Commander Braine showed a little of his own brand at the department and secured De Long's appointment to the *Juniata* as executive officer. Protests erupted that the post should have gone to a more senior officer. The Navy Department, confessing itself "greatly embarrassed," was on the verge of having De Long reassigned when events developed that kept him on the *Juniata* as second in command. The course was thereby set for his first confrontation with the Arctic.

This was summer 1873. The *Polaris* had gone out three years earlier and nineteen of her crew had just returned to civilization. From their account it was evident that Charles Hall's expedition had penetrated farther north than any to date. The *Polaris* had attained the very ice-locked gateway to what so many believed would prove to be an open polar sea. Hall's route had taken him along the upper west coast of Greenland to Smith Sound and beyond Kane Basin, thence into the final frozen channel to the mystery-shrouded polar domain. Civilians, mostly German, had made up Hall's party. The enterprise had enjoyed U.S. government backing, mainly because of the influence of George Robeson, the navy secretary. In recognition of the secretary's help, Hall had given that northernmost passage separating Greenland from Ellesmere Island the name Robeson Strait.

Hall was now known to have died in the Arctic. Rumors circulated about the cause of his death and the assorted circumstances alleged to have foredoomed the expedition. The nineteen *Polaris* men who had come back were told to keep their mouths shut pending formal inquiry, and the Navy Department chartered a Newfoundland steamer, the *Tigress*, to search for their missing shipmates. The *Juniata* was detailed to assist, and on 23 June the sloop sailed from New York with the controversial Lieutenant De Long still on board as executive officer.

At St. Johns, Newfoundland, a week later, the *Juniata* took on stores and had her bows sheathed in iron. She was also joined by a passenger, a correspondent for the scoop-hungry *New York Herald*. When the ship hove to off the Greenland shore, the reporter wrote of its bleakly forbidding aspect. George De Long's initial regard for Arctic regions was equally joyless. "I never in my life saw such a dreary land of desolation, and I hope I may never find myself cast away in such a perfectly God-forsaken place."

Upernavik, three hundred fifty miles above the Arctic Circle, was as far north into drift ice as Commander Braine felt the *Juniata* could safely proceed. More advanced searching would have to be left to the thicker-hulled *Tigress*, which had been delayed at St. Johns. In the meantime, though, Braine could undertake an inshore reconnaissance northward as far as Cape York, using the *Juniata*'s sloop-rigged steam launch, the *Little Juniata*. He placed De Long in charge and gave him another lieutenant, a thoughtful and taciturn young man from Kingston, New York, named Charles Winans Chipp. The rest of the party consisted of an ice pilot, an Eskimo interpreter, and six volunteers, including the *New York Herald* reporter.

The mission had obvious perils. Upon entering the upper reaches of Baffin Bay the *Little Juniata*, a thirty-two-foot coal burner, would be in fogbound waters where entire whaling fleets had been destroyed by bergs calved from Greenland glaciers one mile thick. And unless De Long got back to Upernavik within three weeks he would find the *Juniata* gone, for Commander Braine would have had to retreat for safety's sake before the ice closed in.

The *Little Juniata* pushed away from the mother ship on 2 August with sixty days provisions and towing a ton of anthracite in a dinghy, the coal to be left at some northerly point for the *Tigress*. De Long organized two parties under himself and Chipp and as the ship groped through fog up the tortuously serrated coast they took turns calling at the scattered Eskimo settlements. They ventured farther north than prudence might have dictated, and after leaving the last native outpost the *Little Juniata*'s fuel supply ran low. Maintaining a speed of four knots burned up four hundred pounds of coal daily and that only so long as the boiler was supplied with fresh water, which meant the further expense of making steam to melt the ice. Yet De Long dared not wait for fair winds and the chance to press sail. New ice formed rapidly, "So," he wrote, "kept full steam, grinding and ramming where we could."

Once again De Long felt the weight of responsibility. He listened to the ice pilot's advice and consulted with the calm and reflective Lieutenant Chipp, but he alone had to decide "how far the lives of our little party were to be jeopardized." He found it a burden that "I do not desire to have again."

Forty miles south of Cape York, "where the *Polaris* people might be waiting," the launch anchored to a top-heavy berg and was taking on fresh water when the overhanging mass started to crack. De Long hauled clear scant seconds before a chunk split away and plunged with a roar into the sea.

By now half the *Little Juniata*'s coal was gone. But the ice-encrusted waves rolled before a rising southeast breeze, encouraging De Long's resolve to make Cape York. Under jib and mainsail the *Little Juniata* headed into the northern reaches of Baffin Bay. An ice barrier with bergs a hundred feet high girded the cape but, having brought the steam launch almost five hundred miles from the mother ship and across the 75th parallel, "I was not disposed to quit without a fight."

The elements won. While De Long was looking for a safe lead of water through the pack, the breeze he had prayed for freshened into a gale. It lasted thirty hours, great gusts sundering acres of ice into whirling floes that the waves flung like missiles against the *Little Juniata*'s armor of greenhart planking. The mast and sails providentially held before the wind's fury, but the launch finally staggered into calmer seas with coal bunker waterlogged and firewood soaked. Ice quickly formed again, ahead and astern and on both beams. And the wind, which had shifted, would sweep the *Little Juniata* deep into the new pack if she continued under sail.

Matches were dried by pressing them against one's body. A candle in a lantern was lit and the boiler soon producing steam for the little engine, its furnace feeding on pork fat and oil-saturated cottonwaste. De Long's part in the search for the *Polaris* people had finished. The *Tigress*, which he met on his return south, took over. But there was little cause for regret, much less shame. Considering her size, the voyage of the *Little Juniata*, totalling some seven hundred zig-zagging miles into a legendary graveyard of countless whalers, amounted to a minor epic. If De Long did not infer as much from the compliments of his captain and the cheers of the crew when he reboarded the *Juniata*, on the eve of his twenty-ninth birthday, he was soon to learn of his affirmation as an authentic "Arctic hero" in the columns of the *New York Herald*.

In her memoir, Emma De Long wrote that from this time on "the Polar virus was in his blood and would not let him rest." De Long did not recognize that he had been bitten. In the days immediately following the *Little Juniata*'s exploit, De Long claimed he would have welcomed something of a quiet life. "When we are apart," he told Emma in a letter from St. Johns, "I devise oh! so many schemes whereby we could be happy." It was his present notion to flee with her to some European hideaway "where the Navy Department would not bother me with its orders." He craved a twelve-month furlough and "a little home of our own. Do you think we could do that?" But the desire for tranquility was soon driven from De Long's mind. Within six or seven weeks, while still at St. Johns, he had written another letter, this one to the secretary of the navy, boldly staking his claim to the command of "any expedition that may be sent to the Arctic under government direction."

The *Juniata* returned to New York and hove to off the Battery. In great measure because of the *New York Herald*'s graphic accounts with their half-page maps, De Long had become a focus of speculation as the latest American contender in the fight to reach the North Pole. The *Herald* portrayed him as one of that illustrious company of American polar explorers that included Elisha Kane, Isaac Hayes, and the luckless Hall. He had invaded the same icebound realm as they, defying the northern elements in nothing but a thirty-foot steam launch, and had come back to tell the tale, or, rather, have it told by a skilled publicist. With a fully prepared ship, a loyal and stalwart crew, all necessary equipment, what might he not dare? At this same time, no less an authority than the German geographer August Heinrich Petermann declared that the United States had forged ahead in the international race for what the lamented Charles Hall had reverently called "the crowning jewel of the Arctic dome."

These words from the sage of Gotha, as Americans were wont to call Petermann, first appeared in a private letter to the secretary of the navy following the Navy Department's publication of a preliminary report on the *Polaris* enterprise. Ignoring the rumors of dissidence on board that ship, the report stressed positive results, among them new "evidence" that "the open Polar Sea is . . . a sound of considerable extent." This was music to Professor Petermann's ears for he was prominently committed to the theory that ice-free waters flowed at the top of the world and that the essential Arctic challenge was to navigate their portals. "The Americans have eclipsed all other nations in Polar research," Petermann told the secretary. "The channel now properly named after you, Robeson Channel, is the farthest object known on the globe towards the Pole." Petermann hailed the *Polaris* expedition as the most important yet, surpassing the Arctic voyages of the British, "who talked loudly for nine years, criticizing all other endeavors and opinions, while doing nothing themselves." A continuance of "high-toned acts of the United States government would shame the British into silence." George Robeson's alleged misconduct as secretary of the navy was one of the less spectacular scandals of the current administration, and like every other minister in Grant's cabinet Robeson needed all the kind words he could get. He lost no time in relaying Petermann's to the domestic press.

The pros and cons of the endless arguments among Europe's geographers were unknown to most Americans, Robeson among them. The secretary was doubtless unaware that Petermann had never forgiven the Royal Geographical Society of London for holding his theories up to ridicule, and that the letter was in some degree a product of his anti-British animus. Nor did George De Long thoroughly understand the German professor's analyses and opinions, or he would not have depended on them so completely. On the contrary, Petermann's proclamation virtually asserting America's title to the Pole was enough to set De Long's pulses racing. Almost certainly it helped inspire his application for Arctic command. Should the Navy Department act on the professor's advice and mount its own expedition, the leadership was his by proven right. Quite forgotten now was his proposal to Emma that they seek some distant refuge beyond the department's reach. That poignant notion fled before a glittering new dream that was, perhaps, a resurgence of those adolescent visions which had compelled him to rechristen himself George Washington.

CHAPTER THREE

THE PETERMANN FACTOR

You may rest assured that we shall keep at it as long as the ship floats and we are able to stand up.
        Lieutenant De Long to James Gordon Bennett, 17 July 1879

THE FIRST THREE days outward bound from San Francisco were an early test of nerves. A fierce Pacific blow met the *Jeannette* and raged all that time. De Long and his officers took the weather in stride, but even some of the seasoned mariners among his crew, not to mention the more landlubberly scientists, reeled and collapsed from seasickness. And the storm was a reminder of the ship's overloaded condition. She was so low in the water that the waves crashed over her rails continuously and from every direction.

The following weekend brought brighter skies, light easterly winds, and a calmer sea. De Long had a chance to take up the pen, and into his private journal went the first misgivings. "The performance of the engine and boilers cannot be called satisfactory." He blamed the anthracite they were burning and hoped for a better variety of coal when the ship reached Alaska. For the present, De Long could only comfort himself with the thought that the burning coal steadily reduced the vessel's weight and her speed would pick up as they went along.

After a week at sea, he wrote to Emma in the cheerful vein he knew she expected of him. "Here we are so far on our way to the Pole." He recalled that in their Palace Hotel suite the night before his departure they had joked about the inevitability of their remembering, once separated, words they ought to have exchanged in person. He promised to jot down any that entered his own mind and "wait for my answers when I get back." His constant prayer was that he would prove equal to whatever challenges lay ahead. "I realize I am engaged in a giant undertaking from which neither of us would have me retreat. . . . I must make a good showing."

Of those last letters before the *Jeannette* crossed the threshold of the unknown none could have been more remarkable for emotional intensity and the cataloguing of sober detail than De Long's to James Gordon Bennett. Written nine days out of San Francisco, this letter makes clear that men had bonded the expedition to hazard by basing expectations on flawed theory. It also shows that De Long further risked his expedition, and the lives of his shipmates on the *Jeannette*, by casting his lot with the unpredictable playboy-publisher.

Coping with the varied and complicated tasks of fitting out had prevented him from sending Bennett an up-to-date accounting, but "I was much consoled by the probability of your coming to San Francisco and the chance I would have of explaining everything to you in person." He had savored the anticipation of Bennett's face-to-face approval of how he had tackled unexpected crises and, since the publisher would eventually be billed for them, how he had kept costs under tight control. In addition to this personal review of expenditures, he had looked forward to Bennett's direct endorsement of his plan of operations in the Arctic, and he saw himself proudly acknowledging Bennett's praise before an assemblage of press and public and Navy Department officials from Washington including perhaps the secretary himself, "and finally being sent off with a good word from you to all hands. All this I counted on so long and so much that when you finally telegraphed you would not come it was like a blow aimed right at the success of the expedition."

*   *   *

THE CURIOUS LIAISON between George De Long and the flamboyant publisher can be traced to a dinner gathering at 17 Bond Street, New York, home of the wealthy New York merchant Henry Grinnell on 1 November 1873. Its purpose was to discuss the latest developments in Arctic exploration. Lieutenant De Long, fresh from his accomplishments in the *Little Juniata* and consequently a star attraction, was among those most strenuously renewing the pressure on the wealthy Grinnell to finance another American assault against the North Pole. Grinnell had declined, saying that he had done enough, that the promotion and funding of forays into the uncharted North must henceforth be borne by somebody else. Before the meeting at the Grinnells' home dispersed, there was general agreement as to the only person this could mean.

Through the columns of his widely circulated newspaper, no man had done more than James Gordon Bennett to fix the public's mind on those mysterious areas of the planet that still lured and baffled intrepid adventurers. An instinctive if sometimes penny-pinching investor in daring enterprises, he had most recently sent Henry Morton Stanley to Africa in search of Doctor Livingstone. Bennett, surely, was the man to approach.

De Long had enthusiastically concurred. He knew that if left up to the Navy Department alone, the likelihood of his leading an expedition to the Pole would remain slim. Secretary Robeson had endorsed his application for Arctic command, but despite (or because of) his well-publicized feats in Baffin Bay, De Long still won no popularity prize in certain quarters of the naval establishment, and the Bureau of Navigation's response to his appeal was merely that it would receive "due consideration." Impatiently, De Long got off a letter to Bennett, then in Europe, and the publisher replied at once, from the Hotel Bristol in Paris, proposing a meeting with the lieutenant when he returned to New York.

Bennett, at thirty-two, was already the most talked-about figure in the history of American newspaper publishing. His youth had been characterized by wild escapades that ranged from midnight drives naked in a four-in-hand along New Jersey turnpikes to furniture-smashing sprees in Delmonico's Restaurant in New York. Inheriting unlimited income and absolute control of a powerful newspaper, he found gratification for his lively impulses in the search for scoops and scandals to fill his columns. Critics charged that even his sponsorship of the Stanley-Livingstone expedition was nothing but a grandiose publicity stunt. For all his eccentric behavior, and precisely because of the huge readership his *Herald* commanded, Bennett was avidly courted by Washington politicians and particularly influential in the Navy Department through his regular editorial support of programs for the expansion and modernization of the national fleet.

Bennett's first meeting with De Long took place in January 1874, probably in the white marble *Herald* building at Broadway and Ann Streets. Nothing immediately ensued. A threat of war with Spain postponed serious planning, and De Long received orders to report to the screw sloop *Brooklyn*, cruising the Caribbean. In the fall of 1874, he had the misfortune to stand trial with the *Brooklyn*'s captain before a court martial for having run the ship aground in the Florida Strait. Summoning all his rhetorical skills, De Long succeeded in deflecting blame upon the pilot. A letter the *Brooklyn*'s captain wrote to De Long after the trial, however, implied that the court's judgment in their favor had by no means removed all stigma. De Long never again drew active sea duty, until his assignment to the *Jeannette*.

The year following the *Brooklyn* mishap he was in charge of *St. Marys*, one of four schoolships provided by act of Congress to serve the cities Boston, New York, Philadelphia, and San Francisco. De Long still dreamed of leading an expedition to the legendary Polar Sea and Emma added her bountiful zeal, for all the world as if she would naturally share her husband's command. But American interest in Arctic ventures had waned since the Spanish crisis, and Bennett had gone on to invest in a search for the Northwest Passage headed by the British sportsman-explorer Sir Allen Young, aboard the ex-Royal Navy steam bark *Pandora*. One of Bennett's newshounds accompanied

Young, and his colorful dispatches filled columns in the *New York Herald* even after the expedition had foundered amid the floes of Peel Strait.

Before the failure of the *Pandora* could substantially diminish Bennett's aspirations for a genuine Arctic scoop, August Petermann had arrived in America. The geographer had come over to look at the 1876 Centennial Exposition in Philadelphia. While in New York he held court before deferential reporters at the Brevoort Hotel and addressed the American Geographical Society, newly founded by the Grinnells. Petermann's fascinated audiences did not include Lieutenant De Long, who was on temporary detachment from the New York schoolship for a still less edifying command berth aboard a Civil War monitor laid up and rusting at Port Royal, South Carolina. But the famed geographer's presence in the United States had the effect of rekindling American visions of Old Glory fluttering over the North Pole. And wooing the daughter of New York bluebloods that centennial summer had not so preoccupied James Gordon Bennett that he failed to heed the revival of interest stirred by Petermann's visit and the *Pandora* stories in his own newspaper. Resuming contact with George De Long, he bade him seek a suitable vessel for Arctic exploration.

When none seemed available in North America, the search shifted to Europe. De Long secured two months leave with comparative ease. The Navy Department was alive to his ties with the powerful publisher whose support for naval programs had become all the more vital in a period of rapidly expanding U.S. overseas trade. Swallowing past prejudices, the department prepared itself with effort to henceforth view the self-assertive lieutenant in a kindlier light.

De Long's arrival in England at the close of 1876 coincided with a public postmortem upon the latest British polar venture, led by Captain George Nares of the Royal Navy. His party had struggled far enough north to erect a brass tablet at the lonely grave of the American Charles Hall and then pushed on until an outbreak of scurvy forced it to retreat. Nares had crossed to well above the 83rd parallel, putting his country once more ahead in the international race for the Pole. The British public, however, seemed to De

Long to be more obsessed with failed objectives and the four deaths from scurvy than with the expedition's achievements. Medical experts blamed that sickness on Nares's discontinuance of the lime juice ration to his men when they transferred from ship to sleds. Strong drink was taken to ward off chills, but as the expedition's own physician ruefully stated, for safety's sake, "future expeditions will forget rum, not lime juice." De Long took particular notice of this, and he probably also read with a smile the London *Atheneum*'s appeal for a moratorium on assaults against the North Pole "until we are able to steer through the air to the hitherto unattainable object of our dreams."

At Dundee, Scotland, posing as a gentleman investigating the whale fishery, De Long found a vessel in which "I would not hesitate to winter in the Arctic for ten years," but her owners refused to sell. Whaling was highly profitable business, "something fabulous," De Long told Emma. Unable to get a whaler at a reasonable price De Long had returned to London where he found Sir Allen Young's *Pandora* up for sale for $6,000. He promptly notified Bennett by ocean cable.

While De Long was shopping around incognito in Dundee, his would-be patron in New York had become embroiled in a social scandal as titillating to rival newspapers as any that Bennett's own *Herald* had heretofore featured. At a New Year's Eve party in the stately home of his betrothed's family Bennett had drunk more than could be comfortably held and in full view of all present had urinated into the fireplace. The press baron's mortified fiancee broke off their engagement the next day, and her brother horsewhipped him on the steps of the Union Club where he had fled for refuge. This made mandatory a meeting with pistols. The encounter was staged on the legally safe borderline between Delaware and Maryland. Both duelists aimed to miss, and the matter was formally closed. But this time Bennett had outraged Manhattan's upper crust beyond redemption and he was crossed off every important guest list. A social outcast in New York, yet with scarcely diminished influence in Washington's corridors of power, Bennett decided on indefinite residence across the Atlantic.

De Long meanwhile had examined the *Pandora* at Cowes, the Isle of

Wight. He thought her perfectly suitable for his plans. But by the time Bennett arrived in Europe his furlough was ending. De Long returned home to the supervision of a hundred boisterous boys on the *St. Marys*. It was about then that he learned to his surprise and concern that Captain Henry Howgate of the Army Signal Corps, a visionary whose periodic campaigning for American annexation of the polar lands many viewed as a joke, had actually got a bill before Congress calling for the establishment of a federally subsidized Arctic colony where "coal abounds, game is plentiful, and Eskimos can be had to reinforce the expeditionary force."

This latest development charged the transatlantic correspondence between De Long and Bennett with new urgency. Self-exiled but far from idle, the publisher journeyed to Gotha for three hours' conversation with August Petermann. Petermann no longer felt that the North Pole could be reached by way of Baffin Bay and Smith Sound, a route he accused the British of clinging to only from obstinate pride. The solution to the Arctic Question awaited those bold and resourceful enough to attack it from a different direction. After hearing Bennett's account of his meeting with the sage of Gotha, De Long warmed to the notion of a revolutionary polar route, and by the fall of 1877 his eagerness to set forth was almost uncontrollable.

His impatience might have stemmed in part from a brewing controversy in New York and the Navy Department over his alleged harsh treatment of the boys on the *St. Marys*, a charge he declared based on "falsehood of the vilest kind." But operating most strongly on De Long's mind were reports that Scottish whalers returning home with rich cargoes told of finding the northern waters that season unusually free of floating ice. From this De Long reasoned that the Paleocrystic Sea, as Professor Petermann and others liked to call the great frozen girdle about the Pole, was breaking up and offering unprecedented conditions for solving the supreme mystery.

At De Long's urging Bennett had gone after the *Pandora*. Tightfisted for all his occasional recklessness, the publisher had hired an agent to closely watch Sir Allen Young for some vulnerable moment when he might be talked into lowering his price. So doggedly did Bennett's agent shadow Sir Allen, he might well have lurked among the guests at the supper party which the baronet threw for the express purpose of introducing his friend the Prince of Wales to Lily Langtry. But even when Bennett approached the *Pandora*'s owner in person he "so backed and filled, I was compelled to give him up. It is now too late to think of doing anything this year." And then, even as Bennett's gloomy conclusion sped across the ocean, Sir Allen had an apparent change of heart, perhaps because Professor Nils A. E. Nordenskjöld of Sweden, himself searching for a ship in which to accomplish a Northeast Passage, had decided against the *Pandora*, deeming her of insufficient capacity for carrying coal and supplies. "Our friend has agreed to sell," was De Long's exciting news from Bennett. "Get six months leave immediately." At the same time the publisher ordered his New York editors and the *Herald*'s Washington correspondent to apply all weight on the Navy Department for its cooperation.

Captain Howgate had still to be dealt with. In Congress the Naval Affairs Committee had reported favorably on his projected Arctic colony. "Howgate is going ahead tooth and nail," De Long had warned Bennett. "He means business. However chimerical his plan . . . it is the only one before the public." But with ample furlough, finally free of that ungovernable schoolship, and confident of Bennett's powerful influence, De Long thereafter attacked each obstacle head-on. Before leaving for England he drafted a breathtaking set of requirements for the *Herald*'s top men in New York and Washington to start working on at once.

Their friends in Congress must prepare a bill transferring the *Pandora* to the American flag. She must be commanded and officered by the U.S. Navy, her crew for the Arctic shipped under naval rules and regulations. Appropriate orders must be obtained from President Rutherford Hayes placing De Long in command and granting him authority to call on the secretary of the navy for "detailed assistance." Legislation would be needed conferring "such additional authority upon the commanding officer as will render him able in his isolated position to enforce discipline in extreme emergencies." As well as the Navy Department, the other federal branches must be directed to give unstinting aid in the provision of instruments, appurtenances, stores, and outfit.

Less than a month later the bill to nationalize James Gordon Bennett's North Polar undertaking confronted Congress, and its specifications echoed the lieutenant's sweeping terms almost to the letter.

De Long told Bennett he wanted Charles Winans Chipp, his fellow lieutenant on the *Little Juniata*, for second in command. All it took was a cable from Bennett to the Navy Department and orders were on their way from Washington detaching Lieutenant Chipp from the China Station. But the selection of another officer of the line, a choice destined to cost the expedition dearly, was initiated without De Long's knowledge or consent. It was principally Bennett's doing, and politics were at work.

De Long was supervising the *Pandora*'s overhaul at a River Thames shipyard when he received the first word, in a letter from the U.S. warship *Vandalia*, then off Smyrna. Master John Wilson Danenhower of that vessel had heard about the proposed Arctic expedition and "I want to go with all my heart." In a second letter Danenhower hoped to join the *Pandora* before she left for the United States. Unknown to De Long, the question of signing up Danenhower as the expedition's navigation officer was already pretty much settled. The Danenhowers of Washington had given Grant's administration their loyal support. The ex-president and his wife were on the *Vandalia* enjoying a Mediterranean diversion in their novel tour of the globe, and when news arrived of the passage at home of the Bennett Expedition bill, Master Danenhower had told them of his desire to join the enterprise. Leaving the ship at Naples for some continental sight-seeing, the Grants had promised to put in a good word for him with James Gordon Bennett when they visited Paris for the Great Exposition. Grant told the publisher that although Danenhower might be too young for command, "if anything should happen, by death or accident, to throw him in command, he would be abundantly capable." To which Bennett added his own stamp of approval, thus making a couple of formidable endorsements De Long could hardly have resisted.

He would have preferred more time to consider Danenhower's application. Yet he had no real grounds right then for objecting to the officer, and he wrote him a letter of welcome, which included some necessary advice. The expedition would go for the Pole by way of Bering Strait in "a tidy little ship, thoroughly repaired and put in shape." Danenhower was to read all he could about Arctic exploration as well as study astronomy, magnetic phenomena, and the use of the pendulum in gravity experiments. He must also keep this letter to himself. "We wish to make no splurge and no show, no boasting or promises to achieve wonders. We have plenty of hard work ahead of us and no romance; and while we may be gone three years, we may be gone for eternity."

Bennett had cabled Washington for instructions permitting Master Danenhower to sail for San Francisco as De Long's executive officer. Scarcely hours after the department's consent flashed back across the Atlantic, an officer from an American ship laying in Havre had advised De Long in confidence that Danenhower was once locked up following a mental breakdown. Anxiously discussing this unnerving intelligence with Bennett, De Long argued that if anything was likely to shatter a mind already delicately balanced it would be a long Arctic sojourn. Yet Danenhower seemed fit enough now, or how could the Grants have so heartily recommended him? And would it not settle the matter one way or another to have him on board for the long voyage to San Francisco? If any vestige of his early trouble lingered, it would surely manifest itself before the ship reached America. Bennett at least thought so, and he and De Long agreed to leave it at that.

The *Pandora* had shipped a temporary crew at Cowes and under De Long's command crossed the English Channel to Havre, where she lay for a month while her outfitting was completed. Emma came over from New York, and in the French port where she and her husband had met and were married their reunion had the romantic flavor of a second honeymoon. Bennett arrived on a special train from Paris bringing a swarm of fashionable guests. The rechristening ceremony took place on 4 July. At a special luncheon at Frascotti's Hotel overlooking the harbor, De Long warded off journalists seeking to learn of his plans in detail. Henry Stanley, who had recently published *How I Found Livingstone*, drew smiles by wondering aloud if occasion might not arise for him to produce a companion work, *How I Found De Long*. All had then adjourned to the wharfside where, with De Long's chivalrous assistance, Bennett's sister Jeannette broke champagne against the *Pandora*'s newly painted hull and renamed the ship after herself. One week later the *Jeannette* was at sea.

A storm near the equator snapped the *Jeannette*'s mainboom, making the mainsail unmanageable. All hands struggled to tame the flying canvas and lash down the runaway boom. More bad weather met the *Jeannette* off South America. But De Long wanted to keep a superstitious promise Bennett had drawn from him to avoid any landfall before they sighted the Golden Gate. Three times De Long anchored his wind-battered vessel in the Strait of Magellan but no man went ashore.

As the *Jeannette* passed Cape Horn in continuing rough seas and came about for the northward climb, De Long persuaded Master Danenhower to tell him of his troubled past. Calm under the questioning, Danenhower seemed to hold nothing back. His disturbances apparently began on the *Portsmouth*, cruising Hawaiian waters in 1873. The ship's doctor, unable to cure Danenhower's bouts of melancholia, certified him unfit for duty. He was then furloughed to rejoin his family on condition that he report for medical observation at the Government Hospital for the Insane, near Washington. The authorities there had treated him like a lunatic, locking him up. He had tried to escape, fought with guards, and only when word reached his influential parents was he released from a padded cell. Thus Danenhower's story. "He believes he is mentally sound as any, not for a moment mad," De Long wrote in private. With such candor had the young officer described his affliction, and so commendably had he conducted himself on the long haul out from Havre, that De Long felt able to set his own mind at ease on the matter.

For the balance of the voyage from Havre to San Francisco he and Danenhower mostly discussed plans for the expedition. The ship's library was augmented by Bennett's valuable collection of books on the Arctic, and De Long had obtained "all the charts of the world north of the 65th parallel."

NO POLAR EXPEDITION had gone by way of Bering Strait. Even the region immediately north of this channel had been penetrated only by whalers and English search ships hoping to intercept Sir John Franklin's 1846–48 expedition had it succeeded in making the Northwest Passage. De Long based his decision to break with precedent and take the Pacific route to the Pole on the basis of August Petermann's theories and what he had himself learned about Kuro Siwo, the Black Stream of Japan. The very doctrine of an open polar sea had grown from a conception of Kuro Siwo and the Gulf Stream as mighty twin offshoots from tropic ocean currents, each flowing a changeless course to merge as a single powerful undercurrent far above the Arctic Circle. By rising to the surface near the Pole, these currents were to create a great open lake perhaps "teeming with life."

The best known authority on Kuro Siwo was Silas Bent, who had been a flag lieutenant with Commodore Matthew Perry's 1852 expedition to Japan. Bent had conducted hydrographic surveys in the Far East and after years of further study his conclusions that Kuro Siwo and the Gulf Stream provided "thermometric gateways to the Pole" enjoyed a popular circulation.

While Bent's hypotheses had received Professor Petermann's stamp of approval, other Europeans scoffed that if one took seriously their implication of a safe route northward determined by winter temperatures, all that a vessel needed to reach the North Pole was an ample supply of thermometers. Certainly the Gulf Stream sweeping north from the Atlantic had been of no proven advantage to explorers taking either of the two traditional routes, east and west of Greenland. But what of a third passage, north from the Pacific, between Asia and North America? Typical of such speculation was an article in *Putnam's Magazine*, April 1870, designating Kuro Siwo the "Eastern Portal to the North Pole, the only safe pathway to that mysterious goal of geographical ambition." Still more convincingly, as far as De Long was concerned, whaling skippers he had met in Dundee seemed pretty much in agreement that polar explorers were indeed habitually charging up the wrong ocean. Writing to Emma from Scotland he had quoted one captain to the effect that "the way to reach the North Pole is by way of the Pacific." De Long had added, "Suppose you do get caught in the ice . . . you drift with it forward instead of being set backwards."

Besides that temperate Black Stream thought to sweep through Bering Strait, the eastern route held another attraction. Above the Strait, beyond one or two small islands, more extensive land had been glimpsed, giving credence to old legends among Siberian fishermen and Alaskan Eskimos of a vast continent somewhere to the north. A portion of this land was clearly sighted in 1867, the year Russia sold Alaska to the United States, and was forthwith named Wrangel Land after the Russian baron who had become Alaska's first governor general. Perhaps an island, it was at least equally possible that Wrangel Land was one extremity of a solid tract stretching across the North Pole to become Greenland on the other side. So the tentative plan had formed in De Long's mind, to ride the crest of Kuro Siwo beyond Bering Strait to Wrangel Land then work the *Jeannette* further north along its coast until navigation became impossible, at which point he would take to sleds for the final dash.

The idea of an Arctic continent was not incompatible with August Petermann's supposition of an open polar sea. The land mass might be found to divide the temperate circumpolar basin in half. So ran the convenient surmise. And thus had two romantic theories combined to conjure an altogether fascinating vision: Kuro Siwo, Black Current of Japan, a powerful thermal stream racing northwards through and beyond Bering Strait to the Paleocrystic Sea, melting a breach in that dreaded ice barrier to enter a warm polar basin itself cut in two by a fertile continent layered across the top of the world like a giant scarf.

The day the *Jeannette* had put to sea from Havre, Bennett's *New York Herald* carried the latest interview with Professor Petermann. Holding forth at Gotha, the geographer claimed part of the credit for Bennett's decision to attack the Pole. "I told him last year that after the discovery of the Congo it was the next thing to do."

Petermann had gone on to say that Arctic explorers need have no great fear of the cold. This remark raised few eyebrows, in spite of its coming from a theorist and mapmaker who had experienced nothing more frigid than the winds off the Bavarian slopes. Petermann and Professor Henri Berghaus, whom he had helped prepare the monumental *Atlas of Physical Geography*, were stay-at-homes who nevertheless had secured an international reputation for knowing more about the uncharted regions of the globe than the men who risked their lives to gain firsthand information. After Berghaus's death Petermann wore the crown of geographic omniscience. Stout-hearted explorers had come staggering back from perilous excursions into the unknown only to have their carefully noted impressions challenged by the supreme armchair rover. The wonder is that so many meekly submitted, altering their maps and data without demur.

Petermann's first journey of any distance from his native land had been no further than to Edinburgh where he produced a British version of the *Atlas*. Queen Victoria, probably at the instigation of her German husband, named him the Geographer Royal, raising hackles at the Royal Geographical Society, of which Petermann had become a controversial member. While Silas Bent in America was proclaiming his hypothetical Eastern Portal to the North Pole, Petermann had been as busily developing his theory of an open polar sea reachable by following the Gulf Stream, which he maintained was strong enough in its northeasterly sweep across the Atlantic to overshoot the Arctic Circle (it was indeed to make possible the ice-free port of Murmansk) and flow as a still warm current between Spitzbergen and Novaya Zemlya.

Uncomfortable in Britain, Petermann had returned to Gotha where he directed the Geographic Institute, the world's leading production center for maps and charts, and continued his prodigious writing. It was no secret among geographers that Clements Markham, secretary of the Royal Geographical Society, regarded the so-called sage of Gotha as a self-deluded charlatan whose pretensions to expert knowledge had foredoomed too many brave explorers. But Petermann's phenomenal influence had survived British skepticism, and on his persuasively sagacious say-so expeditions had been mounted and launched into the wilds of Central Africa at first and then, increasingly, into the Arctic. When his theories of a Spitzbergen-Novaya Zemlya route became untenable following too many retreats by explorers attempting it, he had deftly revised his thinking to conform with such American efforts as Elisha Kane's and particularly Charles Hall's to probe beyond Baffin Bay. And his latest fancy was the third route, Silas Bent's thermometric Pacific gateway, the Eastern Portal.

It was, Petermann had told Bennett, the only way to go, and he had pledged Bennett's expedition the use of his charts as well as his inspiration. In that last interview for the *New York Herald* he had struck another passing blow at the British for having "wasted money and lives" in Arctic exercises as futile as their attempts to ascend the cataracts of the Congo and the Nile. The North Pole would be gained, but only "by a navigator who goes to work with the commonsense and determination Stanley showed in Africa. . . . The central area of the Polar regions is more or less free from ice. I am persuaded that it could be navigated by such a boat as the *Jeannette*." Very likely the *Jeannette* would "run into that terrible, hopeless Paleocrystic Sea." In any case, "the cold you can stand and thrive under. It is the long night that tells on body and mind."

That was August Petermann's final interview. The professor had plunged into his own "long night." Just three months after publishing his sanguine endorsement of the *Jeannette* expedition, the *New York Herald* carried a report that ill health and domestic difficulties, unspecified, had driven August Petermann to kill himself. The tragedy at Gotha must have occurred at roughly the time the *Jeannette* was rounding Cape Horn, and De Long got the news of it 27 December 1878, when his ship, after 167 days at sea and with a single bucket of coal left in her bunker, shackled to a buoy in the Mare Island Navy Yard at San Francisco.

CHAPTER FOUR

FITTING OUT

Until I return I shall never know whether I have done as you would wish.

Lieutenant De Long to James Gordon Bennett, 17 July 1879

IN THAT COMPENDIUM of particulars and bitter reproach De Long drafted on the *Jeannette* when nine days out of San Francisco, he deemed it a grave mistake that Bennett had not come over from Europe to bid the expedition godspeed. "We were spending [your money] for you and it was our due that our manner of spending it should have been examined and approved." De Long laid special emphasis on this for it had been at the press tycoon's insistence that he had, from the start of the vessel's outfitting, endeavored to scrimp and save.

Bennett would defray all expenses. That was a fundamental point. Secretary of the Navy Richard Thompson maintained such an arrangement was "the only way to success." The Act of Congress passed 18 March 1878, "in aid of a Polar expedition designed by James Gordon Bennett," had failed to provide for the enlistment and subsistence of a crew and their submission to naval rules and regulations. As Thompson reminded the chairman of the House Naval Affairs Committee, merely registering a vessel under the U.S. flag did not automatically place it "within the jurisdiction of the Department." The officers would remain subject to naval discipline but not necessarily the crew. This complication led to supplemental legislation, approved 27 February 1879, giving the Navy Department complete authority over the expedition's fitting out, manning, and supply. The crew was to be mustered as seamen and paid by the naval paymaster. The ship would sail under naval orders, flying naval colors, her officers empowered "to hold her crew in subordination in the event of any insurrection among them." She would be, to the secretary's satisfaction, "entirely under the charge of the Department and subject to its orders during the cruise." But Bennett would make good to the U.S. government every penny the department spent in the process.

Notwithstanding his enormous wealth and zany reputation, the publisher had a deep-seated fear of losing money to waste and jobbery. This had in turn weighed upon De Long's every decision connected with the manning and outfitting of the *Jeannette*. "My role of conduct is to save all I can," he assured Bennett. The sometimes ruthless economy he practiced very likely enhanced his sense of command over a great national enterprise. Certainly, or so De Long must have calculated, by demonstrating a constant will to keep the costs down he would secure Bennett's continuing support.

He pronounced to the constructors and engineers at Mare Island that, aside from certain modifications for the safety and comfort of his people when they were in the ice, the *Jeannette* needed little in the way of repairs. Within two weeks, however, a four-man board appointed by the navy yard commandant to examine the ship reported that putting her in condition for ordinary service alone would require some $7,500 and more than five times that amount for "an extended cruise in Arctic regions."

De Long reacted with horrified astonishment, fuming by mail and cable to Bennett that the survey board must be out of its collective mind. It wanted the *Jeannette*'s insides ripped out and replaced with a system of stanchions, trusses, and bulkheads, not to mention six-inch planking running the length of the ship. The board even recommended new masts and yards, quite unnecessary in De Long's view for "I saw what they withstood coming around the Horn." The *Jeannette*, as the *Pandora*, had already made three Arctic cruises, and she remained "strong enough . . . to fight her way to the Pole." A little caulking and painting, a fresh coat of tar on the rigging, a prefabricated deckhouse for the crew "when we are frozen in"—these and new boilers were all the ship required. The survey board had condemned the *Jeannette*'s boilers on sight, and on this point alone was De Long prepared to accede.

To Bennett he quickly dictated action: Bennett's agents in America must start hounding the Navy Department without delay. For one thing, Secretary Thompson needed a shove to issue orders placing De Long in command. Only as the *Jeannette*'s official commander could he pursue the Mare Island board's absurd recommendations to Washington and have them quashed. At the moment he was "neither fish, flesh or fowl. I do not carry enough guns to make a noise."

Leaving Danenhower to keep an eye on things at Mare Island, De Long caught the train east. In Washington he discovered how effectively the *New York Herald*'s editor, Thomas L. Connery, and its Washington correspondent, Charles Nordhoff, had carried out his wishes. Receiving him personally in the Navy Department, the secretary seemed only too anxious to cooperate, readily acknowledging that his assessments of the *Jeannette*'s fitness and requirements were superior to those of the Mare Island board. After all, it was more to De Long's interests than the board's to make sure that the ship was staunch and seaworthy. He assured De Long that the ship's command would be his as soon as the *Jeannette* bill passed Congress. (It was also at this meeting that the secretary of the navy informally conferred on the lieutenant the powers of a fleet admiral.) Reporting to Bennett after this first interview with De Long, the secretary promised that De Long's wishes would prevail. "I shall not be inclined to follow the board's recommendations," the secretary wrote. "With her bow solidly filled with strong timber, her capacity for resisting ice will be greatly increased, and even if some of her outer planking should give way at this point she cannot be endangered by the penetration of ice, whereas if she should be so unfortunate as to be wedged in between floating icebergs, she would be crushed however strong her timbers."

In the same letter Secretary Thompson mentioned De Long's request for a naval man-of-war to carry some of the *Jeannette*'s load up the Pacific coast. Thompson would "probably permit this if there is a suitable ship at San Francisco at the time." Here the secretary was more guarded, using words that were not exactly an unqualified pledge. But De Long, perhaps jumping to conclusions as Emma knew was his habit, professed to having secured one, telling Bennett that the secretary had promised a vessel to share the *Jeannette*'s burden "as far as prudent." And Bennett, taking the same presumptuous tack, acknowledged with pleasure the news that "the Secretary will send a steamer to convoy you to the farthest practicable point."

These long-distance exchanges occupied the first month or two of 1879. With respect to cost estimates and the likelihood of a naval escort ship De Long's mind was, for the time being, set at ease. But he could not afford to delay the expedition's departure beyond June. It was in this connection— the urgency of getting as far north as he could before winter—that quite unknown to De Long and initiated where he least expected it, an obstacle was in the making.

In the mid-nineteenth century, several expeditions had sought the Northwest Passage. All had failed, Sir John Franklin's attempt most catastrophically. Now a northeast passage was being explored by Sweden's intrepid voyager Professor Nils Adolf Erik Nordenskjöld. While De Long and the *Jeannette* rounded Cape Horn westward near the bottom of the world, Nordenskjöld on the *Vega* was pushing eastward near the top of the world, hugging the Siberian coast until his ship was frozen in. The last communication from the *Vega*, borne more than two thousand miles up the Lena River to Yakutsk, was that Nordenskjöld hoped shortly to free his ship and "in a few months hail Japan." De Long had told a San Francisco newspaperman seeking his opinion that he thought the growing concern over the Swede's situation altogether exaggerated. "I am as satisfied of Nordenskjöld's safety as I am that tomorrow's sun will shine." He did not know that the faraway James Gordon Bennett, conjuring visions of an Arctic encore to the African discovery of Doctor Livingstone—with Lieutenant De Long, USN, cast in the role of an icefield Stanley—had begun the necessary (and necessarily clandestine) manipulation.

Bennett's move probably had something to do with his lingering resentments in the wake of that celebrated African exploit. All the fame and honors had gone to the journalist-explorer, leaving the publisher-promoter with a sense of having been upstaged, cheated out of his share of international acclaim as the backer as well as inspiration for the successful pilgrimage to Ujiji. Also, Bennett may not have forgotten that the late Professor August Petermann had raised the exciting possibility of a meeting between the *Jeannette* and the *Vega* somewhere in the fabled Polar Sea. At any rate, as early as two weeks after the *Jeannette* had dropped anchor in San Francisco waters Bennett was trying privately to delay a European program specifically under way for the *Vega*'s relief. On 13 January he had written to the Russian merchant Alexander Siberiakoff, who had financed in part Nordenskjöld's expedition and was preparing a relief ship, stressing that the *Jeannette* could be near Siberia long beforehand, "and she will use every means to discover the whereabouts of the Nordenskjöld party and give them needed assistance with as much zeal as any vessel sent for that purpose." Siberiakoff replied that he would pay Bennett's remarks due heed and in the meantime delay his own plans.

Bennett next turned to Secretary Thompson in Washington. While the "ultimate purpose" of the *Jeannette* expedition was to reach the North Pole, "I am sure that you will agree with me that motives of humanity suggest as the very first object the rescue and aid of Professor Nordenskjöld." European search parties were fitting out but the *Jeannette* could beat them to the punch. In an apologetic tone Bennett conceded that his instincts had led him "somewhat hastily, perhaps, into the committal of the expedition to this duty" but he expressed confidence that the secretary would see things in a similar light. That same day Bennett also wrote to De Long. He gave no hint of what he was up to concerning Nordenskjöld.

Mindful of the political dividends to be had by staying in James Gordon Bennett's good graces, the secretary of the navy replied that while the *Jean-*

nette's course would be largely determined by her commander's discretion, "the great object of rescuing Professor Nordenskjöld will be kept constantly prominent." Siberiakoff's steamer, fitting out at Malmo, would depart late and by all accounts take the long way around, through the Suez Canal, into the Indian Ocean, and north from the Sea of Japan. "The *Jeannette* is bound to be far ahead of her. I concur fully in [your] views and beg to assure you that I will omit nothing on my part to carry them out."

The United States Coast and Geodetic Survey had published its opinion, based on consultation with experienced whaling captains, that there was no cause for anxiety regarding the *Vega*. De Long had read this, perhaps with some apprehension that Bennett might start getting ideas, for he promptly wrote him that "there seems to me unnecessary alarm in Europe about Nordenskjöld. He is simply frozen in, from what I hear." This was a month after Bennett had initiated the plan to deflect De Long's aim for the Pole in pursuit of an Arctic scoop as sensational as the one he had engineered in Africa. In the meantime, it being essential to the publisher's scheme that the world fret over Nordenskjöld's safety, Bennett's paper continued to whip up fears. Indeed, in an editorial the *Herald* took credit for having "roused . . . the sympathy of all lovers of science and admirers of heroism," and in the same issue it was reported that the *Jeannette* would do all in her power to find the "missing explorers." This news item was published before De Long's departure from San Francisco, where it might not have appeared. In any event, he was often at this time too busy to sleep and eat, much less glance at a newspaper. He was certainly on the train east when the *Herald* editorialist in New York proclaimed that "the reliance of the Russian government on the American expedition for making a thorough search for the *Vega* will not be misplaced."

In Washington the De Longs put up at the Ebbitt House, Emma "making ready for the Arctic" with scarcely less fervor than if she were going as second in command. De Long needed all the help he could get. While self-convinced that he held Secretary Thompson in the palm of his hand, he found that the carte blanche implied by the secretary's cooperation had limited impact upon the ruling minds at the various naval bureaus, especially with regard to those who did not share Thompson's servility to James Gordon Bennett and who sided with their colleagues on the Mare Island examiners' board.

But De Long had not lost his knack for browbeating opponents with rhetoric. One by one the bureau chiefs gave ground: the head of the Bureau of Steam Engineering, for instance, cabled Mare Island that the *Jeannette* was to have the two new boilers that had been shipped there for the *Mohican*, a vessel under construction in the stocks. Bennett congratulated De Long upon "getting your own way in Washington." Even so, with Danenhower at San Francisco keeping vigilant watch for any slacking or wastefulness, De Long felt he must remain in the east, close to the naval bureaucrats, "prodding them up all the time."

The prodding consumed precious days. After Congress passed the *Jeannette* bill in late February, De Long toiled on with an ever more anxious eye on the calendar. At the close of March—with scarcely ten or twelve weeks left before the sailing date De Long had set himself—Bennett and the secretary of the navy dropped their bombshell. It came as a letter from the secretary stating that, in compliance with Mr. Bennett's wishes, the *Jeannette's* first duty must be to look for Professor Nordenskjöld.

However much he may have feared that something of the sort was in the works, blunt word of it left De Long badly shaken. Although in writing to Bennett he strove to hold his feelings in check, they moved him to a rather caustic choice of words. Supposing the *Jeannette* failed to find the Swede, did Bennett wish her to keep looking until provisions ran out? "If we do find him, do we bring his party to San Francisco if he cannot get south in his own ship? Or turn them over to the first passing whaler and we labor north again?" And this was assuming enough time remained. "We may find them too late in the season for us to work north." Committing the expedition to a detour of unknown length posed a question mark over the amount of time he could safely figure on for voyaging north.

De Long may have hoped that his restrained letter would give Bennett second thoughts and persuade him to get the secretary to rescind or modify the order. He pointed out to the publisher that he, Bennett, was "the head and promoter of the expedition to the end" and, in a daring disavowal of the secretary's authority as final and binding, he told Bennett that "whatever instructions I receive from the Navy Department will be incomplete without yours."

Bennett did not change his mind. And if De Long was in the dark as to the publisher's role, so too was Emma, who half a century later was blaming Secretary Thompson for having jeopardized the expedition by "introducing a hindrance." Neither De Long ever learned that the handicap had come about at the instigation of the expedition's promoter. De Long's only recourse was to pray that within the ever-narrowing time before the *Jeannette* put out news would burst upon a waiting world that Professor Nordenskjöld and his party were safe and sound.

Meanwhile, there were other difficulties to wrestle with. Mare Island threatened to run up a fearful bill. Eight workmen were assigned to the *Jeannette*'s engineering alone. Cost estimates for the boiler replacement had skyrocketed. That the deck amidships had to be ripped open was a foreseeable expense, but it transpired that the new boilers required two new furnaces. This meant that the boilers would have to be practically rebuilt, a job the navy yard constructors calculated would take thirty days. A cable from Danenhower dated April 5 informed De Long that the overall cost of installing new boilers would reach $13,000 as opposed to the $1,600 originally estimated. De Long shot off a message to Charles Nordhoff in Washington: "Stop them, or they will ruin us." When the *Herald* man replied that he had too little grasp of the technicalities to intervene, De Long caught the next train to Washington and descended on the Navy Department.

He wrote afterwards of how he had harangued the secretary of the navy and William Shock, chief engineer. Charging Mare Island with incompetence, De Long told them, "I don't intend to have my professional reputation injured by becoming a party to it." The other two, admitting a possibility of error, cabled Mare Island for confirmation and the navy yard replied promptly with a figure marginally altered, to $11,000. "No," De Long snapped. "The highest I shall go is $2,300." It was not a question of haggling, more than money was at stake. "My reputation means everything to me. I am not going to a private citizen and tell him I am a fool who cannot figure better than that." Chief Engineer Shock argued that his own reputation would suffer if he ordered Mare Island at this point to cease work on the boilers. While the secretary fluttered, Shock proposed a compromise. The installation of the boilers would proceed without interruption but at Bennett's expense only until 15 April, after which the Bureau of Steam Engineering would assume "the entire cost of putting the ship in first-class engineering condition for sea." And thus, De Long crowed triumphantly to Bennett, "from the fifteenth, the boiler machinery and labor will cost you nothing."

This was not all. He had even scored on that portion of the boiler expenses for which Bennett would be liable. " 'Now,' said I to Secretary Thompson [De Long wrote to Bennett], 'What are you going to do about *that* difference [between Mare Island's estimate of repair and De Long's]?' As I had already pushed him pretty hard to the wall and did not want to push him right through, I hemmed and hawed until he volunteered to make it up in many ways like tools, packing supplies. The result? Your bill may be increased a thousand or so and we have gained double the amount in things which would have to be purchased. Had I not interfered, your bill would have soared."

Even allowing for some hyperbole in De Long's description, the encounter over the boilers could have been only a mortifying experience for the secretary of the navy. In the lieutenant's gleeful opinion, of course, the Navy Department's readiness to strike its colors with little resistance whenever he bore down was a measure of James Gordon Bennett's almighty influence. Unfortunately, De Long had little time to reflect that, given the slightest sign of fading interest on Bennett's part, the cooperation wrung from the Navy Department would start to dissolve. His every thought and effort were bent on equipping and manning the *Jeannette* for sea as soon as possible.

The boilers were but one source of trouble; costs crept up in other departments as well. The cabin porch he had proposed? Danenhower seemed to make too much of it. Nothing permanent or elaborate was intended, just a rough shed placed in front of the cabin for winter weather. He doubted the need for a closed-in pilothouse. "I want the man at the wheel to be able to see around him when we meet ice and not be shut up in a glass case." Water tanks? Also unnecessary. The ship need carry enough water for only two or three weeks at a time. A distiller would be employed, and "when we get into the ice, we shall not want for fresh water." And bunks in the forecastle? They took up too much room and were also colder to sleep in than hammocks. "I do not wish or expect to keep up the neatness of a man of war's berth deck. If I can make the men comfortable I am satisfied." He did not rule out bunks and he asked Danenhower for an estimate. He reeled off what he considered a list of necessities, including cooking stoves, curtain rods, fresh bedding, and such items as spare grate bars for the boiler fires. A double Jacob's ladder from the rail to the crow's nest (later rejected as too expensive). A good steam winch, preferably secondhand, to be placed at the foremast for use in warping the ship, hoisting the propeller, heaving anchors. In all this procurement he wanted Danenhower to exercise the strictest economy. "Little things run away with the money and I am more careful about spending money belonging to Mr. Bennett than if it were my own."

Danenhower at Mare Island had shouldered more than enough responsibility for one man. He was obliged to summon great tact, appearing not to interfere with the laborers in the navy yard but at the same time monitoring their work, remaining alert for malpractice. His burden was lightened when Lieutenant Chipp arrived at San Francisco from the China station. By then a ship's engineer was also on the way, George Wallace Melville, who had served aboard the chartered steamer *Tigress* searching for the *Polaris* survivors and in earlier years had been among De Long's shipmates on the sloop of war *Lancaster*. De Long told Danenhower that he would find Melville "a No. 1 man and a brother." An ice-pilot had enlisted, William Dunbar, with recent experience as first mate on New England whalers. As for the ship's doctor, Bennett had talked De Long out of his original wish for two on board, and for a while it looked doubtful whether he would get even one. An expected rush of applicants at the Navy Department's Bureau of Medicine and Surgery had failed to materialize, and James Markham Ambler, at the top of the chief surgeon's list for sea duty, was conspicuously lacking in enthusiasm for an Arctic cruise. Only with reluctance, perhaps to save the bureau from embarrassment, did Ambler finally volunteer. He arrived in Washington following a last furlough with his family in Virginia. Almost immediately he learned from a medical colleague that the man named as the *Jeannette*'s navigation officer had once suffered from "a disordered intellect" and that the condition might recur.

De Long was still in the east, "undoubtedly . . . the place to do most good," he reported. "A word from San Francisco is enough to enlighten me and I immediately open fire on the Department." In the same letter to Bennett he revealed the first symptoms of a special disquiet. "Are you coming over? Pray, do not under any circumstances send me away without a goodby in person."

In De Long's opinion the publisher should have crossed the ocean before this and taken a more direct and prominent role in affairs. He was unaware of Bennett's distaste for showing himself in those circles that had cast him out nor could he guess that Bennett's prolonged self-exile might have been his way of snubbing New York's high society for ostracizing him. De Long never had developed a cautionary perception of Bennett's mercurial nature. Immersed in his struggles with the naval bureaucracy over the *Jeannette*'s fitting out, he did not learn that on the other side of the Atlantic the unmarried press baron was up to his old escapades, flouting convention and titillating gossip. With almost brutal suddenness, De Long felt the first chill setting in at the Navy Department consequent upon Bennett's continued absence. In the lieutenant's retrospective words, "The country was full of rumors about your coming over to start the ship. Everybody in the Department asked me when you might be expected. Of course, I had no answer. . . . The uncertainty of your movements seemed to weaken the ardor."

That was putting it mildly. In mid-April, only six or eight weeks before the *Jeannette*'s scheduled departure, Secretary Thompson notified De Long that he could not spare a vessel to help carry the expedition's coal and supplies. Because of those orders to hunt for the *Vega*'s party, which would use valuable time, De Long's dependence on this help, "promised all along," was all the more acute. An agitated cable to San Francisco brought word that no ship could be chartered there at any reasonable price. "We are beam-ended," De Long told Lieutenant Chipp on 2 May and he hurried once more to Washington, where the *Herald*'s correspondent was finding it increasingly difficult to gain an audience with the secretary of the navy. When De Long finally secured one, he rattled off the names of warships he thought available. By this time, however, Thompson had prompt rebuttals.

The *Alaska*? Already north of Sitka, would return too late. The *Jamestown* at San Francisco? On standby for relieving the *Alaska*. The *Adams*, at sea bound for San Francisco? Scheduled to go out of commission as soon as she dropped anchor. The *Pensacola*? In South Pacific waters guarding American interests during the Chile–Bolivia war. "The whole fate of the expedition," De Long wrote then, "seemed to be hanging by a thread."

The setbacks only fueled an already white-hot determination in De Long. The *Jeannette* would sail even if she had to "paddle off with her rails level to the water." And he had not yet exhausted all his weapons. If Bennett's influence at the Navy Department was waning, that of the chief executive might be brought to bear. On the pretext of wishing to pay his respects to the commander-in-chief, De Long gained an invitation to the White House, where his volubility and Emma's charm were employed. But to no avail. Rutherford Hayes could scarcely have shown less interest in the expedition if he had never heard of the North Pole. Still De Long did not give up. He laid veritable siege to the Navy Department, trapping Richard Thompson on the stairs, in corridors, outside on Pennsylvania Avenue. Forcing an agreement from the beleaguered secretary to restudy the availability of service ships, he also won a promise to follow it up from Commodore William D. Whiting, head of the Bureau of Navigation, seemingly the only senior official

in the department with admiration and sympathy for the tenacious lieutenant.

Scarcely a day had passed without harassing new problems. Danenhower
reported that quantities of the 54,000 pounds of pemmican shipped to the
Jeannette from Baltimore were found to be tainted. The matter was settled to
De Long's satisfaction only after some heated give and take with the con-
tractor.

Recruiting alone would have kept him on tenterhooks. De Long expected
the freedom to pick and choose his men, signing them on in San Francisco
to avoid transcontinental travel expenses. He originally preferred Scandina-
vians, thinking English, Irish, and Scots undesirable and absolutely forbidding French, Italians, and Spaniards. And he wanted a musician. With May
at hand, however, he was informed by Lieutenant Chipp in San Francisco
that good seamen were impossible to recruit locally at navy wages and for
service under naval discipline. Obliged to recruit in the east after all, De
Long secured the agency of a Boston shipping master, but the physical-fitness
requirements imposed by a naval board of medical examiners were so rigid
that with scarcely a month left in which to complete recruiting only a dozen
men had signed up, and these on the promise of a salary slightly higher than
navy scale.

IN THE MEANTIME, Doctor Ambler had discreetly investigated the medical
history of Master John Danenhower. Ambler crossed the Potomac River to
the Government Hospital for the Insane and found records showing Danenhower as being treated there for melancholia, cause unknown, and discharged
four months later as "improved." Danenhower had been sent to the asylum
by an officer of the Bureau of Medicine and Surgery, where he had reported
following his service on the *Portsmouth*. The bureau was Ambler's next stop,
to study the *Portsmouth*'s medical log for 1875. It showed Danenhower as
certified unfit for duty, afflicted with neck abscesses. A notation added that
their origin was not in the line of duty. According to one entry, the patient's

mental faculties had become impaired, he was "gloomy . . . despondent . . . timid for fear of doing wrong." The *Portsmouth*'s medical officer had further written that "brooding over imaginary wrongs, Danenhower had repeatedly expressed to me that he had a strong inclination to jump overboard and end his misery."

James Ambler hurried to De Long at the Ebbitt House and disclosed the results of his detective work. His professional conclusion was that extraordinary privation, the long Arctic night, the desolate surroundings, might well induce a relapse. He felt obliged as the *Jeannette*'s medical officer to recommend that the vessel not sail with Master John Danenhower on board.

De Long had a problem neither his glib tongue nor Bennett's influence could readily fix. Now he was not so sure that Danenhower had been altogether candid with him while coming around the Horn. The immediate question was whether to summarily drop him from the expedition. Not only had his feelings for the officer grown friendly since the departure from Havre almost a year ago, but no one else except himself was so acquainted with the expedition's plans. Danenhower had an excellent grasp of the work ahead, and his latest letters shone with zeal and anticipation. He had indeed become invaluable. "I cannot replace him," De Long wrote to James Gordon Bennett. And if compelled to, what effect would this have upon the man? "To unship him now, if he is at all shaky, might bring about the climax we all desire to avoid."

De Long agonized. Reluctant to remove Danenhower from the *Jeannette*, he also felt he dared not broach the matter with the man himself, "a sensitive officer" liable to break down at the merest hint that his sanity was at issue. He turned to Danenhower's family. Summoning a brother to the Ebbitt House he suggested, as the most tactful and humane course, that the Danenhowers concoct some excuse of a domestic nature and persuade the officer to voluntarily remove himself from the expedition. But Washington Danenhower, a locally prominent attorney, argued that his brother was "bent on going" and that if De Long wanted him off the *Jeannette* he had better be privately advised that his withdrawal was in the expedition's best interests and that an honorable pretext would be furnished in the form of a medical certificate citing some commonplace ailment. De Long opposed such correspondence. "I wanted the whole matter kept in my hands for a while yet."

But Washington physicians who had treated Danenhower in the asylum entered the wrangle. Their opinions were vague and conflicting. Growing desperate, De Long again consulted Ambler, who was by then himself on edge. He had not known Master Danenhower, never set eyes on him, had no reason for believing him at that moment anything other than sane. "But it is my considered opinion that the insidious disease is not unlikely to return after many years." Ambler had spelled out the difficulty in words that left De Long little choice. It went without saying that an ordinary seaman with this medical record would be rejected out of hand. What, then, of an officer who had to shoulder vital responsibilities? It was all very well for Bennett to recommend from Paris that they take a chance on Danenhower's condition. The lives of all hands must be considered. With this fact in mind De Long wrote back to Bennett: "My duty seems clear"—somehow, Danenhower had to be detached from the expedition.

At the height of this crisis, the editor of the *New York Herald* informed De Long by telegraph that Bennett could not reach San Francisco in time to bid the *Jeannette* farewell. Coming on top of the Danenhower problem the news stunned De Long and he implored the publisher in a telegram. "Can you not do it yet?" He would even postpone the sailing date. "I can keep the *Jeannette* back until July 1 and still be in time to dig Nordenskjöld out."

It was late May. De Long had labored long enough in the east, and the time had come to depart for San Francisco. He dreaded the heart-wrenching ordeal of telling Danenhower to his face that he could not go with the ship. But what alternative was there? "It seems almost cruel to . . . make arrangements for Danenhower's successor," he wrote. In the same letter to the Navy Department, though, he explained the responsibility he would have to bear if Danenhower sailed with the expedition, responsibility not only for the officer's own welfare but, above all, for the safety of the crew. He had no choice but to request that Danenhower be dropped.

In the meantime, however, Danenhower's family acted. Insisting that his brother be permitted to remain on the *Jeannette* without further question, Washington Danenhower prevailed on one of the physicians drawn into the fray to pronounce his brother competent and fit for exploring the Arctic or anyplace else. De Long was in Burlington, Iowa, interrupting his westbound journey for a visit with Emma's sister, when the Navy Department's decision caught up with him. And it carried a warning. He was to take "no steps to imply distrust of the ability of any officer to perform his duties when he seems in every way capable." The favorable judgment passed by Danenhower's last promotion board rendered all fears about his sanity "groundless, officially." Reading on, De Long may have grown eerily aware that he, not Danenhower, had become the issue. "Any action on your part not based upon an official opinion expressed in proper form would be an official injustice to the officer."

Then the decision was no longer his. Anything he did to remove Master John Danenhower from the *Jeannette* would invite charges of persecuting a fellow officer. Instead of sailing for the North Pole in command of an exploring ship he might find himself facing a court martial. The situation was suddenly unreal. But he had been freed of an excruciating duty. Bennett's last cabled word on the subject, reinforcing the Navy Department's position, was that Danenhower should remain on the *Jeannette*. That was enough for De Long. Too full of relief to harbor any fears of what now might loom ahead he wired back to Washington: "I shall take no steps towards displacing the gentleman of whose fitness and valor I have the highest opinion. I wanted to be on the safe side."

CHAPTER FIVE

"EVERYTHING BUT SKATES"

*We have a good crew, good food and a good ship. I think we have
the right kind of stuff to dare all that man can do.*
Lieutenant De Long to James Gordon Bennett, 17 July 1879

DURING DE LONG'S frenetic sojourn in the east, mail at San Francisco had
piled up—solemn warnings, earnest counsel, facetious proposals. The expedition must expect to find tropical heat issuing at the Pole from the earth's
hollow center. It should beware of hostile creatures lurking beyond the Paleocrystic Sea. A former messmate who remembered Midshipman De Long's
proficiency on the flute sent one along and urged him to cheer the crew when
the going got rough with selections from *HMS Pinafore*. A young impresario
sought a berth on the *Jeannette* with a view to staging a vaudeville show that
would run through the long Arctic night.

Many of the letters reflected serious hopes for scientific achievement.
James Gordon Bennett, showing more interest in this direction than the
commander, at least at the start of preparations, had invited the aid of noted
scholars and inventors. Professor Spencer Baird, director of the Smithsonian
Institution, suggested to Alexander Graham Bell that the *Jeannette* take tel-
ephones into the Arctic realm. The notion failed to stir De Long until Bennett advised him to cooperate. Jerome Collins, the *New York Herald's*

meteorologist attached to the expedition for "special service," had procured from Bell all the necessary equipment including hundreds of feet of copper wire. Collins then proposed that the battery or generator needed to operate the telephone might also be employed in an Arctic display of the electric light. De Long, more responsive to this idea, wrote to Thomas Alva Edison, "I should like to illuminate the ship from time to time during the long Arctic winter, and subject the crew to the benefits morally and physically arising from that light."

Edison just then was fighting off creditors and making only fitful progress in his efforts to perfect an incandescent electric lamp. The one form of electrical illumination in practical use was the arc light, produced by a current through a gap between carbon rods. Already lighting broad Parisian avenues and installed in British lighthouses, arc lamps had recently been introduced into America and were blazing away in Pittsburgh workshops and above lower Broadway in New York City. Edison advised against the use of cumbersome batteries for the arc light and offered to build De Long a generator powered manually with a wheel and crank. The apparatus would work well, he wrote, "so long as your sailors keep their muscle. You can belt and crank the dynamo on it when you have no steam, and your crew can take a hand driving the machine. It will keep them warm."

Jerome Collins visited Edison's "invention factory" at Menlo Park, New Jersey, and reported to De Long that the machine was indeed a beauty, keeping fifteen lamps burning brightly all at once. But because the men cranking it would quickly tire, Collins recommended that Edison's suggested alternative—that the generator be powered by one of the popular Baxter steam engines in mass production—be followed. "Without it we lose the light," Collins told De Long, who thereupon approved purchase of a two horsepower model. Edison connected his generator to the steam engine. Arc lamps were obtained and on 24 May, as recorded by one of Edison's assistants, "The machine for lighting the North Pole has been sent away."

By then, De Long's own enthusiasm glowed. "Heretofore," he wrote Bennett, "expeditions have suffered and men have pined for light during the long winter months." It might well prove a worthwhile investment. The equipment shipped on board the *Jeannette* promised light exceeding that of three thousand candles and at a cost of only a bushel of coal a day. "Plants have been made to grow by it."

De Long also consulted with aeronauts on the feasibility of taking balloons, one at least, from which when aloft greater distances could be surveyed than from the ship's crow's nest. But this notion he reluctantly abandoned after concluding that to provide the hot air necessary to lift the balloons would require a series of coal mines on the way to the Pole. Even so, "everything the *Jeannette* might need in the polar wilderness seemed to have been thought of. In fact, the only thing I can tax myself with having forgotten is—skates!"

At the time, however, De Long worried that the ship would stagger under the weight of her cargo. Collins had got him to approve the procurement of a well-equipped portable observatory for setting up on the ice and also a portable darkroom for photography. Professor Baird had found the expedition an eager young naturalist named Raymond Newcomb, "a very good collector and taxidermist" from Salem, Massachusetts, and at Baird's persuasion Newcomb filled three trunks with alcoholic tanks, taxidermist tools, dredges and deepsea water cups for hauling up marine specimens. Baird had notified an incredulous De Long that this freight, on its way overland to San Francisco, was but the "massive part" of the naturalist's outfit. Needing more, Newcomb was heading west with "a long list of desiderata which I hope you will permit him to fill as far as possible."

De Long was then in the midst of making extraordinary travel arrangements. Bennett had at last agreed to come over, provided De Long ensured that no word of his presence in the United States be allowed to leak into the papers until he arrived in San Francisco. This was a tall order, but De Long bent to the task with desperate energy. He found that the Erie Railroad could haul a special car from New York only as far as Omaha. But then Union Pacific, which controlled the rest of the westbound rail journey, told De Long that in his case it would waive its rule against hauling a special car carrying fewer than eighteen passengers. Bennett's latest cable had indicated he would leave Liverpool by White Star Line on 20 June, reaching New York in ten days. Would that allow sufficient time?

De Long had just heard that the Nordenskjöld party had safely wintered off the Siberian coast a hundred miles west of Bering Strait. Deciding that "this gives me a little breathing time," he cabled back to Bennett: "You will be in time. Expedition will not suffer." Equally anxious for official navy representation at the send-off, he wrote to Commodore Whiting in Washington that "at my urgent solicitation" Bennett was coming out and Whiting ought therefore to be on hand as well, "not only for my sake, but for the good of the service."

Borrowing a private railroad car for Bennett, though, was proving difficult. One after another, prominent capitalists to whom De Long applied declined with excuses. It began to look as though Bennett might step ashore unobtrusively enough only to find no curtained carriage standing by to whisk him westward unseen. De Long wondered where to turn next when the double-barreled blow hit. Commodore Whiting's telegram reached him at San Francisco just twenty-four hours before the scheduled docking at New York of the steamship on which, until that cruel moment, he had presumed Bennett would be a passenger incognito. For reasons "official and private" Whiting would not be coming to San Francisco to see the *Jeannette* off, and "I have another disappointment for you. I hear Mr. Bennett has not left Europe, so he cannot be there either."

Perhaps the press baron had not received De Long's latest entreaty soon enough. Or he had heard that the *Herald*'s rivals in New York and elsewhere were having a field day with rumors of a Bennett visit, some speculating that the publisher planned to transfer from transatlantic liner to yacht outside New York and steal ashore like a phantom on the New Jersey side. It is just as possible that Bennett had read the news more firmly establishing the *Vega*'s whereabouts and his zeal had ebbed with a fading vision of another Stanley-Livingstone epic, Arctic style. In any event, in the candid letter he wrote Bennett while outward bound De Long recalled the futility of trying to shroud the publisher's movements in secrecy and he professed bafflement over his excessive concern with it. "No matter how carefully you had kept yourself in the background, everybody knew you were sending the ship and paying for the expedition. . . . On my arrival {at San Francisco} your coming was counted on as a certainty. Demonstrations were to be made at the departure of the vessel and a good time generally was to be the order of the day. . . . The papers were full of it."

The press feasted on Bennett's absence on the eve of the *Jeannette*'s sailing time with the same relish it would have done his return from exile. De Long was almost hourly beset by reporters asking him to "tell all I knew about you, the ship, the plan, the cost, myself and everybody. Failing to get what they wanted, they pitched into me." He tried to keep them at bay, refusing interviews, and was attacked all the more fiercely. One local paper denounced the expedition as a fraud, the ship a failure. "On a trial run the other day a tug with a line of mud scows was able to overtake her." As for her provisions, a ton of canned meat brought from the east had so putrefied "it stank for rods around."

The day of this published scurrility had found De Long awaiting answer to his most urgent appeal to the secretary of the navy. The *Jeannette* had 132 tons of coal on board and twenty-two months provisions for thirty-three men. Could not the department yet spare a vessel to carry the balance of provisions and a hundred tons of coal as far as Alaska? The hours passed without reply, and De Long's conviction of what lay behind the secretary's silence grew stronger. As he subsequently told Bennett, "Everybody was waiting to see whether you cared enough for the expedition to come and see us off in person." But it was then the end of the month. Bennett would have needed wings to materialize at San Francisco in the nick of time, and Lieutenant De Long was not one to believe in miracles. He plunged into last-minute tasks, refusing invitations from San Francisco businessmen wishing to honor him with a farewell banquet. On the evening of 27 June he was busy on board when handed the Navy Department's final rejection of his pleas for an escort ship.

The *Alaska* had returned from Sitka and lay to in San Francisco harbor. Off flew more impassioned cables to Bennett, who reacted promptly with renewed transatlantic pressure on both Secretary Thompson and the White House to place the *Alaska* at De Long's disposal. "It would be a great pity," wrote the publisher, "if the expedition is crippled." President Hayes bestirred himself to find out what all the fuss was about, and in a confidential letter to him Secretary Thompson tried to explain. He simply could not permit "the man of war to be used as a tow-ship and freighter." After all that the government had already done for Bennett and his expedition it was unreasonable of him to expect more. "My mind is pretty well made up that if I were to do as he asks, the whole country would cry out against it."

Authorizing De Long to spend whatever it took to charter an escort vessel, James Gordon Bennett added a comment on the secretary's refusal. "If you should happen to meet with disaster, the nice old gentleman will be held responsible." But frivolous threats would not have sat well with De Long just then, and in his embittered retrospection it was only too plain that the secretary's shift in attitude was a direct result of Bennett's indecisiveness or apparent loss of interest. If Bennett had set out for the United States "the Secretary would not have failed to send the *Alaska* or some other ship to carry our stuff to St. Michaels. I cannot help feeling that the impression gained ground that you did not care much about the expedition anyhow, and that there was no use bothering about it." At the last minute De Long was able, through Bennett's backing, to charter a 92-ton schooner, the *Frances A Hyde*, at a sum that both would heretofore have shrunk from. On that occasion, De Long wrote of the publisher in relief and gratitude, "Thank God I have a man at my back to see me through when countries fail."

The *Jeannette* was officially commissioned as a U.S. naval vessel on 28 June. The last batch of recruits arrived, bringing the crew up to full strength. De Long mustered the entire company on the poopdeck. The officers were attired in gold lace and cocked hats and wore their swords. The double rank of twenty-four seamen, clad in navy blues, included Jerome Collins, Raymond Newcomb, and the ice-pilot Dunbar. Their attachment to the expedition had raised questions as to their status on a government vessel. The matter was settled uneasily by shipping them as seamen while according them wardroom privileges on board and paying them more than double a seaman's allotment. Secretary Thompson had decided that this solution would at least subject them to naval discipline. Also on the *Jeannette*'s deck for the commissioning ceremony stood the ship's cook, a steward, and a cabin boy, all Chinese.

With Emma at his side, Lieutenant De Long read aloud part of Bennett's farewell message, as cabled to his *Herald* editor in New York. The expedition should push northward with every confidence. If De Long became icebound, "I will spare neither money nor influence to follow him up and send assistance." And if none returned "the widows of the men will be protected by me." The majority of the listening crew were unmarried.

Emma stepped forward and ran aloft a blue silken ensign she had sewn. De Long closed the ceremony by reciting the Articles of War and reading his official sailing orders from the Navy Department. "As soon as the *Jeannette*, under your command, is in all respects ready for sea, you will proceed with her to the Bering Strait." He was to diligently enquire for information concerning "the fate of Professor Nordenskjöld, as the Department has been unable to have positive confirmation of his safety." If satisfied that the Swedish party was all right, he should continue towards the North Pole. If doubt remained, De Long must shape whatever course he deemed necessary for Nordenskjöld's rescue. That said, the secretary of the navy commended the ship, her men, and the purpose of the expedition to Almighty God.

After thousands of dollars worth of overhaul and repair the *Jeannette* may have been in all respects ready for sea, but there were technicians at the Mare Island navy yard prepared to wager that she would not last long in polar latitudes. Three weeks before her commission, the navy yard commandant had appointed a second board of examiners to see if the repairs and alterations recommended in the original survey had been carried out. Long afterwards, this board's senior members testified in a Washington hearing room that to make the ship strong enough for polar icefields would have meant practically rebuilding her. Even in ice-free waters, heavy waves would so strain her frames she would leak badly. The curious explanation offered, at that future date, for the omission of the latter caveat from the board's report as drafted at Mare Island was that it would have been considered "indelicate" for naval men to find fault with a largely civilian undertaking. It was enough that "those most interested in the enterprise" were apparently satisfied. Yet that second board's report had certainly made no bones about stating that, while everything practicable was done to the ship at Mare Island, "for an extended cruise in the Arctic regions it was not possible, in our opinion, to make her particularly adopted."

Had De Long seen a copy of the second board's report and found time to study it (there is no evidence he did), it would probably have made not a scrap of difference. The *Jeannette* might be "a little small for all I want to carry in her" but otherwise was "everything I want for an expedition." The succession of setbacks and breath-stopping crises had fortified, not enfeebled, George De Long's determination to storm the Arctic in the *Jeannette*. "My heart is set on this thing," he told Bennett. Given his character, the dreams he shared with Emma, the intensity of the struggle he waged to get the ship ready, it is probable that hardly a direct order from his commander-in-chief in Washington, much less the carping of a panel of naval bureaucrats, would have held him back then.

He sent the *Fanny Hyde* on ahead, burdened with her portion of the cargo. The schooner was to sail as far as St. Michaels, a harbor south of Seward Peninsular where the Bering Sea narrowed into the Strait, and there she would await the *Jeannette*. On the way to that rendezvous De Long hoped to have heard that Professor Nordenskjöld was in no danger. Should he learn nothing of his location, or hear anything that indicated the *Vega* was in peril, he would cross the Bering Sea and make enquiries among the Siberian natives. If necessary, the *Jeannette* would skirt the northern shore working westward "until I get some tidings of him."

If there were news at St. Michaels that Nordenskjöld had escaped from the Arctic pack and had safely proceeded southward into the Pacific, De

Long would, of course, pay no more attention to him. His main object was to push on through Bering Strait and perhaps touch Wrangel Land, following its coastal extension as far as could be navigated, seizing what advantages might yet be offered by a waning season and that mysterious Kuro Siwo. "If the current takes me to the west, you will hear of me through St. Petersburg, but if it takes me eastward and northward there is no saying what points I may reach." If the *Jeannette* wintered at Wrangel Land, some of the party would press on by sled. When summer returned, the ship would move still farther north, "wintering wherever God lets us." If, at the outset, the *Jeannette* was forced to winter in the pack, "no one can tell where we will bring up, where to look for us."

So much was uncertain. Forethought could only grapple with supposition. Positive planning was a pointless exercise "when we do not know what we are going to find." But whatever direction events took, "we shall keep at it as long as the *Jeannette* floats and we are able to stand up."

CHAPTER SIX

THROUGH BERING STRAIT

July 13, Sunday. Inspected the ship and crew, and found everything neat and tidy. Had the Articles of War read and the ship's company mustered. Then read divine service, and was much pleased at observing that every man not absolutely on watch voluntarily attended.

Journal of Lieutenant De Long

THE SHIP WAS built at Devonport, England, in 1863 as a gunboat for the Royal Navy and was the latest British vessel (by World War II number ten would be launched) to bear the name of the mythological female empowered by the gods to bring about the ruin of man. When Sir Allen Young purchased the *Pandora* from the Admiralty in 1875 for his first penetration of the icy regions, he had her hull strengthened and her engine force increased to give 200 horsepower at about 60 r.p.m. The *Pandora* had voyaged north of the Arctic Circle three times before James Gordon Bennett bought and renamed her. She was 146 feet long with a beam of 25 feet; fully rigged and loaded, she drew some 15 feet of water. Lloyds Register listed her weight as 244 gross tons. When she set out for the Arctic under Lieutenant De Long's command, her overall condition and fitness to house thirty-three men for three years in a perilous environment were the result of six months of preparation marked by abundant conflict and compromise. The total bill for the

Jeannette's fitting out and manning, as presented to James Gordon Bennett by the U.S. Navy after the ship had long vanished beyond the Arctic mists, exceeded $50,000.

The principal known danger in the polar domain was ice—ice huge and powerful enough even in accessible latitudes to have rammed and crushed entire whaling fleets. With this in mind, the first examiners' board at Mare Island advised construction of four new watertight bulkheads from the spar deck to the keelson, and six-inch planking running fore and aft, as reinforcement for the interior hull. De Long vehemently opposed these recommendations as unnecessary and too expensive. But however adherent to thrift in Bennett's interest, he came to a reluctant conclusion that the work done on the vessel before leaving England was less than adequate for his plans and that substantial modifications at Mare Island were unavoidable. These were carried out. And though the second examiners' board expressed its reservations about the ship's suitability for a prolonged Arctic cruise, the fact is that the *Jeannette* left the Mare Island navy yard more sturdily fortified for ice encounter than any previous exploring ship.

The bow had been filled in solid for a distance of ten feet abaft the stem and from the berth deck down with Oregon pine, bolted through and through. Wrought-iron straps and heavy oak timbers armored the bow's exterior and the lower hull was girded along its entire length by a doubling of three-and-one-half-inch American elm that covered from the waterline down to within five feet of the keel. In the heart of the ship, extra iron transverse beams fore and aft of the boilers would add resistance to the ship's sides when under pressure. Long layers of six-inch timber strengthened the bilge. The two original bulkheads athwartship were left intact. But the Mare Island constructors substituted for their abandoned notion of four new and bigger bulkheads a system of heavy wooden trusswork braced diagonally forward of the boilers. An old iron truss built in during Sir Allen Young's ownership of the vessel was repositioned farther aft. In the space occupied by the engine, boilers, and coal bunkers, planks of Oregon pine sheathed a forty-foot length of each wall.

The new eight-foot-high cylindrical boilers were half the size of those they had replaced, allowing extra space for coal stowage. Even so, the total bunker capacity was only 130 tons. An entire new deck had been laid in place of the timbers torn out for the boiler installation. A pair of steam launch engines was set up forward of the brand-new smokestack and fitted with lines and drums to form a winch for the purpose of lifting the anchor, hoisting the rudder and propeller, or warping the ship ahead. Three new gun-metal screw blades, diameter nine inches, had been added to the three old copper ones of the same size.

The *Jeannette* carried all new sails and rigging and had received a complete new coat of paint. At De Long's suggestion, all exposed ironwork throughout the vessel was felted, the insides of the forecastle and the wardroom likewise insulated, and an entrance porch as wide as the ship and felted all around sheltered the approach to the officers' quarters at the forward end of the poop. A prefabricated deckhouse of two-inch planking was stowed aboard, another of De Long's ideas for the convenience of his men when in the frigid zones. Once erected, measuring forty feet by twenty feet, it would cover the main deck over the forecastle practically to the ship's rails and reaching from the foremast aft to the smokestack. De Long intended it as a place where the crew could relax and amuse themselves.

Among other significant features were a new No. 4 Sewell and Cameron pump and the distilling apparatus assembled in the engine room. The survey board had recommended that the *Jeannette* carry more drinking water, her sole tank having a capacity of only four hundred gallons. De Long had argued that, coming out from Havre, the one tank had sufficed. Moreover, there was no room for additional tanks or barrels, and he felt confident that the distilling system would see him through. He had concentrated maximum thought on precautions against scurvy. It was his belief that the British expedition under George Nares had fallen victim to the disease because of its dependence on salt food and its lack of lime juice. The *Jeannette*'s only salt provisions consisted of thirteen barrels of pork. Canned goods made up the bulk. Also three barrels of lime juice and eight hundred gallons of alcohol, medicinal and refreshment, including brandy and Budweiser beer.

In addition to food and drink, the expedition carried "every appliance for all kinds of scientific experiments. Our outfit is simply perfect, whether for ice navigation, astronomical work, magnetic work, gravity experiments or collections of Natural History." When they were above the Arctic Circle, the portable observatory stowed on board could be carried folded across the ice and easily assembled for use in meteorological observations.

AFTER TWENTY-THREE DAYS at sea the *Jeannette* hove to off Unalaska, in the middle of the great Aleutian chain. The sealer *St. Paul* had just put in from the Pribilof Islands with a multimillion-dollar load of skins, and her captain reported signs northward of an unusually open or ice-free season. Confirmation came from the crew of a U.S. revenue cutter that had steamed as far north as East Cape on the Siberian side of Bering Strait without sighting a floe of any large size.

Such tidings rekindled De Long's bitterness. Since leaving San Francisco, precious time had been consumed in maneuvering the heavily laden ship at a sluggish five knots through dense fog and adverse winds, often at the mercy of rough and uncertain tides. The resentments evoked by the circumstances of his departure gave a jaundiced tone to an official report he drafted for the *St. Paul* to carry south. The past winter had by all accounts been a mild one, offering a golden opportunity now lost. "I can but deplore that the necessity of loading the ship so deeply at San Francisco has made our progress thus far so slow, owing also to headwinds and swell, as to make it doubtful whether we shall be able to profit by the open water in our effort to gain a high latitude this season."

He gave his injured feelings freer rein in the private journal. Had the *Alaska* towed the *Jeannette* as far as the Aleutians, he would have been enabled to set forth from St. Michaels, his final stopping place on the North American continent, with a full ship and "we might have made Wrangel Land by now."

But having to coal again from the *Fanny Hyde* would lose the expedition precious time, he would be lucky to clear Bering Strait by the end of August, which would leave perhaps twelve days to make a good northing. "And this, supposing Nordenskjöld is heard from. If he is not, who can tell where we shall winter?" Furthermore, he had to rely on incomplete and misleading charts. The most reliable one he had of Alaskan waters was thirty years old, issued by the Imperial Russian Hydrographic Office.

At Unalaska the local agent for the Alaska Commercial Company, which controlled the Pribilof Islands fur industry and had aided De Long at San Francisco, supplied the *Jeannette* with a quantity of coal and twelve hundred pounds of dried fish for dog food. On 6 August the *Jeannette* was at sea again, bound for St. Michaels, where De Long prayed he would receive news of Nordenskjöld's safety. If he did, the expedition could make directly for Wrangel Land once the *Jeannette* had taken on the supplies carried up in the *Fanny Hyde*. If no good word on Nordenskjöld awaited him "there is nothing for us to do but go poking over to St. Lawrence Bay for news, and if none, go westward along the Siberian coast seeking him." Fuel, meanwhile, began to pose a problem. The coal received at Unalaska was proving worse than the hard anthracite hitherto used, it "flares up like pitch and is gone." The *Jeannette* burned as much as ten tons in twenty-four hours, the weary men in the engine room shoveling nonstop.

The *Jeannette* took seven days to complete the eight-hundred-mile voyage across the Bering Sea from the Aleutians to Norton Sound. At St. Michaels, nobody could tell him anything about Nordenskjöld. Worse yet, the *Fanny Hyde* was nowhere in sight. De Long vented his dismay on the desolate little trading settlement. "This is a miserable place," he wrote Emma on 12 August. "Exactly four white men here and not one white woman." Something moved him to add, however, that "we may yet look back upon it as a kind of earthly paradise."

Next morning at first light he was on the poop deck with a telescope. Still no sign of the schooner. "Our fine season is slipping away." But the *Jeannette* dared not steam off without those reserves of fuel and provisions.

There was less than eighty tons of coal in the bunkers, and burning like powder it would not last long. "I confess I am seriously embarrassed," De Long wrote to his wife, and he went on to remind her, unnecessarily, that he was not by nature pessimistic nor prone to easy surrender. "In fact, I believe my resolution increases in proportion to the difficulties thrown in my way." But he could not forgive those he considered wilfully responsible for them, and, convinced that the Navy Department had reneged on a pledge to aid him with an escort warship, "I am forced to say (or think) uncomplimentary things of our Secretary."

Sleds were obtained at St. Michaels, also forty dogs. The dogs fought endlessly, and nine would soon die. De Long hired two local natives to drive the dogs and to hunt for some of the expedition's food. Named Alexey and Aniguin, they impressed him as decent, intelligent, and wonderfully clean considering they were Indian, although Aniguin was a sight too disturbingly feminine in appearance and manner. At any rate, "I had them rigged in white men's costumes and they looked very swell indeed." Another sartorial function of De Long's while waiting for the *Fanny Hyde* was to have the reindeer skins shipped aboard at Unalaska tailored into warm clothing for the crew. The men were already equipped with canvas suits, woolen lined, and Captain Howgate, a good loser, had donated to the *Jeannette* party all the fur suits made up for his own Arctic enterprise, which Congress had rejected.

After five days the *Fanny Hyde* finally crawled into St. Michaels. Working at a fever pitch, all hands transferred her cargo to the *Jeannette*. Toward the end, De Long calculated that the schooner had brought up twenty tons more coal than the *Jeannette* could safely ship just then. But rather than leave it at St. Michaels he decided that it would serve to replace what they burned crossing to Siberia. This meant he was not yet finished with the *Fanny Hyde*. The two ships left St. Michaels on the night of 21 August, when the commander wrote with renewed confidence, "If God will only give us fair winds and let us save our coal until we are through Bering Strait, we may find Nordenskjöld and reach Wrangel Land before the ice freezes us in."

George De Long was never to know that even as he penned those words

Professor Nordenskjöld and the *Vega* were far to the south of him, safely in North Pacific waters and approaching the Kuril Islands above Japan. After months of waiting for the ice to break on the northern coast of Siberia, the Swedish explorer had at last reached Bering Strait, triumphantly completing a northeast passage. This was about the time the *Jeannette* was groping northward toward Unalaska. The *Vega* interrupted her voyage through the Strait with a landfall at Cape Prince of Wales, the westernmost tip of Seward Peninsula, and then continued due south, making no other call along the Alaskan coast. Somewhere in the fog-wreathed Bering Sea between the Aleutian Islands and Norton Sound, the USS *Jeannette* and the ship she was supposed to look for passed each other on opposite courses. And as Lieutenant De Long embarked upon an ordered deviation from his original dream of a polar dash, the explorer he conscientiously sought savored the anticipation of an imminent anchorage at Yokohama and the applause of a world agog with news of his safety and success.

Had De Long made directly for Bering Strait from St. Michaels, confining his enquiries to the Alaska shore instead of crossing to Siberia, he would have learned of the *Vega*'s call at Cape Prince of Wales and satisfied his mind as to Nordenskjöld's situation. But the luck that could toy so callously with him had taken another perverse turn. It was the same with his prayers for fresh breezes, anxious as he was to conserve fuel. The wind certainly freshened, running the ship at five or six knots. But before long, the sea was breaking in from all directions, and on the starboard side where De Long's room was located huge waves stove in the window. Dozing in his chair, he awoke to find himself awash in foam and shattered glass. He rushed to the deck with orders that the *Jeannette* lay to, and she rode out a storm that lasted almost thirty hours.

The *Fanny Hyde* had also survived. When the two ships put into St. Lawrence Bay after the three-hundred-mile crossing, the elements had subsided. A few Chukchi natives paddled out in walrus-hide kayaks to beg the strangers for bread. All that De Long could get out of them, using the dog-driver Alexey as interpreter, was the tantalizing intelligence that some three months ago a ship had anchored outside the bay unable to enter because of ice, and that her captain, who had a white beard, said they were bound for home. De Long thought this over. If that crude translation of "three months" was anywhere close to the truth, the visitor could hardly have been Nordenskjöld, for he would undoubtedly have reached civilization long before this, the news of his safety telegraphed worldwide, while the *Jeannette* still lay at San Francisco. Unless, of course, the Swede had run short of coal and resorted to sail, in which case he might still be somewhere in the North Pacific. But then again, if the white-bearded captain had been Nordenskjöld, would he not have left some written message with the Chukchis? It was a binding tradition among Arctic explorers, indeed plain commonsense, to leave word at every place of human habitation, however remote or primitive. Nordenskjöld would surely have done so, even without knowing that an American explorer was about to jeopardize his own chances of a successful mission in polar seas to search for him.

De Long determined to see the task through. After dismissing the supply schooner he would follow the Siberian coast a hundred miles or more as far west as Cape Sertse Kamen, the last place at which Nordenskjöld had been officially reported. Fortunately, this would not take him too far off the direct course to Wrangel Land. If he learned at Cape Sertse Kamen that the *Vega* had left there safely, "we will go on our way rejoicing." With 160 tons of coal in the bunkers the *Jeannette* could afford to steam for a considerable distance. But it was impossible to foretell how long the seas would remain navigable, even at these comparatively low latitudes. "Whalers say some good weather is experienced in September. We will do our best to make the most of it." He still cherished hopes of a landfall at Wrangel Land before going into winter quarters, and if this proved out of the question "we may winter in Siberia and risk everything in a dash next spring and summer."

In a final letter to James Gordon Bennett he railed once more against the Navy Department. Its failure to send a ship with the *Jeannette* had cost the expedition at least three precious weeks. "Instead of commencing our voyage proper at as high a latitude as it was prudent for us to be accompanied, with a full ship and choc-full of enthusiasm, we were made to begin it really at San Francisco." What particularly angered him was the fact that in 1871 the *Polaris*, under civilian command, had enjoyed the escort of the largest steamer in the U.S. Navy as far north as 70 degrees latitude. "By contrast, the *Jeannette*, officered and manned by the Navy, is turned adrift at the 38th parallel." He expressed his regrets to Bennett for not having advanced "with the dash that usually characterizes everything you undertake." On 27 August, he wrote his last letter to Emma. "Goodbye, my precious darling, with a thousand kisses. With God's help I shall yet do something to make you proud of bearing your husband's name. Do not give me up for I shall one day or another come back."

He entrusted the *Jeannette*'s mail to the captain of the *Fanny Hyde*. Also transferred to the supply ship was Ah Sing, "our smiling angel of a Chinaman." Enlisted at San Francisco as cabin boy, Ah Sing had proven himself quite useless, breaking dishes and spilling food, yet invariably reacting to cuffs and curses with serene unconcern, that cherubic smile of his finally getting on De Long's nerves. The two other Chinese, a cook and a steward, were altogether praiseworthy. But he had determined that Ah Sing return to San Francisco on the schooner. The Chinaman left the *Jeannette* with, wrote De Long, "the same childlike and bland smile that ever characterized him, accepting the inevitable as a philosopher." That was one way of interpreting it. When the two ships parted company on the evening of 27 August, their crews waving farewell to each other, Ah Sing stood motionless at the rail of the homebound vessel and his smile, conceivably, was broader than ever.

TWO DAYS LATER the *Jeannette* anchored off Sertse Kamen, an ice-cluttered bay whose east and southern shores were lined with crude huts and skin tents. Lieutenant Chipp took a party ashore in the *Jeannette*'s whaleboat but made little headway with his enquiries among the villagers until they produced an old squaw to whom Alexey made himself understood. She affirmed that a ship had wintered at Kolyuchin Bay, a further seventy-five miles west.

De Long rewarded the natives' information with bread, tobacco, and a sailor's cap, embossed with the *Jeannette*'s name in gilt, for the village chieftain's wardrobe. Another forty-eight hours and the ship had hove to in Kolyuchin Bay. This time the shore party brought back tangible evidence—Russian, Danish, and Swedish uniform buttons. This satisfied De Long, for other than the *Vega*, no ship had recently carried officers from those nations into this corner of the world. It was Sunday, the last day of the month. De Long held divine service in a spirit of special thankfulness, with a conviction of duty faithfully discharged. He could now forget Nordenskjöld with an untroubled conscience, strive to make up for the time lost in seeking him, and bring all his faculties to bear on the original purpose of the *Jeannette*'s voyage.

This much seemed certain: The season was too advanced for the expedition to accomplish much of a noteworthy nature before winter set in. As De Long later expressed it, so much time had been consumed "we could have no choice of starting points or trails in various directions in quest of the most promising route. As the commander of the Polar expedition my chief desire was to get north, and I had already come so far westward in carrying out the Department's orders that the sooner I started northward the better." De Long's immediate target, now not much more than two hundred miles away, had become Wrangel Land, "Though seen, never landed on, and which some geographers assumed a second Greenland, if not an extension of the original across the Pole."

He shaped course accordingly, the ship proceeding at full speed. For two or three days after leaving the Siberian coast, she made good progress. Loose ice, though often a nuisance, was no match for the steamer's reinforced bows. The big question was how long would the ice remain fragmented. To an undetermined extent, or so De Long presumed, the answer depended on the accuracy of the hypothesis that the Kuro Siwo, flowing out of the Pacific, ran north through Bering Strait with enough strength left to warm the polar waters. De Long told himself he would have to wait and see. In the meantime, on board the *Jeannette* all seemed well, a gratifying harmony forming among "my little family."

On their last night together in San Francisco's Palace Hotel, Emma had advised De Long to secure the trust and respect of his men as early as possible. To this end, as the ship steamed through an expanse of broken floes, he felt assured of success. "I try to be pleasant and agreeable without being familiar," he had told her in one of his last letters, "gentle but firm in correcting anything I see wrong, and always calm and self-possessed. I feel my responsibility and care and I hope I appreciate the delicate position I am placed in of leading and directing so many people of my own age."

Excluding the crew, George De Long's "little family" numbered seven: Fellow lieutenant Charles Winans Chipp, his executive officer; Master John Danenhower, navigation officer; Engineer George Melville; James Ambler, ship's surgeon; the ice-pilot William Dunbar; and the two civilian scientists Jerome Collins and Raymond Newcomb. Chipp had favorably impressed De Long during the hazardous cruise of the *Little Juniata*. On this more ambitious and risk-fraught undertaking, De Long anticipated Chipp's full support and understanding. His opinion of him was as "ever true and reliable" although he "smiles rarely and says very little." Chipp's unruffled demeanor, the methodical proficiency with which he performed his duties, boded well. But that reticence was all too apt to prevent the kind of intimate affinity between a commander and his executive officer that can work wonders in tight spots.

De Long's and Chipp's living quarters were in the forward end of the poopdeck cabin, the front most exposed to the elements, which is why the commander decided to have an entrance porch built. Chipp's room was on the port side, De Long's the starboard. Aft of the former had been rigged Doctor Ambler's dispensary and next to that, in the chartroom area, were work spaces for the naturalist and meteorologist. Fetching up last, against the bathroom and water closet, was a darkroom for photography. The midship portion of the poopdeck cabin measured thirty feet long and nine feet wide, extending from the bulkhead to the propeller well, and was used as the officers' mess and general conference room. A pantry stood at the forward end, against the bulkhead, with the companionway to the wardroom below immediately aft of it. Light filtered into the cabin through a small octagonal skylight abaft the mizzen and through the five small ports along each side, with ordinary Walton lamps or candles providing nighttime illumination. The lamps smoked badly.

The wardroom directly beneath the poopdeck cabin contained four small rooms and two berths, sleeping quarters for De Long's three other naval officers, ice-pilot Dunbar, and the scientists Collins and Newcomb. Born in New London, Connecticut, and at forty-five the oldest of the *Jeannette*'s company, William Dunbar had been a whale-hunter most of his life, in the Antarctic as well as the Arctic. Something of a sobersides, Dunbar was not wholly at ease with his station on the *Jeannette*, having no particular love for naval authority of whatever allegiance. This prejudice dated from the wartime destruction of his whaling ship, the *Elizabeth Scott*, with thirty-three similar craft, by the Confederate privateer *Shenandoah*. That exercise in mass burning afloat was probably not far from Dunbar's mind in the first weeks of the *Jeannette*'s voyage, for it had occurred in the Bering Strait.

The youngest of the wardroom company was Raymond Newcomb. (He was not the youngest on board, a distinction shared by four members of the crew, each twenty-one.) The son of a Salem, Massachusetts, businessman, Newcomb had won over Professor Baird of the Smithsonian Institution with his boyish enthusiasm for taxidermy and ornithology. His active experience in these fields had consisted of a single summer cruise. Baird wanted Newcomb, in the Arctic, to "pay attention to animals, plants, minerals, fossils and ethnology," a formidable injunction to carry out. To help him, the Smithsonian had furnished him, to Lieutenant De Long's private alarm, with an elaborate outfit replete with cups, seins, dredges, taxidermist tools, and countless bottles and boxes of every shape and size.

The tone of certain entries in his private journal and final letters to Emma suggests that De Long was unaware of the kind of psychological threat that under rare and peculiar circumstances can develop out of the most innocent human indulgence in leg-pulling. From the outset, and for all the initial good feeling that De Long was pleased to note, there was a good deal of banter, scorn even, leveled at the landlubberly scientists by the seamen. De Long himself, in a letter to Emma, described with barely concealed derision the helplessness of the two civilians during their first attack of seasickness. (Neither had he spared the Chinese cook, when similarly afflicted, "a shadow of his former self, long pigtail flying to the wind.") He did little or nothing to check the almost constant teasing of Raymond Newcomb. With no hint of the trouble that such behavior might store up for the expedition, regretting only that the naturalist was so young and immature, he wrote of how even Surgeon Ambler and Engineer Melville amused themselves by poking fun at Newcomb's eager anticipation of capturing rare birds and of demonstrating his expertise in skinning and mounting. Newcomb reacted to their wisecracks with an increasingly withdrawn manner, a deeper engrossment in his assigned tasks, moving De Long to record that with manifestly no ideas outside natural history, and thus having "nothing to advance, [Newcomb] may be deemed to be our silent member."

Newcomb's earnestness attracted attention if not the admiration it merited. He had no sooner got to his feet after the first bout with *mal de mer* when he began baiting lines over the side. The first bird he caught was an albatross with a seven-foot wingspan. He set to work at once, skinning it for mounting, paying no heed to the jokes and sniggers about "Ninky and the goose" from Engineer Melville and certain of the crew.

"More and more a treasure." This was De Long's early assessment of the *Jeannette*'s engineering officer, a thirty-eight-year-old New Yorker who had spent one-third of his life afloat. George Melville's most conspicuous assets were an unquenchable breeziness and a high degree of professional skill. The *Jeannette* had only just cleared the Golden Gate when one of her pump rods broke and Melville could justifiably have recommended that they haul about for the repair at Mare Island. Instead he had insisted on pushing ahead, and had pledged in his cannonading voice that come the first landfall, he would make not one but fifty pump rods with his own pair of hands. Such lusty good humor and roaring self-esteem De Long considered a godsend to the expedition. As for Melville's ingenuity, De Long wrote, "I believe he could make an engine out of a few barrel hoops."

Melville's naval record was spotless. He had served commendably during the Civil War and in the official report of the *Tigress*'s efforts to find the *Polaris* survivors his contribution as senior engineer on that chartered search vessel was invaluable. Melville's domestic life, on the other hand, was a story of dark discontent with occasional violence. He had married a pretty but eventually unstable woman who bore him three children and for one reason or another had taken to drink. The whole melancholy business would ultimately break into public view with charges and countercharges involving pistols and hallucinations. Melville would review life with his wife Henrietta in a storybook cottage at Sharon Hill, outside Philadelphia, as little short of a nightmare from which his long absences at sea (in fifteen years of marriage he was home for only four) offered the only escape this side of death. It would be said of George Melville that while he served on the *Jeannette* "the secrets of his home and fireside hung over him like a cloud." They were not perceptible to Lieutenant De Long, who wrote of his engineering officer as the ship plowed northward that "he sings well and brightens everybody. Already I consider him one of the strong points of the expedition."

Melville's singing was much easier on De Long's senses than the labored puns of Jerome J. Collins. But perhaps there was little love lost between the commander and the meteorologist from the start. De Long seems to have had an old-fashioned skepticism for modern ideas and gadgets (a trait perhaps inherited from his staid, church-going Huguenot parents), with corollary misgivings about the brainy individuals who produced them. So as not to aggrieve James Gordon Bennett, who had personally selected Collins for the expedition, De Long had at the outset assured the publisher that he was "very much pleased" with his choice, adding that "[Collins] has a large fund of general information and will make a name for himself in the Arctic."

Collins was born in Cork, Ireland, where he had served as the city corporation's assistant engineer, supervising river and harbor construction. His career in the United States began inauspiciously with the failure of a New

Jersey marshland reclamation project for which he had energetically canvassed support and funding. Thereafter, Collins's interest in "science" was that of a dilettante. Although he lacked the imaginative daring and experimental genius of such popular inventors as Edison and Alexander Graham Bell, he believed himself as gifted as they with zeal and insatiable curiosity, and he had no compunction about calling himself a scientist. (Among his various undertakings was the clandestine one of a study into the possible use of submarines by U.S.-based Sinn Feinians in a long-dreamed-of assault against the English.) Specializing in meteorology, Collins wrote regularly in Bennett's *New York Herald* and in 1877 he inaugurated a system of cabled storm warnings to Europe, which earned him a place of honor the following year at the Meteorological Congress in Paris.

His principal task during the *Jeannette*'s fitting out had been the procurement of such instruments as hydrometers, pocket aneroid barometers, anemometers, thermometers, telescopes, and compasses. De Long had armed him with letters of introduction to the Smithsonian's Professor Baird and the heads of naval bureaus, and with these, not to mention his enthusiasm and a sense of humor more aggressive than subtle, he managed to secure numerous donations. Thus engaged, Collins had been in his element. He coaxed a theodolite out of a Coastal Survey professor who told him (he wrote gleefully to De Long) that "if we never return from the Arctic he will regret losing the theodolite very much." When the government failed him, he was always quick to appeal elsewhere. Informed by the Navy Department that it could spare no chronometers for the expedition, he obtained from Tiffany and Co., at a good price, three silver lever watches, which De Long agreed would serve just as well "for hard sledge travel." He talked publishing houses into contributing books on anthropology, exploration and medicine, and scores of romantic novels. Entrusted with the purchase of photographic supplies and equipment, it was Collins who had advised De Long that the *Jeannette* should take a portable darkroom for icefield camera work.

The seeds of future rancor between Collins and De Long were sown during a press interview the lieutenant gave at the Ebbitt House in Wash-

ington at the close of February, scarcely a month after writing of the mete-
orologist in moderately glowing terms. Never at ease with newspapermen,
De Long fielded most of the questions but to one he gave a hapless response.
What would be the ship's total complement? About thirty-three men in all.
And would De Long take any scientists or specialists? "No. I think the
American navy can furnish the talent to produce all the scientific information
the expedition can develop. It may be that some specialists will be invited
or permitted to accompany us, but they will be simply accessories, without
any independent functions." These words appeared next morning in the
Washington Post. Collins immediately interrupted his scrounging and shopping for the expedition and fired off a letter to Bennett, then in England,
demanding to know where he stood. Bennett attempted a soothing reply.
De Long would of course be in command and all on board subject to naval
discipline. But the lieutenant would, "for my sake as well as for the credit
of the expedition, afford you every facility for your work." In a separate letter,
Bennett gently reproved De Long and advised him to steer clear of the press.

Later, in San Francisco, De Long made a great point of parading the
meteorologist before civic organizations as the *Jeannette*'s prize scientist. This,
though, had only intensified Collins's unease, nor was his mind set at rest
when the *Herald*'s editor in New York, in a further effort to mollify, told
him of the lieutenant's earlier words of praise, written to Bennett. Collins
preferred to doubt De Long's sincerity, suspecting that he was simply making
sure that he remained in the publisher's good graces.

That interview continued to rankle. Three weeks before the *Jeannette*
sailed, Collins and De Long were guests of honor at the annual meeting of
the California Academy of Sciences. The highlight of the program was a
discussion of the Arctic Problem. De Long had accepted the invitation only
on the understanding that he would not be expected to say any more than
politeness required. After a welcoming burst of applause he did little more
than emphasize that Bennett's expedition would be the first to try and reach
the North Pole by way of Bering Strait. "We shall begin our work at the
seventy-first parallel. Beyond that, all is unknown." But Collins then got up,

unable to resist the opportunity to publicly offset any lingering impressions from that still-galling press interview. Collins made what he subsequently described as "some rambling remarks based on the supposition that I was more than a mere accessory." He told the Academy that his capacity on the *Jeannette* would be twofold: as a specialist in meteorology and as representative of the press.

After the meeting, De Long invited Collins to his room at the Palace for a nightcap. But those "rambling remarks" only heightened the tension then simmering between the two men. When Collins brought up the *Washington Post* article, De Long would not deny that he had been accurately quoted. "Instantly, I saw the trap," the meteorologist was to tell De Long at a time all too harrowingly late for either's escape. "Not set by you, for from the start you did not want any but Navy people, as you showed even when I first met you in the *Herald* office. The trap was set by circumstances." Having volunteered in a dangerous enterprise, he could hardly retreat without the slur of cowardice inevitably cast upon one who backs out at the last minute. When De Long told him after that unfortunate interview that he was not to take it too seriously, that he would indeed be more than "a mere accessory," he was half inclined to believe him. But those assurances, too, Collins came to believe, were offered only to please James Gordon Bennett and "I saw that I had been betrayed. . . ."

As THE *Jeannette* steamed northward through steadily amassing ice, the semblance of shipboard tranquility prevailed. Jerome Collins persisted in manufacturing puns, getting some of his material from the names of shipmates, Sweetman, Cole, Starr, even that of the captain. "For a while," wrote De Long, "we steadfastly refused to see them." Perhaps these included Collins's assertion that the *Jeannette* would never want for fuel as long as Cole remained on board. "Now, though, we let him pun away, praising the good ones, condemning the bad." Most of the crew, like Engineer Melville, appeared to have good voices and a few were capable musicians. Besides such games as dominoes, cribbage, cards, chess, and backgammon, the *Jeannette* carried enough musical instruments to equip a small orchestra, most audibly two accordions, bones and tambourines, and at least half a dozen harmonicas. Music echoed almost nightly in the early weeks, competing with the howling of the dogs who had free run of the ship and added their inescapable reek to the pleasanter shipboard smells of tar and timber, salt spray and steam, and the warm odors from the Chinamen's galley.

De Long wrote that to all intents and purposes his officers were sublime. As far as Danenhower was concerned, a calculated gamble had been taken, not exclusively De Long's. All De Long could do was pray that time and events would justify the chance-taking, that however delicate John Danenhower's mental balance, his sanity would no more succumb to the strain of northern latitudes than the *Jeannette*'s ironclad bows crumple under the impact of ramming heavy ice. Still, misgivings lingered. In his last words to Emma on the subject, the commander wrote of feeling that "there is something about [Danenhower] which I cannot fathom. I cannot yet bring myself to have that *implicit* confidence in him that I would like to feel."

As for Surgeon James Ambler, he stood as ready to dispense cheer and inspiration as salve, bandage, or quinine to each morning's sick parade. He put De Long in mind of Dickens's eternally optimistic Mark Tapley. Ambler was a tall Virginian who had fought in the Confederate cavalry and in peacetime, as a civilian, had practiced medicine for three years before entering the navy as assistant surgeon. His unfailing jollity in the first months of the *Jeannette*'s cruise might have been in part due to his rigid avoidance of canned meats. "He abhors our hash, lives mostly on vegetables." Also, Ambler could feel confident that whatever else awaited the men of the *Jeannette*, they would at least enjoy immunity from the kind of medical problem encountered by Captain Nares. Scurvy had defeated that expedition because of its dependence on salt food and lack of lime juice. De Long and Ambler heeded the lesson of the Nares disaster and drafted their shopping list appropriately.

With De Long's knowledge, the ship's doctor had struck up a special acquaintance with Master Danenhower, the better to keep him under close and benign watch. There seemed, however, nothing to fear. The *Jeannette*'s navigation officer went about his tasks competently, regularly writing up his log or making astronomical observations. Ambler acted with discretion, to prevent Danenhower from suspecting that he was under surveillance. As things transpired, there was pretense on both sides. Even if Danenhower had learned that Ambler had investigated his medical background, he could feel secure that not everything about his state of health had been discovered. He alone knew the full truth about himself. His commanding officer remained in ignorance. So did Doctor Ambler. And thus was fixed a crucial element in a stage set for tragedy. De Long had been impressed by Danenhower's candor while coming around the Horn on the *Jeannette*'s maiden voyage. More might have been revealed, but Danenhower could or would not speak. Neither Lieutenant De Long nor the expedition's astute and experienced physician knew anything of John Danenhower's darkest secret. Neither one had any timely forewarning of the gross circumstance over which Danenhower himself had no control and which was fated to manifest itself with the grimmest consequences.

CHAPTER SEVEN

CUL-DE-SAC

September 6, Saturday. This is a glorious country to learn patience in. As far as the eye can range is ice, and not only does it look as if it had never broken up and become water, but it also looks as if it never would.

Journal of Lieutenant De Long

ALTHOUGH DE LONG found the notion of a thermometric gateway to the North Pole attractive, he had never devoted much time to a critical evaluation. Because Professor Petermann, among other scholars, had robustly endorsed the idea, he concluded that there must be something to it. The same distractions that denied him enough time for careful appraisal may also have prevented him from reflecting that the program he had set for himself would put Petermann's theory to the test. That test can be said to have begun when De Long observed that the ice through which the *Jeannette* steamed grew heavier by the hour.

By heading deeper into the icefield, De Long was not taking an unprecedented gamble. Among Arctic explorers, imprisonment in the pack was an habitual risk. Clements Markham, Britain's eminent authority on exploration (and Petermann's inveterate critic), had declared, "The first Arctic canon is 'Never take the pack if you can avoid it, but stick to the land floe.' The second is 'Reach the highest possible exploration by sledge travelling.' " It was argued with equal authority (and would be repeated in De Long's defense) that only by putting one's ship in the pack could one hope to reach the Pole. In any event, once De Long acknowledged the damage to his time-table caused by, first, the refusal of the Navy Department to grant him a convoy, and then the detour in search of Nordenskjöld, he knew he might meet the pack at a dismayingly low latitude. The question was whether he could reach Wrangel Land before the sea had frozen hard enough to entrap him.

As September began he calculated that the southern coast of Wrangel Land stood no more than a hundred miles to the northwest. But a frozen expanse steadily formed in the *Jeannette*'s path. He tacked to the northwest, constantly on the lookout for promising leads. Yet any such leads cracking open in the ice were themselves potential traps. The *Jeannette* would enter one only to have a man on watch aft yell that the riven floes were rejoining in the ship's wake. The *Jeannette* would then have to come about in a hurry to escape being sealed in or "nipped," to use the understated jargon of whal-ing crews.

"We observe a gradual closing in of large floes around us." The ice seemed to be gathering in defense of Wrangel Land, like a vast glittering shield crowding him off eastward. But De Long, now set on forcing a passage, pushed ahead at full steam and carrying all sail, testing every channel with the slightest northing to it. He was so engaged when the *Dawn*, the *Helen Mar*, and the *Sea Breeze*, part of a homebound whaling fleet, sighted the *Jeannette*'s black smoke. Lookouts on the whalers, their gazes fixed on the constantly shifting plume, reported the distant ship to be close-hauled, first on one tack then another. She must be fighting the ice, they thought, probing for a safe avenue to Wrangel Land. The *Sea Breeze* kept her smoke in view until fog spread across the horizon. When it cleared, not a trace of the *Jean-nette* could be seen.

At roughly the same time that the captain of the *Sea Breeze* logged the last sighting of the *Jeannette*, a hydrographic research branch of the U.S.

government was preparing to repudiate the hypothesis that had so inspired De Long. Of this theory, the *New York Herald* had dogmatically reaffirmed its belief, the day after the *Jeannette*'s departure from San Francisco, in fact, by declaring it "undebatable that a warm current of water from the Pacific flows into the Arctic Ocean at Bering Strait." Now, the U.S. Coast and Geodetic Survey had just completed an Alaska-based study of Bering Sea currents, which proved that the Pacific's Black Stream was cooler and of smaller volume compared with the Atlantic's Gulf Stream. The Kuro Siwo sent no perceptible branch northward between the Aleutians and Russia's Kamchatka Peninsula. Except for a modest flow from neighboring rivers and adjacent sounds whose waters owed their heat to the sun's rays, no warm currents from the Bering Sea entered Bering Strait. Said the official report: "The Strait is *incapable* of carrying a current of warm water of sufficient magnitude to have any marked effect on the condition of the Polar Basin just north of it. . . . Nothing in our knowledge offers any hope of an easier passage to the Pole. Nothing in the least tends to support the widely spread but unphilosophical notion that in any part of the Polar Sea we may look for large areas free from ice."

The thermometric portal was a myth, as was the warm polar sea. Doctor Thomas Antisell of the U.S. Patent Office, in an address to the American Geographical Society, drove the point home. "The North Pacific Ocean has, practically speaking, no northern outlet. Bering Sea is no real gateway into the Arctic Ocean. It is instead a cul-de-sac."

DE LONG DECIDED that on reaching Wrangel Land he would explore it to the best of his ability and would study its life forms, all the while working northward by ship or sled toward the Pole, beyond the limits of known land as shown on U.S. hydrographic charts. On Wrangel Land he would leave a cached record of his progress every twenty-four nautical miles. As the commander looked at the solid covering of ice, his faith in the Kuro Siwo as a warming influence in higher latitudes probably started to crumble. But his basic optimism was shored up by recalling whalers' stories that tell of these waters sometimes basking in an Indian Summer in late September and early October. At all events, if not this fall then after wintering in the vicinity of Wrangel Land, he would settle in the following spring and summer the question of whether that terrain was an island or one extremity of a great land mass whose other end was Greenland.

The ice continued to spread and thicken. On 3 September William Nindemann, ship's carpenter, climbed seventy feet of rigging to the foretopgallant mast, squirmed through the trap door into the crow's nest, and, using binoculars as well as the long glass, surveyed the *Jeannette*'s surroundings. The German-born Nindemann was no stranger to ice. He had been a member of Captain Hall's ill-fated expedition, and, when ice first threatened to crush the *Polaris*, he had crawled to a berg in the teeth of a blizzard and by securing ice-anchors and hawsers had saved the ship from disaster.

Crouching now in the *Jeannette*'s wind-whipped tops (the crow's nest was essentially an open cask four feet wide), Nindemann saw no substantial break in the icefield stretching northwest. He thought, however, he detected open water northward and eastward. Descending, he reported accordingly, only to be told by De Long, "Nindemann, we are not going north and east. I intend to make Wrangel Land."

De Long ordered engines slowed that night and allowed the ship to circle idly, just clear of the pack. At daybreak he spread all fires and worked up a full head of steam. The fog had cleared. Again the *Jeannette* charged the pack, her solidly timbered bows and iron-belted sides grinding through young ice. She reached a wide lane that seemed to run clear to the west horizon. De Long himself took the crow's nest. He was heartened by the sight of several shimmering pools, some as big as lakes and beckoning from a distance of three or four hundred yards. But even as the *Jeannette* strained toward each in turn, the temperature plunged, the enticing ponds shrank, froze over, vanished. De Long was forced to swallow his words and again bear eastwards.

He did not give up. At 4:00 A.M. on 5 September the *Jeannette* steamed west-northwest in yet another attempt to reach Wrangel Land. The ship made five miles with relatively little difficulty until brought up by hummocky, or ridgelike, ice as much as fifteen feet thick. But the vista still contained enough of tantalizing promise to lure the lieutenant into further effort. "Though our lead had terminated at a wall of ice" there were ponds and pools on all sides "which any movement of the ice might unite into a lane of navigable water. Waiting, therefore, with what patience we had, we succeeded during the afternoon in advancing another mile or two." Fog fell and the *Jeannette* tied up alongside a floe. When visibility returned, the ship rang with shouts. What looked like a range of snowcapped sugarloaf hills hung above the frozen undulation of the northwest horizon. A mirage, thought De Long, but Surgeon Ambler felt sure they had sighted "mountain peaks of Wrangel Land." The doctor had just distributed smoked goggles to all hands "as we are in the ice pack and bright sun." But if what the men of the *Jeannette* saw through shielded eyes was in fact a mountain chain on Wrangel Land, it was as close as they would ever get to that fabled *terra incognita.*

The ice had staved off the siege for Wrangel Land. De Long bowed to reality and shifted objectives, determining his winter quarters would be the waters off Herald Island, a barren and insignificant nub fifty miles east of Wrangel Land. (The name had nothing to do with Bennett's newspaper. A British captain who first saw the island in 1849 named it after his ship.) The steamer resumed its laborious selective advance, ramming and coming about and ramming again, each time thrusting the ice wide enough apart to squeeze through. When the ship had no room to be turned with the helm, De Long would snub her bows into a weak place by use of the steam winch. But the ice coalesced on both beams and ahead faster than the vessel made progress.

The *Jeannette*'s navigation officer, John Danenhower, was to recall that on 5 September "a very good chance" had remained of withdrawing from the pack. "Our commander did not take advantage of it for the reason, we supposed at the time, that he wished to make a daring and magnificent attempt to reach the North Pole. He seemed to have confidence that the *Jeannette* was strong enough to resist any ice she should meet." By midday on the sixth, however, after the ship had lodged herself in a crevice between floes, it was obvious that the young ice forming on all sides froze fast to the old fragments and cemented the vast misshapen mass into an impenetrable new pack. And by nightfall the *Jeannette*, listing five degrees to starboard, was sealed in the middle of it as tightly as a fly in amber.

After ordering the fires banked and lanterns lit, De Long retired to his room and summed up the situation. Judiciously ramming under steam and sail for half a week, "twisting in and around all sorts of curves," the ship had penetrated sixty miles of ice, to be brought up within a maddeningly scant twenty miles of dry land. In a more detailed review composed later, De Long told of having "followed up the only water lane and come to the end of it. My choice of plans was limited. To advance was impossible; to retreat disagreeable, though in fact we could not have gone more than a mile; and our holding our present location meant wintering in the pack and drifting we knew not where, the ocean we had left behind . . . as much out of our reach as if a continent had intervened. There seemed nothing left but making a virtue of necessity and staying where we were."

He had resolved all along to winter in the pack "should no favorable opportunity occur for advancing." He had made no attempt to withdraw his ship from the ice, a "disagreeable" alternative and by then an impracticable one. He had probably given scant thought to it, unable to contemplate returning empty-handed to face Emma, Bennett, and his peers and superiors in the U.S. Navy. Retreat would have been unthinkable at such an early stage, especially to the officer who, in command of the *Little Juniata*, had declared himself not disposed to quit without a fight. Moreover, in the first hours of entrapment, De Long half hoped that the season had not begun in earnest. The prevailing conditions might prove only temporary. "I consider it an exceptional state of ice we are having just now, and count on September gales to break up the pack and perhaps open leads." Or that "Indian Summer" he had heard so much about. Three more weeks would pass before De Long accepted that the *Jeannette* was in the ice to stay. By then, his expectation of autumnal gales or vestigial summer warmth removing the frozen walls of the ship's prison had led him to take a calculated risk.

She listed to starboard, jamming her rudder hard over. The strain thrown upon the pintles and gudgeons could be imagined, and De Long was tempted to unship the rudder and trice up the propeller. Though the rudder weighed two tons, to unhang it was relatively simple. And that modified propeller could similarly be hoisted up. But new ice would form in the space they had left under water and prevent their prompt reinstallation, keeping the ship immobilized when the hoped-for mild spell or rising winds parted the ice and offered escape. So De Long opted for leaving the propeller and rudder in place, gambling on the chance that they would not suffer irreparable damage in the meantime.

That same trust in the approaching disintegration of the ice pack had also determined him against sending a sled party fifteen miles or so to Herald Island in search of driftwood. Should the ice break up during the men's absence he might never get them back. Then dawned, however, a day of crystal-clear visibility, making Herald Island appear seductively close. With visions of unlimited driftwood awaiting collection, De Long changed his mind and ordered a sled made ready. To a scattering of cheers Lieutenant Chipp and Engineer Melville, with Alexey driving the eight-dog team, left the ship on 13 September. They were to gather up as much driftwood as could be carried and conduct a hasty reconnaissance for a winter harbor but would have to be quick about it. De Long had estimated their traveling time as twelve hours each way and he wanted them back on board within forty-eight.

The danger he had first feared intervened. Chipp's dogsled party gliding across the glacial hillocks had reached just six miles short of Herald Island when a spiderweb of cracks split the ice ahead, spreading fast on both flanks and rearward as if to cut them off from the *Jeannette*. Chipp permitted himself a rapid survey of the island through binoculars. He saw no driftwood nor anything like a snug harbor. The ice fracturing on all sides, he ordered a fast turnabout. And the party made top-speed back to the ship, a widening swarm of fissures at their heels.

Time and again, suddenly obvious realities altered De Long's plans. There was, for instance, the matter of sea water. He had supposed that in freezing it lost its salt, which was why the already overloaded *Jeannette* had not taken on substantial reserves of water at San Francisco. De Long had in fact retained a clipping from *Galaxy*, June 1875, that quoted Petermann's *Mitteilungen* and which he had underlined at the words "Beginning at a certain thickness the ice is almost free of salt." Doctor Ambler and two seamen had to venture three miles from the ship before they found a supply of ice that, once melted, was relatively saltfree, and this soon ran out. With dread De Long contemplated the necessity of distilling, for the process would consume precious fuel. But though Ambler conducted regular tests of the surrounding surface ice by applying a silver nitrate solution to melted quantities, "we could find no ice that would yield palatable water." That frozen seawater lost its salinity and had only to be melted to provide an unlimited source of liquid sustenance was thus another preconception shattered.

The pack seemed momentarily to slacken, then tightened again. It drifted with its prisoner west-northwest at a rate estimated by John Danenhower as about three miles a day. De Long attributed the drift to some prevailing current. This was another point on which he would soon find himself in error, for the movement of the ice was actually more dependent upon the winds. But the main thing was, the *Jeannette* could not budge. In the privacy of his stateroom De Long chafed as he reflected upon the more promising starts gained by Arctic explorers with only sailing ships at their command. "Here we are on a steamer, beset in the pack before we are two months out of San Francisco. My disappointment is great, how great no one else will probably know. I had hoped to accomplish something new in the first summer out and we have done nothing."

The *Jeannette* remained heeled to starboard, squeezed between floes almost twenty feet high in places, and young ice forming beneath her had begun to disturb the old pack. De Long ordered attempts made to right the ship by getting up masthead tackles on the port side with their blocks tautly attached to heavy ice-anchors 150 feet off. This operation failed, chiefly because of unstable ice. The danger to the ship's rudder and propeller intensified, the opposing pressures of old and newly formed ice threatening to wrench and carry them away. A day was spent trying to blast the ice from the rudder with small explosive mines made by Lieutenant Chipp. Defective fuses or leaking electric current defeated each attempt. And when shifts were detailed to saw away at the ice around the stern, this move produced nothing but bent saws. Again De Long reversed himself, partly at least, by ordering the rudder unhung. After it was triced up to its davits across the stern he was about to hoist in the propeller as well when Engineer Melville pointed out that any damage to the propeller could most likely be repaired, that left in place it protected the otherwise exposed rudder post. So the propeller stayed where it was, ready to spin should the ice relax its grip.

That blessed event seemed further off than ever. The morning after removing the rudder, as De Long paced the creaking deck, pitch and oakum oozed visibly from seams in the planking. His ship was being steadily throttled. Deep within her, leaks might spring at any moment. Anxiously he scanned the heavens and prayed for signs of an approaching storm.

Freed to roam the ship because tied up they howled interminably, the dogs befouled every nook and cranny. De Long turned them loose on the ice, to give a sanitary detail the chance to clean and fumigate, and there was a nasty oversight. The men had put out bear traps the previous night, using as bait the entrails of a seal Alexey had shot. The inevitable happened. "Today we caught something—one of our finest dogs." The traps were brought in at once. Reset when the dogs were back on board, however, one trap almost immediately vanished, leaving a trail of blood. The crew was so excited it was all De Long could do to keep them from stampeding off on the hunt. Armed with Winchesters and Remingtons from the ship's sizable arsenal, De Long himself, with Lieutenant Chipp and the ice-pilot Dunbar, led a party across six miles of ice. They found a male and a female bear, the male dragging the chain. A couple of rifle volleys secured the expedition some thousand pounds of bear meat. Also busy at the trigger that day, Raymond Newcomb added four ivory gulls to his ornithological collection.

The winds freshened toward the close of September but forced only feeble cracks in the ice. So firmly was the *Jeannette* wedged, De Long told himself it would take an earthquake to liberate her. Clearly, neither gales nor Indian Summer could be counted on for succor. It was altogether too late for such wayward optimism. On the twenty-fifth of the month the ice appeared wholly still. From the crow's nest, commanding a view of ten miles radius, all was frozen solitude. To Newcomb's disappointment even the birds had gone. Their number had steadily diminished with the growing scarcity of pools on the surface of floes. On the twenty-ninth, De Long wrote: "Seeing no chance for any further navigation, we set to work preparing for the winter."

HIS PEOPLE APPEARED in tolerably good condition and not greatly dismayed by the *Jeannette*'s early besetment. To ensure their continued high morale and physical well-being he paid almost fussy attention to certain matters. When the original cookhouse on deck was demolished at Mare Island to remove the old boilers, its stanchions were sawed through and it could not be put back. But a galley below had since proved a nuisance, so De Long had a new one built on deck under Melville's supervision. This had to be kept spic and span, and the berth deck where the men slept kept warm and dry. Also, De Long ordered regular exercise spells on the ice and organized games (the ship's recreation gear included several footballs), a routine which gave the cleaning detail better chance to mop up after the dogs. When Doctor Ambler's tests for carbon dioxide in the crew's quarters showed disturbing amounts De Long ordered the doors leading from the old galley room to the berth deck kept open night and day for proper ventilation. The men soon complained of the cold and De Long had the doors shut again, with tiny air holes drilled in their lower panels.

For all his hopes of escaping a winter in the pack, he had not neglected plans for eventualities. The ship's engines, which he had decided not to dismantle for laying up, were given a protective coating of tallow and white lead. When the first snow fell, the men were issued their fur clothing, and De Long had all hands employed in building up heavy banks of snow around the ship, until it was soon as high as the rail. This would help reduce the loss of heat from within, also the sloping sides would serve as a ramp for sleds should any need arise to leave the vessel. With this same possibility in mind, De Long ordered the steam cutter moved to the ice and five sleds positioned on the poop for an immediate getaway, fully loaded with sleeping bags, tent gear, and forty days' emergency rations for thirty-three men and about as many dogs. The men were told off into five sled parties, each to be commanded by an officer.

Work began on one of De Long's pet projects—the felt-lined deckhouse prefabricated at Mare Island. Two hundred yards off the ship's starboard beam, the canvas observatory was raised and lashed down to ice-claws. Jerome Collins took daily soundings through a hole chopped in the ice and recorded water temperatures. Master Danenhower maintained an astronomical fix on the ship's position; the pack had veered south from its northward drift, and this encouraged De Long to send out hunting parties for game that might be found in those lower latitudes. Raymond Newcomb dredged the depths for samples of marine life, and in the cramped quarters reserved for his studies and taxidermy he set about mounting the score or more birds he had downed. Newcomb was especially proud of one he identified as a Ross gull, a rare capture, for there were no specimens in any U.S. museum and only one such stuffed bird in all Europe.

In the early weeks of the *Jeannette*'s icy imprisonment the humdrum hours had their intervals of relief. The diet was good, Sunday dinner always looked forward to, the two Chinese who had prepared it basking in the praise lavished on them for their labors. The menu for the last September sabbath featured oxtail soup, roast bear, pork, string beans, potatoes, beets, jelly, hard bread, raisins, duff, and coffee. The ship's provisions included a large quantity of fresh potatoes, somewhat fewer carrots and onions. To keep them from freezing, all vegetables were stowed in the coal bunkers. In the brief daylight hours the subfreezing air around the *Jeannette* rang with shouts and songs and the thud and rasp of hammers and woodsaws. The ship trembled when a heavy wind gust descended, otherwise was "as steady as if in a drydock." At night, peace enveloped her, except in the forward section where laughter echoed and occasional snatches of melody from a violin or harmonica could be heard, until nine o'clock when the berth deck lamp went out, captain's orders.

CHAPTER EIGHT

No Place for a Ship

November 11, Tuesday. At 6.10 A.M. awakened by the trembling and creaking of the ship. The ice was again in motion, grinding and crushing. I know of no sound on shore that can be compared with it.

Journal of Lieutenant De Long

FAT LAMPS WERE all very well, but it was time to try out the Electric Light. As soon as the carpenter's portion of the deckhouse was completed, De Long ordered sixty carbon lamps hoisted aloft and strung between the maintop and the mizzentop. He was anxious for the experiment to work, imagining sustained and artificial illumination to be an ideal morale-booster for the crew.

Success with the light was even more vital to Jerome Collins. It was he who had waxed most enthusiastically over the notion of lighting up the ship (if not the North Pole) electrically, he who had initiated discussion on the subject with Thomas Edison, and he who had finally gotten De Long to authorize purchase of the necessary apparatus. For Collins, a decisive moment had arrived. Electricity was science. Nothing would more solidly affirm his status on the expedition as "scientist" instead of "mere accessory" than a brilliant and permanent electric-light show. Success was all the more imperative because his professional status, if ever seriously acknowledged by his commander and wardroom colleagues, had suffered marked erosion as a result of the missing developer.

Photography was a branch of "science" in which Collins had expected to excel. During the expedition's fitting out, he had been entrusted with the purchase of all necessary equipment. From Bradley and Rulofson in San Francisco he had bought for $65 a Double Swing Cone Camera made by the North American Optical Company. He had also obtained five hundred dry plates. The camera was first used in St. Lawrence Bay to photograph natives. "Mr. Collins engaged in making sketches and taking photographs," De Long noted on that occasion. And on 17 September, after a bear hunt, "We had the two bears photographed by Mr. Collins."

According to John Danenhower's subsequent recollection he had at that time assisted the meteorologist, "took the things on the sled and carried them out for him." But Collins produced no chemical developer, and after every box of plates had been thoroughly broken open still none could be found. There were plates of a different type on the *Jeannette*, called Beachey plates, and Collins experimented with the developer for these. All to no avail.

The only testimony afterwards elicited about the failure of the expedition to maintain a photographic record of events was one-sided and patently self-serving. De Long's journal provides no adequate information. The commander was not conversant with cameras and perhaps his lack of expertise on the subject (if not plain disgust at yet another frustration) accounted for the omission. The deliberate implication of that future testimony was incompetence on Collins's part for having failed to ensure, at the time of purchase in San Francisco, that the plates were accompanied by proper developing materials. The question of whether any of the photographic plates could have been developed when the party reached home was left unsettled.

So it was that by the time the electric light was to be tried out De Long's disenchantment with Collins had almost certainly intensified, and equally so the latter's sense of a need to prove himself. Showing some of his old zeal, heightened with a new urgency, Collins set up the Baxter steam engine in the deckhouse.

Manufactured by the Colt Arms Company of Hartford, Connecticut, Baxter steam engines were in worldwide use driving a variety of devices that included coffee grinders, lathes, sewing machines, and printing presses. In the *Jeannette*, the steam engine, a two horsepower model, was to both warm the deckhouse and keep the masthead lights ablaze. Collins had it belted to Edison's generator, a contraption whose most conspicuous feature was a pair of heavy field magnets about five feet tall, and steam was raised in the boiler. The engine started up and proceeded to run smoothly. Edison's generator did not.

De Long and Collins would not have known, of course, but one of the reasons the wizard of Menlo Park, after a year of constant experimenting, had not perfected a usable incandescent light by the summer of 1879 was his lack of a good dynamo. Edison (or, more accurately, his most skilled assistant, Francis Robbins Upton) did not effectively improve the generators at Menlo Park until about the eve of the *Jeannette*'s sailing, too late for De Long to have derived any benefit. The generator that Edison furnished the expedition with failed to respond, the galvanometer needle scarcely twitching. The mast-high necklace of lamps gave not a glimmer.

"Collins hopes to make it work yet," wrote De Long, little realizing with what agitation the meteorologist did so. The commander's worry was over his crew, whose spirits might be more sorely damaged by another bout of dashed prospects than the bright lights aloft would have buoyed them. Collins's fear was that the moment he slackened his efforts in uncertainty or defeat Engineer George Melville or others would take over the job. A few of Collins's puns might have helped relieve the tension just then, but he was evidently beyond any and instead found himself wrangling with the officers as to why the generator would not work. Melville and Master Danenhower argued that it must have gotten wet during the stormy crossing from Alaska to Siberia and its wires chafed of their insulation. The more the officers persisted in their opinion that the apparatus ought to have been given longer to dry out, the sharper grew Collins's resentment, as if he took their remarks as saddling him with responsibility for the generator's failure.

If anybody could get the generator working, George Melville was the man. De Long thought this, having repeatedly voiced amazement at the engineer's resourcefulness and ingenuity. Among his latest accomplishments were the design and construction of a shoe crimper for the footwear De Long had set the crew to making, along with clothes, out of the spare skins on board. "Among the natives, crimping is done with the teeth, but Melville has supplied a more effective apparatus." He had also just perfected a new and improved method for recording wind velocities by combining the Morse Telegraph Register with the anemometer.

Melville attacked the stubborn generator with characteristic gusto, completely unreeling the coils and reinsulating them. This and the rewinding took days. But despite all the effort, a new trial brought no results. Mindful of the fuel consumed for these experiments, De Long ordered that the Baxter's firebox be fed with walrus blubber instead of coal. This produced a terrible stench in the deckhouse. And still no spark of electricity. "I am afraid Edison's generator is irretrievably useless," De Long wrote on 15 October, "and our electric light has remained, not gone, 'where the woodbine twineth.'" Neither was Lieutenant Chipp having any better luck in his attempts to link the ship by telephone with the observatory across the ice. He had the instruments set up and the lines laid, but bare copper wire in the snow lost its conductivity. At the close of that last October week (the precise period when Edison, in faraway Menlo Park, secured incandescence in his lamp long enough to triumphantly declare electric light a reality), Lieutenant De Long wrote, "The hunters brought in three seals today, as a pleasant thing to contemplate after being disgusted with electrical experiments."

In the midst of those disappointing essays, De Long began one of his daily journal entries with the words: *"Collins' birthday"* (emphasis in original). Nothing follows in that penned record to explain why. Other than his own, De Long made no written references to the birthday of anyone else on the *Jeannette*. Collins's own thoughts on this particular anniversary can be imag-

93

ined in the light of subsequent events and declarations. He was convinced of having become usurped as the party's chief scientist. He had come to believe, following the episode of the "missing" camera developer and the failed electric light, that De Long had consciously embarked on a practice of assigning scientific tasks rightly his to others, leaving him to "infer by the withdrawal of instruments from time to time that I have either neglected or do not have the ability to use them." All of which adds a touch of mystery to the commander's terse but emphatic reference to Collins's birthday, something he was to repeat, leaving a minor puzzle that stirs conjecture and is not without pathos.

Man's efforts to generate electricity in the icefield having come to nought, the hyperborean elements staged a show of their own. This, at any rate, was the gist of the curt explanation volunteered by a still-smoldering Collins for the radiant ball seen at night first by Raymond Newcomb and later by some of the crew. The naturalist sighted the fireball as it hovered above the ice half a mile from the ship and thought it pulsated gently. It looked big as a full moon to one half-scared seaman, barrel-sized in Dunbar's awed estimate. The strange sphere would work to within five hundred yards of the ship, increasing in brilliance and swaying slightly, then retreat, sink to the ice and vanish. In the poopdeck cabin and in the wardroom beneath it, Collins's theory of a natural phenomenon was thoughtfully discussed. In the forecastle the sighting had inspired nervous jokes about signs and portents. After the berth deck lamp had gone out, more than one superstitious mind fell prey to uneasy thoughts.

ON ONE OF the last days of the month (a red-letter day for the ice-pilot Dunbar who shot three large walruses), clear skies gave Master Danenhower excellent sights for ascertaining the *Jeannette*'s position. She was drifting northwestward again. One thing De Long could congratulate himself on having settled: Wrangel Land did not extend across the top of the world. The *Jeannette* had more than half circled it, not from any design of the commander's, but in the process proving that Wrangel Land was not part of a transpolar continent. It was an island.

Now occurred De Long's first direct embroilment with Jerome Collins. The commander had issued new medical orders, feeling it essential that he be kept fully informed on the physical state of all in his charge. His self-sworn duty was to "regulate or remove any source of evil, whether arising from lack of variety or any quantity of food, insufficient ventilation, excess of labor, exposure to cold, or other circumstances." Consequently, he told the ship's surgeon to conduct monthly physical examinations of every man on the *Jeannette* "starting with me." This latter egalitarian gesture made no manifest impression on Jerome Collins. Already a severely hurt man, his pride scarred, he thought that having to strip down and be poked at by Doctor Ambler was an indignity which, as Bennett's handpicked civilian specialist and representative on the expedition, he should rightfully be spared. With concentrated patience, De Long explained the purpose of his order. Collins finally complied but with unconcealed sourness. De Long kept his temper throughout the incident, which he could have regarded as no more than a spat within his "little family," dismissing it from his mind, but which he would recall when it proved a foretaste of more serious trouble.

From such disagreeable tensions De Long sought relief in solitary nocturnal strolls on deck or across adjacent ice. Once he stood muffled in furs near the foremast, marveling at the awesome combination of spectacle and silence. The temperature had fallen to ten below zero, a balm compared with what he knew the deepening winter would bring. The moon hung full in a blue-black sky fulgent with stars. Against this shimmering background stood the *Jeannette*'s thickly frosted masts and shrouds in stark geometry. On such occasions De Long would wish that he could have shared the scene with Emma. Since he could not, the spell it cast upon him had usually dissipated by the time he returned to his quarters. "The pack is no place for a ship," he wrote, "and however beautiful it may be . . . I wish with all my heart that we were out of it."

Even so, De Long felt challenged to describe the natural wonders in his journal. Each attempt taxed his vocabulary. "These poetical outbursts are too much for me. I commence them and cannot finish them. I seem to know the tune but never remember the words." He wrote that the distant horizon was "clearly defined as a knife edge, the delicate new moon a little above it" and that his ship, every rope and spar swollen and fluffy with rime, looked as if "she had dropped out of fairyland." The soundless phenomena he witnessed on those glacial promenades—the visions of auroral radiance, of rippling streamers and ribbons, of meteoric streaks and flashes, all rainbow-hued and mirrored in miles of ice—stirred sensations within him for which it seemed no language was invented. What further distracted him from adequate expression was the *Jeannette*'s canine complement. He would try to find the right words to "express my feelings suitably. But a lot of dogs wrangling over an empty meat-can drag me down to plain matter of fact. So I take my half-frozen nose tenderly in hand and lead myself back on board ship." De Long's wry humor had evidently not deserted him.

It was a pity he could not record, to his own satisfaction, the emotional impact of the wonders he beheld, while he still had the chance. For those aesthetically overwhelming excursions on the ice were about to be cut short by outbreaks of nature's fury such as no man who had never experienced them could possibly have imagined, much less put into words.

It BEGAN 6 November "a day of extraordinary interest and some anxiety." Giant leads split into view with the noise of gunshots. On every side, black channels appeared as by magic, some racing to the far horizons and ramifying into a vast crazy network. Severed floes rammed and wrestled each other. Everywhere the pack seemed to be breaking up. De Long ordered the steam cutter hoisted in and came near to losing the observatory when a huge fissure appeared as if aimed right at it. Widening as it formed, the lead zig-zagged between the tent and the tripod. Only in the nick of time did a ship's detail dismantle the tent, gather up the thermometers, dip-circle, anemometer, and other instruments and scramble up the gangplank. An outhouse spun away on a floe. That night, like so many to come, rest was ruined by the incessant snap and screech of ice on the move.

De Long wondered if the sudden upheaval could be due to tidal action under some unpredictable lunar influence. But he had little time for hypothesizing. The ice basin cradling the *Jeannette* had begun to crumble. And although the first glacial spasms were for the most part at a safe distance from the ship, in the second week of the month hillocks of ice reared and crashed scarcely two hundred yards away. The turmoil was interrupted by sudden lulls of unforeseeable duration, themselves harrowing to the nerves because of the constant expectation of resumption.

Taking advantage of one such respite, De Long's men missed a brilliant aurora that their commander and Raymond Newcomb dutifully recorded. De Long thought the colorful sight began with "swirling tails" rippling across the firmament from north to east. The naturalist saw "six arches intersected by cirrus clouds near the horizon covering almost half the heavens. Throughout, the stars were twinkling beautifully. Some perpendicular rays near the horizon, the whole display full of majestic power. One could almost feel the electricity." The coruscating sky show was an overture to fresh turbulence much closer at hand.

At 4:00 A.M., 12 November, shouts from Newcomb arousing De Long were almost immediately drowned by the scream and thunder of convulsing ice. De Long doubled to the deck and climbed on the roof of the deckhouse, where he could hardly believe his eyes. All along the horizon, floes were on the march, in apparently random directions, at varying speeds and at odd angles, some overtaking those ahead and mounting them to form fantastic scalloped pyramids. Most of the *Jeannette*'s crew were quickly on deck, and, though shocked by gusts of the bitterest cold, they braced themselves to watch the distant tumult in silence and without panic. The men appeared to De Long as if mesmerized by the spectacle, furclad onlookers at a pageant, even as what was left of their ship's ice-cradle gave way more rapidly under the renewed and progressively fiercer reverberations.

By afternoon disaster seemed imminent. An icy column of thirty-foot-long slabs, which De Long likened to "a marble yard adrift," bore down on the vessel with the sound of artillery. It approached at the slow-torture speed of a man's walk. Sometimes ceasing to advance, the floes tossed in ferment as though they had paused only to fight among themselves. One such halt lasted long enough for De Long to think that the cruel game was in abeyance, that the diabolical intelligence controlling the ice had enjoyed its caprice for the day. But, in fact, lulls in the frozen bedlam were murder on already frayed nerves, and it was an almost merciful relief when the ice again ran riot. Gathering bulk as the floes telescoped and mashed each other, an enormous wall of dully gleaming white rolled head-on for the *Jeannette*. Its approach shook the vessel from truck to keelson. De Long had ordered stand to and the crew obeyed, but many now shrank before a storm of ice splinters. To the elemental din, worsened by the howling of frightened dogs, was added the murmur of human prayer.

The more stalwart of the *Jeannette*'s company shouldered past their trembling shipmates to join the captain and Lieutenant Chipp on the roof of the deckhouse. De Long grasped a mainstay, gave a last cry for all hands to hold firm, and before the first giant floes came thundering across the old ice under the *Jeannette*'s head-booms, officers and men alike had lunged at the nearest shrouds and were hanging on for dear life. The *Jeannette* shuddered as if possessed. Her decks bulged. The men clinging to ropes were tossed to and fro. Some were struck by hurtling cakes of ice, for as if alive the floes seemed attempting to board, leapfrogging each other to scale the ship's hull, wedge and hang above the bends or crash through the light upper bulwarks to whirl and skid down the sloping deck.

The assault ended as abruptly as it had begun. But the ice had not finished with the *Jeannette*. Besieged a further week or ten days she took repeated blows, broadside, port, starboard and sometimes on both beams at once. Shortlived spells of quiet provided no relaxation, for false alarms kept everyone on edge. The men remained fully clothed. Whenever peace descended it was too often shattered by unholy whoops and groans from the pack. Even when the ice seemed to tire of its tumbling and tossing, it was insidiously at work, squeezing the ship. Repeatedly the pressure started the deck from its beams, raised the timbers, forced pitch and oakum out of the seams. As De Long strode fore and aft, comforting his exhausted, shivering, and bleeding men, there were moments when he expected the deck to burst upwards in his face. But warped and bruised though she was, the *Jeannette* yet endured. De Long could now concede, however grudgingly, that the naval constructors back at Mare Island had known their business. Had they not reinforced the vessel internally as well as externally she would, before this, have collapsed amidships, cut in two.

One new morning revealed that the main body of the pack had retreated, gone raging off into the southern gloom. Some of the floes piled up against the *Jeannette*'s hull had slipped away in the night, so stealthily that four dogs asleep or moping alongside were lost before their howls could attract attention. The pressure on the ship noticeably lessened. De Long tried to calculate what next might occur, telling himself that as long as Bering Strait remained ice-free, there would be scope for the icy fist enclosing the *Jeannette* to relax its grip. But when that far-off channel froze over, bottling up the ice north of it, the pressure on the ship would surely increase. "Whether by wind or tidal action, the humping and piling up will go on around us. . . . Truly this is no pleasant predicament. Wintering in the pack may be a thrilling experience to read about alongside a warm fire in a comfortable home, but the actual thing is sufficient to make any man prematurely old. . . ."

The ice reformed around the ship. "We are again surrounded." But for all his anxiety he could still feel himself fascinated by the juxtaposition of hovering peril and indescribable grandeur. "While the great ice tables on the one hand tower above us to prevent our egress, the huge blocks on the other also clearly indicate 'No Thoroughfare.'" The ice continued its war of nerves. "The steady strain on one's mind is fearful. Seemingly we are not secure for a moment, and yet we can take no measures for our security. A crisis may occur at any moment, and we can be thankful in the morning that it has not come during the night, and at night that it has not come since the morning. Living over a powder mill waiting for an explosion would be a similar mode of existence."

But on 24 November he was able to write, "It has come at last. We are broken adrift from our floe! Our snug cradle of two and a half months split and shattered. . . ." Certainly that massive ice collar had finally disintegrated. Ice glued itself to the ship's sides now only as great scabs. Thus barnacled the ship spun before light breezes through "a kind of canal . . . sluiceway of running ice." Moonlight refracted by ice crystals and snow dust suffused the scene in a golden glow, and De Long thought he was "looking into fairyland." But this proved no pleasure cruise. The wind freshened. Freezing squalls struck the *Jeannette*, whirled her about until she scudded stern-first, "pushed, forced, squeezed, driven . . . amid a grinding and groaning of timbers and a crashing and tumbling of ice . . . fearful to look at. . . . All hands were on deck, grouped upon the deckhouse roof and the poop, while we were running this gauntlet." It was a nightmare ride through that frozen fairyland, the vessel at the mercy of the winds and charging ice, her captain and crew crouching and hanging on. It seemed an eternity but was only a matter of hours before the *Jeannette* broke through a breastwork of floes and hurtled into clear water.

The ship would be spared any further battering. The elements at last had spent themselves. "Even the distant ice-gorge that had force-ejected us out of it seemed to have come to rest." The lake into which the *Jeannette* had been catapulted quickly froze, ice pressing up against the sides until once more the ship's frames complained and the deck buckled. But nature had settled into frozen repose. "We hope to freeze in solidly for the winter that has already long since begun." The *Jeannette*'s people were all right, shaken but physically ship-shape except for cuts and sprains, to which the ever-patient and paternal Ambler attended. The surgeon, also Chipp, Melville, Dunbar and the scientists, appeared none the worse for their experience. And Danenhower? Often during the glacial onslaughts and that climactic wild ride De Long may well have glanced apprehensively at the navigation officer, alert for any manifestation of his former brain trouble. Doctor Ambler, back in Washington, had dutifully warned De Long that it might reoccur. But Danenhower seemed to have come through the strain and terror without unpleasant aftereffects. He, in fact, looked a lot healthier than the ship's surgeon. That, Lieutenant De Long might have told himself, was something to be grateful for in a situation where hazards abounded, prayers fell on deaf ears, and blessings were too few to be counted.

CHAPTER NINE

Danenhower's Secret

December 1, Monday. A halo about the moon. A mirage to the
southward of an open water space very clearly defined in the sky.
The usual monthly examination of officers and men was begun to-
day. I shall notice with much interest the result. I can see no change
for the worst from ordinary observations.

Journal of Lieutenant De Long

HARDLY A DAY passed that De Long failed to discuss the crew's health with
Surgeon Ambler. It was the commander's firm resolve that if disaster should
strike the expedition it would come from without, not from any neglect or
oversight in the medical department. Above all, De Long feared scurvy. The
scourge of polar exploration, scurvy had been most recently blamed for Sir
George Nares's failure to penetrate the Northwest Passage. De Long had
studied the proceedings of an official inquiry into that 1875–76 expedition
and noted the continued British emphasis on lime juice as an effective antiscorbutic.

Nares's mistake had been to depart from tradition by discontinuing the
issue of lime juice to his sled parties. De Long placed more reliance on good
nutrition than rations of lime juice as the best defense against scurvy. But
he soon felt that his party's daily diet of meat, fish, butter, milk, vegetable

juices, and fresh bread was of little avail if the water they all drank was insufficiently purified. "In my judgement, the primary and predisposing cause [of scurvy] has been the habitual use of water containing too much salt for a healthy condition of the blood." While unconvinced of the efficacy of lime juice, he knew "the importance attached to it by Arctic medical authorities and Arctic voyagers generally [and] did not care to depart from an established custom." In the first week of December, after consultation with Doctor Ambler, he ordered the daily issue of one ounce of lime juice per man, the antiscorbutic sugared for tastes that balked at its acidity. But he fretted more and more over the scarcity of drinkable water. Not much snow fell, and what little accumulated in the vicinity of the ice-locked steamer was soon consumed. De Long's crew had scraped clean all the floes that could be reached. He had put off distilling in order to economize on fuel. "If we have to distil water with the main boiler we shall use up a fearful quantity of coal." With distilling now the only recourse, he asked Melville if it could be done without using the main boiler. Melville thereupon resurrected the Baxter engine from below, where it had been stowed with the disgraced electric generator, and improvised a distilling system with it in the deckhouse.

The first yield tasted almost as salty as melted floe ice, a mystery quickly solved by the dependable Melville. The boiler fed through an iron feed pipe from a tank or starting tub on the roof of the deckhouse, and the seaman who hauled up the water from a hole in the ice alongside the ship occasionally spilled his bucket as he poured. In the subzero temperatures his clumsiness was perhaps excusable. At any rate, seawater splashed down and found its way to the two condensing coils, trickled into the fresh water cask, and contaminated the contents. Melville's remedy was to place a pan over the cask so that it caught the salty drops.

Even then, when Surgeon Ambler tested the water before its transfer to the galley, his silver nitrate continued to show up an unacceptable salinity. Melville promptly dismantled the whole system. Again his painstaking investigation pinpointed the trouble. Pumping cold water too quickly into the hot boiler caused a vacuum in the steam space, and the water then bubbling up threw a steamy salt spray through the distiller and into the water barrel. Melville repositioned the feed-pump at a safe distance from the steam space and made certain other adjustments to prevent too sudden or too vigorous an operation. When the boiler was next refilled and fired up, all worked well. The evaporator produced some forty gallons of salt-free water daily. The process did not drain as much fuel as the main boiler would have done. Even so, De Long wrote on 9 December, "it takes two pounds of coal for every gallon, will ruin us at this rate."

The year was ending. Before a new one had far advanced, De Long would be stunned by the virtual loss of that member of his team, his "little family," whom he had once described as irreplaceable. But he had no hint yet of that impending bombshell. In the middle of December, the source of his most acute exasperation was what he presumed with dismay to be an irreversibly churlish streak in the personality of the meteorologist, Jerome J. Collins.

De Long had decided that following their recent experiences, the physical tone of the *Jeannette*'s people could be fully restored, their ravaged nervous systems healed, by the resumption of daily exercise on the ice. He issued appropriate orders. Except for the duty watch, everybody had to be off the ship between 11:00 A.M. and 1:00 P.M. so long as it was not snowing and the mercury no lower than minus thirty degrees. All had obeyed with easy grace or, at worst, mock grumbling. All save one. De Long wrote of the unpleasantness in a report destined to surface under mournful circumstances. "From the earliest date Mr. Collins showed a disposition to disregard this order. At first he was merely reminded by me of his failure to obey and advised to be more careful in future." This had no effect. Collins would get up and breakfast late, and when his absence was noticed on the ice a man had to be sent to fetch him. He would stretch out his routine noontime task of making and recording meteorological observations as far as he could in an effort to dodge the exercise period.

De Long might have correctly diagnosed that Collins's attitude was related to the diminution of his standing in one area of "science" after another.

But the commander had little aptitude and no time for playing psychologist. One morning, when the men trotted dutifully down the gangplank onto the ice with Collins not among them, he strode to the wardroom and shook the meteorologist awake, reprimanding him "for repeatedly evading and disregarding my order." Collins at once "became impertinent and disrespectful, saying he took more exercise than any other, that he had his own opinion as to the wisdom or necessity of my order." Collins continued in this vein until De Long finally snapped, "I shan't tell you again. If you persist in disobeying my order, I shall be forced to take disciplinary action."

Considering the situation of his ship and crew, Lieutenant De Long probably had little clear notion of what form such action might take and hoped it would be unnecessary for him to elaborate. Collins doubtless sensed the other's dilemma and was tempted to take advantage. In a show of studied insolence he kept De Long in suspense for several more minutes before silently dressing himself and joining the men on the ice.

THERE SEEMED NO rhyme or reason to the *Jeannette*'s drift. At one point Danenhower reported that his observations indicated a triangular course, the ship fetching up at the same position she had occupied weeks before. They had crossed to well above the 75 degree line, were about 500 miles north of the Siberian coast and drifting in the pack further northwestward on a leisurely zig-zagging course. De Long was baffled. Nightly in the wardroom he conferred with his officers and the increasingly withdrawn Collins. But no amount of debate over pipes and brandy could break the uncertainty, pierce the curtain shrouding whatever lay in store. In the meantime, De Long had issued orders putting the ship on stand-by for emergency. The men must remain dressed at all hours, their outside furs within easy reach. Provisions, arms, and ammunition were to be kept on deck with the sleds and the dogs. Harness and traveling gear were conveniently tethered and stacked. And the boats were made ready for instant lowering.

Should the ice jaws begin finally to crush or devour no time must be lost in abandoning ship. None of the *Jeannette*'s company could foretell when the ice would turn on them again, perhaps for the *coup de grace*. In fact, De Long suspected, it had already resumed its assault in clandestine fashion, strengthening its stranglehold. For even as it carried the vessel along with it the pack was steadily thickening, crawling up the hull. He told off a detail to monitor its ascent and soon discovered that the ice was climbing the sides of the *Jeannette* at an average rate of an inch a day.

"We live in a weary suspense." It was telling more and more on the nerves. Card games, chess or backgammon in the wardroom, reading, smoking and chinwagging around the stove, nodding to the strains of a violin or harmonica from the forecastle, all were diminishing in the measure of relief they offered. The enforced familiarity was itself becoming a burden to the spirit. "We seem to get in each other's way." They had warmth and a degree of comfort in their cramped quarters, "but we would like to be able to go somewheres." Unable to foresee from one hour to the next whether the ice would remain quiet, De Long had decided against rebuilding the observatory. Detailed astronomical and magnetic observations were suspended. Meteorological sightings were still made and recorded, usually by Master John Danenhower since De Long could no longer count on a cooperative Jerome Collins.

Of the ship's company, only Dunbar and William Nindemann had spent a winter in the pack. The ice-pilot's sojourn was in Cumberland Gulf, his whaling ship "nipped" tolerably close to dry land. Nindemann never talked much about his service under Charles Hall at Thank God Harbor, an experience, it was suspected, he would sooner forget. Before the *Jeannette*'s season was half over De Long had formed his own view of wintering in the pack: Providence could never have conceived a harsher test of a man's temper or physical endurance. What rankled the lieutenant more than anything else in his specific circumstance was a manifest futility: "We are consuming provisions," he wrote on 9 December, "wearing out clothing, and burning coal to no good purpose."

But he had not lost his capacity to delight in the surrounding grandeur, the overhead magnificence. One night he watched a rainbow form above the moon. It expanded and became "a lunar halo in which all the prismatic colors were visible. Then flared up an auroral arch which absorbed the halo," and an hour later "the auroral arch became an auroral curtain, floating sheets of trembling flame down to the horizon. Our whitened ship, already agleam in the moonlight, reflected all these colors." The cosmic display ran its course in total silence but for the far-off rumble of restless floes and, now and then, the grimly familiar gunshot report as a metal bolt or other fastening sprang from wood frames deep within the trapped ship.

WITH THE COMMANDER'S permission Master John Danenhower announced to the crew that he would begin classes in elementary navigation. The response was enthusiastic. De Long was especially heartened for it was not merely a splendid idea. Danenhower had himself thought it up, further evidence if needed that his mental ailment was a thing of the past. De Long had already concluded as much, impressed as he was by the officer's demeanor during the tensions and terror of recent weeks. And he regarded it as infernally bad luck, nothing more, when Surgeon Ambler reported to him a few days before Christmas that the navigation classes would have to be postponed, Danenhower having developed an inflammation of the left eye that would require him temporarily to wear a blindfold.

De Long first noted this in his journal on 22 December, adding that the eye condition "is of no very serious character." The commander's recorded anxiety that equinoctial day (celebrated celestially by "a display of auroras far exceeding anything previous") dwelt chiefly on the extreme fatigue which several of the ship's company were feeling. Doctor Ambler's initial diagnosis of Danenhower's complaint was "a slight conjunctivitis . . . caused by the inferior light we are obliged to use." The navigator had been working from 5:00 A.M. daily, engaged in prolonged meteorological sightings and close paperwork by candlelight.

The passing of the shortest day touched off an appropriate optimism.

Signs were sought of returning daylight. Even as the Christmas week began, twilight was perceived as slightly stronger than moonlight—De Long noted with elation that "our shadows are faintly cast on the ice." But Christmas Day dawned without a semblance of good cheer. Clouds hung low and a light snow fell. Breakfast in the wardroom was bereft of ceremony, memories accumulating in the silence. In the privacy of his stateroom that morning De Long was unable to cast his eyes on the photograph of Emma and their seven-year-old daughter Sylvie over his bunk without emotion. Christmas threatened to be "the dreariest day I have ever spent."

Dinner in the wardroom, in substance quite a grand banquet, would have been a happier occasion "were it not that one of our mess did not appear at the table," an allusion to Collins, whose resentments had evidently become too much for him this holiday. As for the men, there had been talk of getting up a minstrel show, but this seemed to have fallen through. The day drew to its close with little enough done or spoken to mark its significance. Then De Long reminded himself that it was his duty to guard against lowered morale no less than scurvy. He ordered three quarts of whisky sent forward to the crew. In the forecastle at least, a toast would be drunk to distant loved ones. Happily, more toasts followed. De Long had achieved his purpose, "to inject conviviality." Led by Boatswain Jack Cole (recruited to the *Jeannette* from one of James Gordon Bennett's yachts), the crew came aft to wish the officers a merry Christmas and invite them to the deckhouse for some impromptu entertainment.

It was a hastily rigged affair whose main event was what De Long presumed to be a native Alaskan dance, performed by Alexey and the girlish Aniguin or "Queen Anne," as he was sometimes called. This gaiety inspired the crew to dust off earlier plans for something more elaborate, to be presented on New Year's Day.

At midnight on New Year's Eve the ship's bell welcomed 1880. The men were fortified by the four quarts of brandy De Long had ordered dispensed. The long-suffering band of thirty-three, which George De Long, with undiminished pride and feelings of close kinship, now wrote of as "our little colony," gathered on the quarterdeck in a temperature of 40 below and shouted three cheers for the *Jeannette*. Their voices echoed in the Arctic sky, which responded in its own matchless fashion, with auroral ribbons and a mock moon clinging to a blood red halo around the old one.

The following night at 8:30 when the officers entered the deckhouse they found the forty-foot-long timbered and felt-lined shelter converted into a theater, with flags, footlights, and a drop curtain. All available talent had been recruited. Even Collins had made the herculean effort of casting aside his obsessive grudges. He had composed a prologue in rhyme, humorous and sentimental and twenty-two verses long. It was now recited by Fireman George Boyd. Albert Kuehne and Adolph Dressler, two of the four seamen on the *Jeannette*'s muster roll with *no one* registered beside their names in the "next of kin" column, performed solos on the violin and accordion. Fireman Boyd and Seaman Henry Wilson sang and exchanged humorous insults. The cook and the steward, Ah Sam and Charles Tang Sing, had been armed with knives and poles and cajoled into what was announced as a demonstration of Oriental martial arts. Boatswain Cole danced a jig with, De Long thought, "the gravity of a judge." *Tableaux vivants* wound up the program, such pieces as "Sailors Mourning a Dead Marine"—two seamen mute with grief over an empty brandy bottle—drawing loud and boisterous laughter.

Master John Danenhower attended the concert with a bandage over his left eye. Surgeon Ambler sat beside him. Both officers applauded as vigorously as any in the audience, nothing in their manner betraying the oppressive secret these two shared that festive night and withheld from their commander.

Ambler, suspecting there was more to the navigator's optic trouble than at first appeared, gathered some facts in the dying hours of the year. He had been treating Danenhower for a conjunctival condition, affecting the inner surface of the eyelid, when he discovered that the iris looked sluggish, was contracted, and had a muddy color. He asked searching questions to which Danenhower, seemingly afraid of no more than that Ambler would certify him unfit for duty, gave hesitant responses. The doctor persisted—"received a history of his case"—and before the dawn of the new year had diagnosed Danenhower's complaint as syphilitic iritis.

Ambler was by no means inexperienced in these sorts of cases. He treated Danenhower with mercury for his general condition and began a routine of frequent atropine drops in the eye. These drops were to keep the pupil dilated and prevent or break up the glutinous exudate which, if allowed to accumulate unchecked, would adhere the iris to the lens of the eye and threaten blindness. It was essential to keep out even the limited Arctic light. Ambler ordered that a canvas screen be draped over the window and Danenhower confined to his quarters.

Why the doctor did not immediately report his discovery to De Long can be deduced from his medical journal. Danenhower had confessed that he had engaged the services of a private physician in the United States. Thinking that this treatment had cured him or would do so, he had sailed on the *Jeannette* without telling either the ship's medical officer or its commander of his infection. From what Danenhower had told him, Ambler decided that the doctor back home, probably some quack, had given him bad advice and the wrong medicine. Most worrisome, however, was that he, Ambler, had perforce assumed the burden of sharing Danenhower's secret. The doctor's dilemma can be imagined. Duty and compassion were in conflict. If he gave De Long the whole story right away, the commander would be compelled to take stern action against the navigation officer. Even were he not such a stickler for discipline, this must be De Long's solemn course when notified by the ship's doctor that Danenhower was diseased, had known it when the ship left San Francisco, and had deliberately kept the fact to himself. But there was Danenhower's old brain trouble to consider. What the man was already going through might be enough to bring on a recurrence. To add more could prove disastrous. A harsh reprimand from De Long, the inevitability of a court-martial once they were all returned to civilization, would prey cruelly on Danenhower's mind and perhaps plunge him back into that suicidal depression that had driven him from the warship *Portsmouth* into a padded cell. Reasoning thus, Surgeon Ambler took a gamble. With a few more days and a measure of luck, his administrations to the sick man might at least stabilize or control the condition. A full uncovering of the details to the commander could therefore be deferred.

So it was the doctor's turn to maintain sealed lips. But if providence rewarded his humane motives, the harrowing quandary would not persist. Ambler did go so far as to warn De Long that Danenhower might lose the sight of his left eye but withheld a complete explanation. De Long received the news with great distress, "for Danenhower is highly prized by all of us . . . his efforts have kept us many an hour from moping. He is now shut out from all participation . . . and we can do nothing but go down occasionally to sit and talk with him in the dark. He is cheerful enough, however, and having great force of character, has made up his mind to accept the situation and fight it out patiently."

As the days passed, though, Ambler was unable to report any improvement in Danenhower's condition. On 4 January, a Sunday when "a very brilliant meteor shot in a curved line from south to southeast and exploded like a rocket showing red, yellow and blue colors," Danenhower, huddled in his blacked-out room, suffered intense pain. Ambler increased the dosage of atropine to six drops an hour. One week after his grim diagnosis, when Danenhower's eye had become too sensitive to tolerate further drops, Ambler strove to relieve the patient's discomfort by applying lint soaked with opium. He had discontinued the mercury treatment when Danenhower complained of aching teeth and gums, the drug's adverse side effects. The atropine drops were resumed with still greater frequency, but the adhesion between the iris and the lens steadily thickened.

THE ICE HAD moved very little in weeks. It began to stir again, and the men of the *Jeannette* could hear its familiar grinding and booming. The commotion sounded so close to the ship that De Long, accompanied by Alexey with a lantern, set forth to gain some idea of where the new turbulence was centered. They trudged a thousand yards over the ice, the noise ahead swelling into a combination of "the howling of a gale" with "the beat of the paddlewheels of a hundred steamers." Then the lantern went out. The floundering return in total darkness, with the ice sometimes splitting underfoot, thoroughly dissuaded De Long from further inquisitive forays. It was safer to "await events nearer home." But he continued to wonder what the gelid world would do next.

If this uncertainty could play havoc with the nerves, just as unbearable to Surgeon James Ambler was the weight of the secret he shared with Master Danenhower. That maintaining silence conformed with the principle of confidentiality between physician and patient was all very well. But Ambler and the men for whose continued good health he bore official responsibility were adrift in the Arctic, not at home in civilization where such ethics could be obeyed with little risk or inconvenience. He could not, in any event, have indefinitely withheld the truth from De Long. Nothing in naval rules and regulations justified keeping one's commanding officer in ignorance regarding something that might affect the successful discharge of his duties. Besides, Danenhower's condition was becoming pitiably conspicuous. Mucous sores appeared in and around his mouth and erupted on both legs. On 17 January the doctor fully informed De Long about their navigation officer.

It was the coldest day the expedition had yet experienced, three thermometers capitulating at 42 below and a more robust model continuing to register an additional drop of six degrees. Lieutenant De Long's reaction to the doctor's story was a sorrowful resolve to bring formal charges against Danenhower at the first opportunity. He did not tell the afflicted man, doubtless at Ambler's persuasion. But he made a significant note in his journal: "Doctor Ambler reported to me a fact in connection with Danenhower's case, which I do not mention here, making this record merely to establish the date of the report in case of necessity for further reference."

The commander's innermost thoughts at that distressful moment can be guessed. Certainly the practical consequences of Danenhower's disability loomed large. For an unknown period De Long must be denied the services of a most valued officer. He and Lieutenant Chipp, Melville too, would have to shoulder some of Danenhower's duties. Others he would assign to Mr. Collins, whether that gentleman liked the idea or not. And so serious was Danenhower's affliction that it would command most of Ambler's time and labor, inevitably depriving the crew of the doctor's services. It is also inferable that the lieutenant felt himself double-crossed by an officer whose interests and well being he had always sought to protect, not the least energetically when he had struggled with the dilemma arising from Doctor Ambler's confidential report in Washington on Danenhower's past mental breakdown. Following that crisis, De Long's relationship with Danenhower had been nothing less than brotherly. All the more unforgivable, then, was Danenhower's willful deception.

Next day was a Sunday. De Long inspected the ship and read divine service in the wardroom. In Danenhower's darkened quarters the doctor had been applying atropine drops to the morbid left eye at an almost frantic rate. In addition he tried to stem the growth, at the same time lessen Danenhower's agony, by taking blood from his temple, using the artificial leech— scarifier and suction-cup—that was part of his medical kit. The doctor could only grope at his delicate tasks, for with light unwelcome he had to labor in the feeble glimmer of a candle. And because his hands had to be ungloved, he was obliged to repeatedly flex his fingers lest they grow numb in the cold that penetrated every corner of the ship.

The turbid substance in Danenhower's eye continued to thicken. Concentrated in the anterior chamber it had now begun to glue the iris to the lens. And this frightening development confronted the doctor with another decision, one he had scarcely bargained for and could not safely postpone: whether to cut directly into the eye and try to relieve it of that sight-threatening viscidity.

On Monday morning James Ambler had something else to contend with, as did every man on board the *Jeannette*. The hummocky ice welded to the ship's reinforced hull heaved into life. De Long had awakened much earlier, aroused after midnight by a bang like gunfire from somewhere abreast his room. Racing on deck he had seen nothing amiss and concluded that the sound was of a timber cracking under pressure or a contracted bolt or rivet bursting from its seat. He was again on deck five hours later, and this time faint reflections danced amid the ice, sure proof that it was moving. Before noon the disturbance subsided as suddenly as it had begun. The crew relaxed, deeming it another false alarm, only to have their complacency shattered by a breathless report from Walter Sharvell, coal heaver, that while passing through the engine room on a routine visit to the ship's bunkers he had heard the splash and gurgle of water in the forward bilges.

The *Jeannette* had sprung a leak. The latest spasm of squeezing upon an already strained internal structure had imposed fresh longitudinal and transverse stress. Despite the solid timber girding the *Jeannette*'s bows against the shock of ramming ice, the sea beneath the frozen crust had found an entry. Water stole through cracks somewhere in the blackness of the inner bows. A detail De Long rushed below with lanterns discovered a rising slushy flood already eighteen inches deep in the forepeak and steadily infiltrating the storeroom and forehold abaft of it. Even as De Long ordered the deck pumps manned and the port boiler fired to run steam pumps, water came swirling across the floorplates of the *Jeannette*'s engine room.

CHAPTER TEN

AGAINST THE SEA

Thursday, February 19. All our hoped-for explorations and perhaps discoveries, this coming summer, seem slipping away from us. I do not like to contemplate any further accidents although in our position almost anything might happen.

Journal of Lieutenant De Long

THE FIGHT TO save the ship became a complex exercise in quick thinking and improvisation, doughtiness, and technical ingenuity. As an urgent first step, the men removed all provisions from the forehold. Hundreds of pounds of flour, beans, oatmeal, and cornmeal were already spoiled and fit only for dog food. The main task was getting up steam to drive the pumps. Manual pumping alone could not contain the flood. In this regard, George Melville's abundant self-assurance and mechanical skills were tested as never before.

He had to activate one of the Sewell and Cameron steam pumps in the engine room, where the freezing inflow threatened to engulf the furnaces before either pump could be started. De Long had the gates of the forward watertight bulkhead shut tight in the nick of time, this being done by turning a control rod extending up through the spar deck. The seacocks were frozen fast in their seats, so the boiler could not be run up in the ordinary manner. Buckets of water had to be scooped from the fast-freezing bilge and poured from above through the manhole plates. Soon, Melville reported, "the steam giant was casting out water."

In reality the process was nowhere near as smooth or initially as successful as those subsequent words of Engineer Melville's might have implied. The steam pump's suction was on the port side of the ship. But because the vessel listed to starboard, the greater volume of water came off the starboard side, and the steam pump worked only when the water rose above the keelson and washed over to port. This had some advantage. The water was forced up through a fire hose to the spar deck and via a scupper to the ice outside. The hose kept freezing, and the interval of waiting each time for the flood to come under suction allowed it to be thawed out.

But the icy sea stole into the ship at a rate of sixty gallons a minute and would have to be pumped out directly and continuously instead of inter-mittently. On Melville's initiative, the men dismounted the other Sewell pump and carried it forward to what had been the ship's galley prior to its relocation on the spar deck. This was immediately above the flooding forward store room. They secured the pump in place against the berth deck bulkhead with a suction to the water below and connected it aft to the main boiler by lengths of piping. In De Long's words, "as the water won't come readily to the steam pump, we must get a steam pump forward of it."

The outside temperature had fallen to 40 below. The water froze in the forehold and threatened to choke up the limbers and pump suctions. "We certainly had ice enough to contend with outside, without having it inside as well." The mercury stood at 30 below in the engine room early next morning when the steam was turned on, and the pipeline had frozen and had to be taken down again for thawing out. The pump worked well on the second try, but the suction pipe proved too small. Melville replaced it with the bilge-suction pipe from the ship's main engine. Much of the work in-volved handling iron, painful labor in such terrible cold. By forenoon, though, everything seemed to be functioning well. De Long had earlier or-dered holes drilled in the forehold bulkhead to allow a freer flow of water aft to the engine room where the first steam pump could seize and expel it.

This had enabled the weary men on the hand-pumps to enjoy a breathing spell, with hot coffee prepared by the Chinamen and, at Doctor Ambler's insistence, a special ration of two ounces of brandy each. Once the flooded forepart of the ship was directly accessible to steam pumping, De Long had those holes plugged.

By the third day of the sea's invasion the two steam pumps—one working part-time in the engine room and the other fully operational in the old galley—were clamorously keeping pace with it, each at about forty strokes a minute. Even Edison's generator finally made a contribution. Melville had taken out the shaft and was using it as a countershaft for the pumping. But this very success added to De Long's chronic anxiety. Working two steam pumps simultaneously made alarming inroads on the *Jeannette*'s already-depleted fuel stocks. Again Melville cudgeled his brains, soon coming up with a more economical way of steam pumping than by wholesale use of the main boiler. Since the failure of the electric light experiment, the two-horsepower Baxter engine originally shipped on board as part of that project had served for water distilling. Melville now devised a gearing by which the Baxter could be adapted for running the hand-operated spar deck bilge-pump. This was no overnight job. Proper forgings and fittings had to be made at the blacksmith's forge, the Baxter disconnected from the condensing coils, pipelines and attachments rigged and tested, and hoses repeatedly thawed out. In the meantime all hands bent to save the ship, and none more unflaggingly than the carpenter William Nindemann and his mate, Alfred Sweetman.

De Long concluded after inspecting the flooded forepeak that the "solid filling" put in the bows at the Mare Island navy yard was "no more hindrance [to water] than that offered by the meshes of a sieve." Given his feelings just then the exaggeration was excusable. Theoretically, at least as De Long understood things, the filling had been intended to "make just so much solid bow to the vessel that the stem or forefoot might be sliced off"—which he surmised had in fact occurred—"and yet leave a waterproof surface." But because the filling extended only to the ceiling of the bows, it had no effect on the space between this and the bow planking. The calked close timbering and deadwood of the bows' extremity might have been expected to constitute a reliably tight and solid mass for that narrow area. But such was evidently not the case, water pouring from the seams of the "solid filling" and through countless unseen cracks and orifices. De Long had thought the situation called for an additional bulkhead, speedily built across the forepeak to seal off the incoming water and keep it under control of the steam pump overhead.

For this purpose Nindemann and Sweetman were assigned to the forehold. But the sea gained too rapidly, and instead of building a bulkhead the two men found themselves standing hip-deep in ice-clogged water for hours on end frantically plugging leaks with oakum, tallow, ashes, and felt pickings. The new bulkhead, of heavy oak, was to go up abaft the bow filling. De Long planned to let the space forward of the bulkhead fill and be carried as a watertight compartment. The possibility of its contents overflowing into the berth deck above had not escaped him. "Should we get under way again [we could] stanchion down the berth deck to prevent it springing up by pressure and the motion of the mass of water beneath." But it was clear that no matter how strong or how many, bulkheads in the present situation were no sure defense. Water found its way in and around the frames and through the flooring alongside the keelson abaft of the original forward bulkhead. By continuing to ram oakum and white lead and other materials into every leak their sleepless eyes fell upon, the indefatigable Nindemann and Sweetman succeeded in reducing the flow to tricklets, but no sooner had they begun to cut and fit planks for the extra bulkhead when water burst upon them from the seams of the ceiling on each side.

The two men waded through waist-deep slush to the hatchway and climbed to the berth deck where they crawled under the lower tier of berths and cut through into the saturated ceiling. They shoved quantities of cinders, tallow, even oatmeal, deep down, pushing them into the furthermost recesses, "filling every nook and cranny." Still the leaks persisted. De Long feared that so much of the outside planking had been torn aside that some of the ashes and other materials were falling into the sea below. Nindemann and Sweet-man returned to the forehold, managing to complete the extra bulkhead. After the calking was done, they began ripping away the ceiling above and below the bilge strakes to cram yet more filling among the icily sodden timbers. The lower part of the ceiling was teak and had literally to be splin-tered out.

Hour upon hour, for almost three weeks this hardy twosome, "N & S" in De Long's journal, toiled in near darkness, standing in ice-choked water seldom below their knees and enduring a temperature never above minus 30 degrees. (De Long made a special notation recommending to the secretary of the navy that the pair be awarded Congressional Medals of Honor.) A barrel of plaster of paris shipped at St. Michaels for Raymond Newcomb's natural history work was broken out, De Long hoping that if this too was thrust down between the frames it would mix with the incoming water and form an impassable barrier. He had ceased to believe that a forepeak bulkhead would stem the flood. Under present conditions the perfect bulkhead would have had to extend to the ship's planking and rest against a frame on each side, and the cutting of bilge strakes that this would entail might fatally weaken the ship. Hence the carpenters' desperate improvisations in the for-ward depths. "Unless we can unite all the materials rammed down into the interspaces into a watertight cement, and so prevent the ingress of water, all the bulkheads . . . that could be built in our forepeak would not prevent the water from flowing aft."

For ten weeks the sun had not appeared. But working in the dark had more than one meaning for the men of the *Jeannette*. Their commander was constantly perplexed, chafing against enforced ignorance. Melville and the two Alaskan hunters had tried chopping the piled-up ice from under the ship's headbooms in an attempt to reach the stem and search for the injury. But water kept breaking through the intervening layers to fill each excava-tion, promptly freezing to form new ice. De Long could only suppose that the forefoot was broken, that some of the ship's planking had sprung. Whether the practice of stuffing the vulnerable spaces with what he half-humorously described as "Arctic concrete" could be finally effective depended on how much of the ship's frame was exposed to the sea by the damage to garboards and outside timbers. For all he knew, the keel was broken along a considerable distance and the garboards wrenched open, the sea creeping in along half the length of the keel or more. He could do little more than speculate, and inwardly rage at the enveloping ice that could both wound his ship and brutally deny him any means of ascertaining the nature or extent of her injury.

But he was profoundly impressed and gratified by the crew's showing in this latest crisis. Nindemann's and Sweetman's conduct and devotion to duty were beyond praise. All hands from the berth deck had proved their mettle, and De Long was pleased to construe this as vindication of the policies and practices of command which, not always surefootedly, he had pursued. "Everything is carried out systematically," he wrote. All showed grit and good humor even though each watch, piped below in turn, regularly found the berth deck too cold and waterlogged for comfort. The incessant noise alone would have destroyed sleep. If the ship had to be abandoned, sleds were waiting on the poop, packed with forty days provisions. The ship's two cutters and the whaleboats were ready to lower, and two dinghys secured to their sleds. Every man had his knapsack and sleeping bag on hand "and our records and papers [are] in condition to seal up in a box." De Long and Lieutenant Chipp each stood twelve hours watch and the ice-pilot Dunbar, oldest of the party, more than pulled his weight. As for the ship's engineer, "when Melville does go below, instead of sleeping he lies awake planning some [new] means of pumping a ship by steam." De Long added: "Danenhower is, of course, out of the case altogether. A very disagreeable feature in connection with our trouble is that we have a sick man on our hands . . . unable to help himself in . . . an extraordinary emergency."

Danenhower's private ordeal reached new heights of intensity even as momentum had gathered to drive out the sea. On 22 January Nindemann and Sweetman were in the forehold at their valorous attempt to build a bulkhead. Water flooded the *Jeannette* at a rate of three thousand gallons an hour. The ship rang with the clank and shudder of manual and steam pumps. At this tense juncture, Doctor Ambler told a fatigued De Long that unless surgery was performed at once on Master Danenhower's left eye, its sight would go. Despite the artificial leeching and the atropine, the gummy adhesions of the iris to the lens had multiplied. They could be broken down only by cutting through the cornea into the anterior chamber. Considering the difficulties under which he would have to work, Ambler could offer no assurance that the operation would be successful. The attempt might make matters irretrievably worse. De Long responded that the patient ought to have a voice in deciding whether or not to risk it. After some imaginable mental agonizing, Danenhower gave his assent.

With Danenhower stretched on his bunk before him, Ambler went to work. Limited quantities of brandy, opium, possibly morphine, were all he could utilize to deaden the patient's pain. They would not be enough, and he could only pray that Danenhower might draw on superhuman powers of toleration. In the absence of an ophthalmoscope the doctor had to make do with a magnifying glass. His only illumination was candlelight, his only warmth what filtered into the curtained room from a dying wardroom stove. He had to shut his ears against the rhythmic clamor of pumps, the incessant splash and drip of water. Two seamen gripped his patient's arms, a third the legs. Knife and probe held between half-numbed fingers, Ambler proceeded to puncture the cornea, then to delicately explore the inner eye. In the *Jeannette*'s medical kit were an aspirator to evacuate pus and a bougie, the flexible wax or india-rubber type of probe. The record Ambler made in his journal was tersely professional: "Performed paracentesis corneal and let out a lot of turbid fluid, operating on the temporal side." Lieutenant De Long occasionally looked in, and the commander's disgust with Danenhower was momentarily tempered by awe and respect. The operation was "beautifully performed by Doctor Ambler and borne with heroic endurance. I hardly know which to admire most, the skill and celerity of the surgeon or the nerve and endurance of Danenhower."

* * *

As the main event of 26 January the commander recorded the reappearance of the sun. He ordered all hands except Danenhower to turn out and briefly enjoy the pleasurable novelty of capering in genuine solar shadows. Even Nindemann and Sweetman were permitted on deck to expose their bleached faces to a few minutes sunlight before hurrying back to their vital post below. Save for this break, nothing interrupted the critical routine. The day after the sun's diffident return all effort was brought to bear on the Sewell pump in the engine room, and for a time it ran at a lively fifty strokes a minute, ejecting a thousand gallons of water an hour. Also working well was the Baxter engine Melville had rigged to the spar deck bilge-pump, although the boiler had to be blown dry every twelve hours to prevent it from choking up with salt. During each delay (the fires having to be hauled, the boiler emptied then refilled, the coals relit), pipelines froze and more water accumulated in the forward section of the vessel.

Still, the Baxter engine proved as adaptable to driving the hand bilge-pump as it had in the distillation process, now the work of the main distiller in the engine room. Depleted coal bunkers remained De Long's nightmare. Anxious to do away with fires under the main boiler, he had Melville seek ways of connecting the steam cutter's engine and boiler with the bilge-pump attached to the main engine. "If the steam cutter's engine will do the work aft," he wrote, "with the Baxter boiler forward doing its share, our fuel will last twice as long." The cutter's boiler and engine were duly removed to the engine room but a new gearing had to be made to facilitate a connection. Wrote De Long on 6 February, "To bring our main engine bilge pump under control of the steam cutter engine Melville goes on with the work of converting a circle piston pump into a 3-inch plunger pump." When this task was completed and the cutter's boiler filled to supply the steam instead of the main boiler, its furnace was found to be too small to keep up a continuous pumping. Melville cut down the bridge wall of the furnace and replaced its 9-inch grate bars with spare ones twice as long, thus increasing the grate surface. Further dogged and intricate labor was required from Melville's "engineer force" before success was achieved, De Long meanwhile marveling that at no setback did George Melville register the slightest discouragement.

By the middle of February the *Jeannette*'s expertly rigged emergency pumping system was in full and economical, if precarious, operation. The sea had by no means capitulated. It continued to steal in through the ship's bows. But flooding the forepeak it came within suction of the Baxter-driven spar deck bilge-pump, and what escaped aft kept the steam cutter engine running. This combined operation reduced and then eliminated dependence on the Sewell pumps, also rendering hand pumping all but unnecessary. Water purification too—the work of the main distiller in the engine room since the Baxter boiler was fired for pumping—could henceforth be performed by the steam cutter engine when it was not pumping the bilge out. To his overwhelming relief, De Long was able to haul fires under the main boiler and record that the flow of water into the ship had fallen from a peak rate of 4000 gallons an hour to 1650, and fuel consumption for pumping alone from 1500 pounds a day to 400. Less than a hundred tons of coal remained in the *Jeannette*'s bunkers.

There was no opportunity to celebrate even had De Long a mind to. In the third week of the month water broke in on the berth deck, frothing out from beneath the bottom bunks. The cause was apparent. The berth deck lay below sea level. The filling thrust down between the frames had cemented as intended only too well. Sealed off at that level the water had mounted to force an outlet above it. Once more the services of "N & S" were summoned. The pair drilled holes in the berth deck floor to let the incoming water drain off into the forepeak then sprawled themselves under the lower tiers plugging cracks with their "Arctic concrete."

Meanwhile, water for cooking and drinking had acquired an unpleasant taste. The reason for this was quickly obvious. As the steam cutter's boiler fed from the bilge, the yield from distilling came of water that had poured into the ship. "With sea cocks frozen solidly in their seats, getting a supply directly from the sea was no easy matter and a thawed valve soon froze hard again." Not until Engineer Melville managed to get a Kingston valve open did they feed the little boiler from pure salt water. De Long had never ceased to regret the necessity for distilling. As he now noted, "One of my ideas, that fresh water . . . could always be obtained in the Arctic regions, has been thoroughly exploded."

The *Jeannette*'s thermometers registered February's average temperature as minus 30 degrees. The many thousands of gallons of water pumped out of the vessel froze at once, and by 6 March "we had manufactured so much ice by our own steady pumping through the scuppers that it stood level with our rail on the starboard the length of the ship." The accumulating ice added more weight to what already held her down. The heavier the ice, the lower the vessel sank in the water. Clinging to the ship's side, the ice tended to drag her down with it. And the lower the ice sank, the more it was bound to increase the water pressure against the ship's bottom and thereby intensify the leak. By their very success in a desperate bid to keep the *Jeannette* afloat, her people were strengthening the jaws of their own ice-trap. Measures for self-preservation had thus acquired a suicidal cast. It was a diabolical predicament, and De Long realized that only the early advent of spring could bring salvation. He and his shipmates were in a race against time, for the *Jeannette* might not last that long. If she were not dragged under by the ice, it might crush her to pieces. Every so often it took two men to open the poopdeck cabin door and the poopdeck bowed out of shape, unnerving evidence that the ice intermittently squeezed as if testing the *Jeannette*'s ability to withstand a death grip.

The temperature refused to rise. Now the ice towered above the starboard rail. De Long had his men working in shifts, chopping at the surrounding mass with pickaxes and crowbars in an effort to get down to the sea for a direct discharge of the pumped water. But cast-iron striking the ice simply split or blunted. "A piece of walrus liver frozen at this temperature stripped the edge of a razor as if the blade were made of plaster." Not until the second week in March did the mercury climb, and then no higher than to 20 degrees. But the men had succeeded in hacking out a trench four feet wide and twenty-five feet long along the port side, relieving some of the pressure on the ship. Their task revealed awesome visual evidence of how tightly the ice had encased the ship: In the glacial blocks riven clear of the hull not only was every seam shown, the very fiber of the elm doubling had left its imprint.

De Long decided against reassembling an observatory on the ice, because a sudden breakup might result in the loss of valuable instruments. The expedition's astronomical observations were therefore confined to the determination of latitude and longitude with sextant and artificial horizon. Care was necessary to get the sight quickly before the mercury froze, and as one's fingers were "like sticks," they could not readily manipulate the tangent screw. By the time this could be done the horizon glass and the index glass had frosted over and one had then little recourse but to retire to the wardroom or poopdeck cabin and thaw out.

Usually Lieutenant Chipp took the observations, a duty formerly that of Master Danenhower, still "hors de combat . . . [his] sickness throws the work out greatly. With our small number, one less affects us seriously."

As the month of February closed, the navigation officer writhed in pain. Ambler had repeatedly to cut into the eye, tapping the cornea to prevent or control the deadly agglutination. At times, Danenhower had fought off the doctor as he approached. For a while Ambler himself had endured pain, that of neuralgia, and was then "afraid to trust my hand or eye." But neither could he relax his struggle against the recurrent adhesions in the left eye of his patient. In the next six months he would operate on it fifteen times. On 3 March he performed the seventh incision; forty-eight hours later the upper portion of the cornea had refilled with purulent matter and had again to be pierced and drained. "The knife and probe are regular things in his case now," wrote De Long. "There is no improvement. He bears his confinement and the pain of the operations heroically. But he will never be of any use to the expedition and I seriously fear can never be of very much use to himself."

*   *   *

LIEUTENANT DE LONG'S own eyesight was far from perfect, having been defective since his youth. Now he noted a curious means of improvement. When their velvet-rimmed snow-goggles frosted up too quickly, some of the men had resorted to horsehair eye-guards. De Long tried them and "found my nearsightedness was consistently overcome . . . enabling me to see farther and clearer than with the naked eye. It is worth investigating by an oculist some future time."

De Long's quickness to recognize novelty and variegated phenomena was as a restorative whenever his spirit succumbed to the depressing realities of the *Jeannette*'s situation. "The amount of care and anxiety in my mind," he wrote in those late winter weeks, "trying to plan all things for the best, will last me for a lifetime." Yet he could find cause for relief if not rejoicing in the fact that "since January 19, when we were injured, we have had no serious conflict with our enemy."

He was aware that the "enemy" still besieged the ship, at intervals ominously stirring. But the morale of his crew, as far as he could detect, remained high. This was all the more gratifying when one compared living conditions in the sopping berth deck with those of the relatively dry poop-deck cabin and wardroom. De Long had heard no significant grumbling among the men. They seemed only too grateful that the ship was being pumped out by steam instead of their overtaxed muscle. Also, De Long could commend himself on having maintained safe and sound discipline, in no small part through an adherence, as far as was practicable, to proper naval routine and tradition. For instance, Sundays would see a general muster when he would read the Articles of War "with all the seriousness that would prevail in a frigate. The clause providing that all offenses committed on shore shall be punished in the same manner as if they had been committed at sea is read with as much impressiveness as if we were in a port, full of sailor temptations." Then would follow divine service in the cabin, his congregation seldom more than five "although there was no fear of my taking up a collection." On the birthday of his boyhood hero, George Washington, he had ordered his icebound ship dressed with American ensigns at the mastheads and a Union Jack forward.

But it was frightening to discover, with the onset of spring, how the ice, as if defeated in an overt attempt to destroy the ship, had reverted to more insidious tactics. It wormed its way through the ship, formed in every crack and keyhole, found dark corners in which to swell. The officers' quarters aft had not escaped infiltration. Bone-dry compared with the forecastle, this area appeared now to be a furtive and fertile breeding ground for ice. In De Long's stateroom, ice glued his secretary bureau to the wall; a slab almost a hundred pounds in weight took possession of a lower drawer, and he had to attack it with hammer and saw to get at a pair of pantaloons.

The cold held apparently no terrors for two of the ship's company for whom, next to his adroit engineering officer and the carpenters "N & S," De Long had the greatest admiration. They were Ah Sam and Charley Tang Sing, an unfailingly polite and imperturbable pair who could go bare-armed in subzero air to throw away their dishwater with never a frostbitten finger or even chapped hands. Their two berths curtained off in the galley were models of neatness. As soon as the weather permitted, they were on the ice flying colorful kites, a sport from which they derived such glee it was an entertainment for the rest of the crew to watch them. When working, they would leave their kites still aloft, strings tied to a boat davit. They were "impervious to all . . . ever cheerful," had apparently "no concern for the future, no cares for the past." De Long wrote of the attributes of these two disarming Chinese at considerable length and with a transparent envy.

Lieutenant Chipp flew kites too, but his purpose was scientific research. He was a student of electrical phenomena and had had experience with torpedoes. Combining these two interests, he discussed with De Long the possibility of making mines out of small kegs and powder that could be used to blast away the ice between the ship and any lead that might appear at a reasonable distance off. Auroras fascinated Chipp, and acting on a recommendation from the Smithsonian Institution he had kept a detailed record of galvanometer readings during periods of peak activity. Chipp's attempts to provide the expedition with telephonic communication were unsuccessful as were those he made to free the ship with torpedoes, but not for the want of effort.

About twenty dogs remained on the *Jeannette* and had become pets or companions more than creatures of servitude. In this latter respect, when the infrequent opportunity arose they had hardly performed with bounding devotion, yet even then they provoked as much amusement as exasperation. De Long and Melville hitched a dozen up to a heavy sled for a cruise. The commander wrote afterwards, "I had almost believed I knew how to manage a dog team but changed my mind today." Ignoring the whiplash the dogs preferred to frolic and in a comic reversal of roles were half dragged by the two officers for about half a mile, at which point the dogs "had it all their own way . . . tore us back to the ship."

The animals had suffered badly from the efforts to pump the vessel with a minimum fuel consumption. While the main boiler was activated, it had been possible to steam the concentrated dog food shipped at St. Michaels, but once the fires were hauled the food was put out brick-hard. Toothless dogs struggling to masticate with gums were robbed by those with sound jaws. De Long drew the problem to Melville's attention. The engineer quickly rigged a pipeline from the Baxter boiler, carrying steam into a barrelful of dog food and thawing it.

Some of the dogs had been christened: On 17 March "put green ribbon around the neck of a dog named Paddy." Snuffy was a less fortunate member of the pack, having had his nose bitten and broken at St. Michaels. But so bravely had he survived, so solicitously was he cared for by another dog, Jack, who "watches him, protects him from the others, leads him . . . cleans him," that although infection had caused his head to swell about twice normal size, no one had the heart to shoot him. When Snuffy's condition so worsened that his continued existence would have been inhumane, De Long ordered him shot and wrote a twelve-line requiem to which, perhaps suddenly reminded of how his own spiritual condition threatened to deteriorate, he added, "Again, I say, how long, O Lord, how long?"

The dogs threw themselves with snarling vigor into bear hunts and chases, as if aware that they would partake in the resultant feast. Polar bears supplied the expedition with its principal sustenance in those first months of 1880. Some of the bears were themselves starving. One attempted to board ship, attracted by the meat of an earlier kill hung up to a girt line. The bear first tried to climb the ship's side and reach the deckhouse. He fell back, recovered, and was shambling up the gangplank when Dunbar felled him with Winchester fire. So large grew the stock of bear meat on board that even the imaginative cooks ran out of menu ideas. Chipp produced a recipe for sausage balls, mincing pork with bear meat and adding powdered herbs, but "bears are becoming so common now we feel we want some ducks by way of a change."

Above all, the commander longed for motion. Four months ago at winter's beginning he had hoped that "December will drift us quietly and peaceably nearer the Pole and bring us to some land where we can have at least the merit of discovery if not of exploration." This had not come about. His hopes revived with the new spring. Calculating from the positions of the sun at noon and Venus in the evening, he determined that the ship had lately drifted northeast. At the same time daily soundings showed an increasing depth to sixty fathoms or more. Perhaps the *Jeannette* was destined for a northeast passage instead of to the Pole. "My prayer is that we may go on until we come out into the Atlantic Ocean." The ice had started to melt but was "wasting too slowly for me."

April had brought eighteen hours of sunlight daily and six hours twilight, in all enough light to navigate the ship "were we only free." Lanes opened in the ice but too few, too short, or too far off. The most coal De Long expected to have on hand come summer was about sixty tons, at least half of which must be held in reserve for a possible second winter in the pack. The leak had been reduced to some two hundred gallons an hour, but pumping continued to deplete his fuel supply. He had ruled out hand pumping except as a last resort, convinced that constant manual labor would enfeeble the crew. He began wondering aloud about using wind power to drive the pumps and was not entirely surprised when Melville interrupted with a confident, "Can do it."

Before the end of the month Melville's windmill, mounted on a plywood tripod, rose above the starboard side of the *Jeannette*'s bridge. It connected through the deck to a bilge pump in a corner of the engine-room hatch, and its sails, made of hammered-out tin cans with a total surface area of thirty-six square feet, rattled merrily in the lightest breeze. Working the pump at forty strokes a minute in an 8 m.p.h. wind, it was a contraption "worthy of being handed down to posterity." When the crankshaft broke in a sudden strong gust Machinist Walter Lee improvised a new one from portions of Edison's already well-cannibalized generator. By the middle of May, Melville's windmill powered practically all the pumping.

Summer began. "To have come so far and accomplished nothing is very trying," De Long wrote on 20 May. "Something must be done, for we cannot rest content with a blank score. It is terrible for me to contemplate that the *Jeannette* has traveled so many thousands of miles under my command only to overwhelm me with confusion." The drift of the ice and its captives had once more veered northwest. Because of the ship's ever-changing position magnetic observations of any value were difficult to obtain. Yet in all other respects a steady and emphatically reassuring routine was upheld, even though every book had been read, all stories told, and games of cards, chess and checkers long since abandoned, in the officers' quarters at any rate. Over breakfast, the officers would relate dreams and theories, the wardroom complement smoking afterwards (De Long puffing on a cherished meerschaum he had recently lost on the ice and Dunbar had found). Chipp would get a sounding, announcing a drift southeast—backwards—"and we growl thereat." Melville might sing and Danenhower, unable to see who if any were within immediate earshot, "talks incessantly, on any and all subjects, with or without audience." Doctor Ambler moralized, Newcomb made his preparations for dredging and "Collins has not appeared, his usual hour being 12.30."

As the ice wasted, more of the vessel emerged into view. She was losing her ice shroud and "we have noticed she has come up, cradle and all." The men cleared her wet and cluttered decks and suspended themselves over her sides, scraping and painting "as if we were in harbor with other ships to look at us." Once the ice allowed them to hang the rudder again and make sail, "we will have the old girl in fine cruising order."

The ice about the ship emitted uncanny noises as it waned before the sun: a prolonged buzzing, an occasional scream, the boom of a cannon. It was treacherous to traverse, although Raymond Newcomb ventured forth daily to chase a lone raven or return with a handful of dead mosquitos, "the first entomological specimens," he wrote on 20 June, "collected after we entered the Arctic Circle." In subsequent weeks he would add jaegers, kittiwakes, and phalaropes to his other trophies and another rare Ross gull. "Natural History is well looked out for," De Long noted. "Any animal or bird that comes near the ship does so at the peril of its life." This, of course, excluded the dogs, "our hoodlum gang," sprawling in the accumulated ashheaps all day or fighting among themselves. A scientific routine was rigidly adhered to, the dredge regularly lowered and hauled, soundings taken, and specific gravities, wind force, and temperatures logged. Astronomical observations were made and positions computed, dip and declination of the needle observed and recorded, "everything we can do is done as faithfully, as strictly, as mathematically, as if we were at the Pole itself."

Supper followed the posting of the ship's position in the cabin and "when the noise subsides and those who can are asleep, I write up the log and my journal." Meteorological observations were made at midnight, and nocturnal watches the commander shared with Collins, the doctor, Lieutenant Chipp, and Melville. Sometimes the silence was so painful that a promenading De Long would retreat to the cabin "where my kind could be seen and heard." In the solitude of those Arctic nights he could reflect that there had indeed been accomplishments, if of a negative nature. Someone had once told him that no sledding could amount to anything over the rough ice to be encountered north of Bering Strait. This he would have now only too readily confirmed. "If anything should force us to abandon ship, we would be unable to drag enough provisions to enable us to reach Siberia." He could also have boldly stated that Arctic explorers who looked to melted ice as a reliable source of drinking water courted disaster. With equal emphasis he could claim to have proven that Wrangel Land was not joined to Greenland in a single transpolar continent. Several tantalizing glimpses of its shore due south had convinced De Long, correctly, that Wrangel Land was an island.

And there was that magic thermal current. The *Jeannette*'s erratic movement was the result of winds. The Austrian explorer Carl Weyprecht had stated that instead of the Gulf Stream out of the Atlantic regulating the limits of northern ice, it was the ice, set in motion by winds, that dictated the limits of that mighty current. De Long now thought Weyprecht probably correct. As indicated by the *Jeannette*'s present plight, this certainly seemed to be true of the opposite side of the Pole from the Atlantic. "No current of regular direction or velocity exists this far northwest of Bering Strait." Any warm stream up through Bering Strait would have been the Kuro Siwo, out of the Pacific, and he had found not the slightest evidence of any such current reaching the high latitudes. In a most decisive and risk-fraught fashion, the *Jeannette* party had ratified the findings made public at home in a government report that the expedition's leader was fated never to read. On the night of 3 June 1880, bent over his journal in the quiet of the state room, De Long himself made no bones about it. "I pronounce a thermometric gateway to the North Pole a delusion and a snare."

But most nights before falling into an uneasy slumber, De Long would stubbornly insist to himself—ascribing the inner voice to "a certain indefinable, inexplicable something telling me"—that "all will come out right yet . . . [that] this can hardly be the ending of all my labor and zeal."

CHAPTER ELEVEN

ANOTHER LONG NIGHT

Sunday, September 19. We shall stick to the ship as long as she sticks to us.

Journal of Lieutenant De Long

PLUCK AND INVENTIVENESS had combined to meet the sudden crises of the *Jeannette*'s first winter in the ice. With the passing months of 1880 a special brand of fortitude, consisting of patience, loyalty, and sufferance, had more and more manifested itself. The men held on, thinking that the warmer temperatures of summer should melt the pack and bring on liberation. They could, in fact, see the ice begin to shrink, at first leaving slush then pools on the surface of floes. Yet, even by the middle of June, the ice, as measured at a sounding hole a hundred yards on the ship's starboard side, was still four feet thick.

The *Jeannette* shone in the sun, her decks scoured and squeegeed, her sides newly scraped and repainted. But with each passing day it became clearer that the ice was not melting fast enough. Winter would catch the *Jeannette* still icebound. Her bunkers held perhaps fifty-six tons of coal, thirty of which must be kept for warming, cooking and distilling. The remainder De Long calculated would permit five days steaming, if such opportunity arose. "And with this I have to make the Pole, accomplish the Northwest Passage, or go back emptyhanded. It makes my heart sick to think of it."

He would have been comforted somewhat had the ice carried them toward their goal. But in this regard his meteorologist had made an accurate forecast, for which he was in no mood to give the man credit. Earlier in the year, Jerome Collins had predicted that the fresh winds that were then pushing them to the northwest would persist only until June, when the winds would veer from the southeast to the northwest. This had proved dismally true. And the sun, ordinarily inducing cheer as a source of light and warmth, cast its own mockery, "for as observation of that luminary determines our position, we are informed on each occasion how far we have gone backwards, how much nearer we are to the South Pole and how much farther from the North Pole."

A change crept into the style of De Long's journal entries, reflecting something of the mortification he felt at his lack of success. More and more his subjective references took a plural form. "Some of us think the food we eat and the coal burned to cook it are utter and absolute waste. Of what avail are health and energy if we can make no use of them?" Notwithstanding their best efforts he could perceive no outcome but that, instead of adulation and a proud place in the history books, "we and our narratives [will be] thrown into this world's dreary wastebasket and recalled . . . only to be vilified and ridiculed." And again, "The knowledge that we have done nothing [is] almost enough to make me tear my hair in impotent rage."

De Long's use of the first person plural echoed the spirit of fraternity in which he had once written of "my little family" and "our little colony." But now it also served to emphasize his awareness that the torments of frustration were not exclusively his. A sense of futility must also burden the men he led. Had led them where? The question alone was enough to make him shudder. Facing his men daily had become an acute humiliation. And he was apprehensive lest the atmosphere of failure and pointlessness nurture dissension. None of his crew was a regular navy man. Mustered into government service for convenience's sake, the crew members had never been exposed to naval discipline, had no grasp of naval tradition. De Long believed that he had secured their trust and respect early in the voyage (as Emma had advised him to). But that was when all hearts were full of hope and bold expectation. Could he still count on their unswerving loyalty? Doubts, if not already entrenched, must have gathered in his mind the morning James Ambler reported to him that Nelsk Iversen, coal heaver, had brought the doctor a semi-coherent story that a mutiny was being plotted in the forecastle.

Iversen was a powerfully built thirty-year-old native of Denmark who had worked in the cryolite mines of Greenland and had made strenuous efforts to sign on with Bennett's expedition. A butcher by trade, he had earnestly described himself in the letter in which he had sought a berth on the *Jeannette* as "quick and hardy . . . never had a day's sickness." In his agitated account to Doctor Ambler he named Seaman Walter Sharvell, another coal heaver, as a ringleader in the plot. He added that he was afraid for his own neck in reporting it, for he had hesitated to fall in with the others and was thus suspected as one who might betray his shipmates. He believed himself under watch. During the interview with the doctor, Iversen several times broke into tears.

De Long had Sharvell brought before him. The seaman denied Iversen's charge and countered that the Dane was not right in the head, having frequently disturbed the berthdeck with fits of hysteria. This explanation De Long was only too eager to embrace, a mutiny being the last thing he wanted to deal with. Doubtless with equal relief, Doctor Ambler accepted Sharvell's word and that of other seamen that Iversen must have imagined things, and he decided that all the situation called for was a daily check on the man's condition and his removal from tasks of responsibility. After all, Seaman Sharvell seemed an innocent type, in De Long's words "a mere lad." The commander went on to write in exasperation, "First a blind man and now a crazy man." Very likely he offered a silent prayer as well that it truly was hallucinations and not a genuine threat of mutiny that explained the case of the distraught Dane.

"Our glorious summer is passing away." From the crow's nest in every direction stretched ice, rugged masses of it, an endless and misshapen desert of pale, gleaming whiteness broken here and there by black pools but with no leads accessible to the ship, no avenue for her safe advance or retreat. Pond-pitted and hummocked, the ice would have been "as easy to travel over as to go through a city over the housetops." This inescapable ice, De Long wondered, did it itself never achieve an outlet? "Is this always a Dead Sea?" What lay to the northward? "It is hard to believe that an impenetrable barrier of ice exists clear to the Pole." And to the southward? "I should not be surprised if the ocean had frozen over down to the equator."

Were there any tides? Before she was icebound, the lunar influence could be registered, but now, with the ship drifting aimlessly, reliable tidal measurements were out of the question. "Full moon or new moon, last quarter or first quarter, the ice seems as immovable as a rock." Such contemplation invariably deepened his gloom. "My pleasant hope, to add something to the history of Arctic discovery and exploration, has been as ruthlessly shattered . . . as my greatest enemy could wish." But De Long's claim to optimism ("And yet my motto is 'Hope on, hope ever,' " he wrote after recording a backward drift of eleven miles) was no desperate boast, judging by the frequent juxtaposition of good humor with anguished laments. Comparing himself with Job, who bore his many trials and tribulations with patience, he wrote, "But so far as is known, he was never caught in pack ice." The spark of whimsy flickered on, De Long musing that, of course, Job's "may have been an anteglacial period." De Long could feel proud of having bested the sea. Once rushing in at four thousand gallons an hour, it was now controlled by the occasional whirr of the windmill or a dozen strokes of a hand bilge-pump.

Once the *Jeannette* floated again he would be "the happiest man north of the Arctic Circle." Yet the inevitability of another winter in the pack was absorbed with a brave face. The preparations—the reassembly of the deck-house and its addition of a new porch, a renovated galley, and various modifications intended to reduce condensation and improve ventilation in the berth deck—all wrought such a scene of shipboard construction that "when our winter housing is complete we will have quite a village on deck" and later De Long announced "our township . . . ready for a charter." He ordered an issue of rum weekly to all hands. "Gives them something to look forward to." In the wardroom "two glasses of sherry on Sunday is the extent of our tippling."

Despite the warmer temperatures ice still girdled the ship, in places ten feet thick. Anxious to inspect the propeller for damage, De Long asked Lieutenant Chipp if his torpedoes could blast through floes glued to the stern. But this posed too great a risk of injuring the vessel, so they decided to use the ice-saw. This itself might have appeared a herculean task, but Chipp rigged a combination of tripod, stout rope, and a large saw hung vertically, weighted by an eighty-pound anchor. The executive officer, kneedeep in water, guided the saw by means of a crowbar through its handle. After hours of labor had shorn away heavy cakes of ice it was possible to trice up the screw. To his relief De Long found it as perfect as when it was first attached to the shaft. It was again lowered to its seat.

Perhaps partly because of that manual displacement of ice from her stern, the ship appeared to shake herself and suddenly reared upright. The event was totally unexpected, and all hands rejoiced that she was once more on an even keel. No longer was it necessary to move about at an awkward slant. Dishes remained in place on the wardroom table when Charley Tang Sing set them out. "Our ship stands upright," De Long wrote on 1 September, "with her nose well up, like a horse eager for a start. But, poor lady, she has no chance . . . yet."

Indeed, De Long had forced himself to confront the possibility that the *Jeannette* might have to be abandoned. But "I abhor the idea. We have come through so much." He equivocated, telling himself that the *Jeannette* would leave her people before they left her. As long as there remained something of the vessel to cling to, living on that fragment would be preferable to camping on ice. He dreaded the possibility of their having to try to make Siberia, which he estimated at least 250 miles away, hauling their boats and heavily laden sleds, the "winter's cold sapping one's life with every step." A seaman had just slipped and broken an arm. "If disaster strikes the ship we have the contemplation of dragging him and Danenhower," not to mention taking along a score of unruly dogs.

If Engineer George Melville and others favored consideration of abandoning ship while the vessel was still intact, as they later testified, they appear not to have pressed their views. Perhaps they feared the commander's stubbornness on this point. He may have told them, as he wrote, that "in some respects we are better prepared for [our second winter] than for our first. We are tolerably certain of being quite as comfortable aft, and we are sure that the men will be more comfortable forward." He had of course to make ready for a sudden departure from the ship. Seeing that the sleds procured at St. Michaels were probably too frail for carrying boats, men, and gear, he had stronger ones built on board. Haversacks were packed as before and everything placed as far as was practicable for a quick and trouble-free getaway. De Long prayed it would not be necessary.

John Danenhower's purgatory continued. He had been allowed on deck only on rare occasions during the warmer weather and then with the affected eye padded and the other goggled. Doctor Ambler hoped he was controlling the affliction by periodic cutting and draining, using the condenser of his microscope for close examination, but he wondered how long his patient could bear up mentally or physically. Permitted out of his curtained room only at mealtimes, Danenhower was also overexposed to the carbonic fumes from the lamps below. Wrote Ambler on 30 October, "It would hardly be possible to have any patient under worse conditions for the treatment of an eye disease." Danenhower could not be considered for any kind of work, even light tasks. And his needs and treatment all but monopolized the doctor's every hour. De Long drew only limited consolation now from Danenhower's consistent display of stoicism. However brightly the stricken man talked of soon returning to duty, the commander firmly ruled otherwise. It was "not a pleasant thing for me to realize that my work is thus increased, my care augmented and the general strength and efficiency of the ship's company crippled by the action this officer saw fit to take without my knowledge or the knowledge of the surgeon."

The long night returned. Before November closed, the temperature had plunged below zero. On the day De Long recorded the advent of winter "the ice began its horrid screeching and grinding . . . as if in celebration." Once a strange musical humming filled the ship. Lieutenant Chipp finally traced it to vibrating wires and diaphragms in the unused telephone equipment. Chipp explained the phenomenon as the effect of electrical radiation from particularly intense surges of aurora.

The heavens, when cloudless, were brilliantly clear. The region was in truth an astronomer's paradise, except for the extreme cold. De Long ruefully decided observations were unreliable, as sextants were never designed for such low temperatures: the mercury on their index and horizon glasses cracked and split. He tried to obtain satisfactory lunars against which to check his chronometers but got hopelessly varying results. He wondered if he would not do better with the zenith telescope, and was at this instrument in the deckhouse late on 14 November looking for an occultation or transit of one of Jupiter's satellites when Dunbar, the ice-pilot, stepped in and asked if he were aware that ice had again begun to squeeze the ship. "I was watching Jupiter so intently that I made some such indifferent answer as 'heard it some time ago.' He possibly thought I was taking things easy. But the fact is, I have long since concluded to borrow no trouble. We cannot prevent any disaster that may befall us, and we have made all possible provision for its arrival."

The unrelieved suspense produced troubling psychological effects. In the poopdeck cabin and wardroom an irrational discontent had taken hold, a vague feeling of mutual distrust. As implied in testimony long afterwards, somber little cliques developed, the commander, the doctor, and Lieutenant Chipp forming their own secretive knot. In the unnatural atmosphere even George Melville's heartiness and unfailing proficiency might have become suspect, making him something of an enigma to his colleagues. Raymond Newcomb clung increasingly to his taxidermist's bench, the boyish tight-lipped naturalist in proud and silent communication with the birds he methodically stuffed, especially the rare Ross gulls he dreamed of displaying before the world's scientific assemblies. And Collins was a man quivering with resentment, his pride severely bruised and about to receive a final blow.

At the close of the frustrating summer De Long had served each of his scientists with peremptory orders. Newcomb, "without unnecessary delay," was to draw up a list of the number and kinds of "birds and other articles now in the collection belonging to this ship." The order to Collins, also demanding instant compliance, required him to supply meteorological data for the last twelve months including complete temperature and barometer readings, tables of wind directions and mean velocities, "descriptions of any storms of marked importance," monthly precipitation totals, moon phases at intervals of the severest cold, "and any other phenomena which have fallen under your observation." Following this, an acrimonious showdown between the commander and his embittered meteorologist was inevitable.

At midday on 3 December, when all but Master Danenhower and the duty watch were taking exercise on the ice, Collins went back on board and entered the poopdeck cabin to record his noon observations. Danenhower had just come up, blindfolded as usual. It was his winter routine to remain below in darkened quarters until the cabin lamps were extinguished, at about 11:00 A.M. daily. Collins made his entries in the port chart-room by candlelight and then, instead of returning to the ice, lighted his pipe and was chatting leisurely with the disabled navigation officer when De Long entered. The commander asked Collins why he took twenty minutes to perform his duty. Collins's brusque reply was to the effect that he did not know his movements were being timed. Sensing trouble Danenhower descended to his curtained room, where he plainly heard the harsh exchange above him. Also, De Long left an account of it, word for word. Charging Collins with insubordination and discourtesy, De Long said: "You seem to assume that you are to receive no correction, direction or dictation from me."

"I came here supposing—"

"Never mind that. You *are* here and we will deal with the fact. Great allowances have been made for your ignorance of naval regulations."

"When you accuse me of disobeying your order, I deny it."

"Are you beside yourself? You contradict me flatly. Have you lost your senses?"

"I am perfectly calm and collected."

"That's enough, sir. Situated as we are, this matter cannot be conveniently dealt with now. But upon the return of the vessel to the United States, or her reaching some point of communication, I shall report you to the Secretary of the Navy. Meanwhile, you will perform no further tasks beyond completing the work called for in my written order of September 1. You have done your last duty on this ship."

DESPITE THE ACCUMULATING tensions, or because of them, the denizens of the *Jeannette* indulged in the traditional December festivities with fierce gaiety. After Christmas dinner, topped off with mince pies De Long thought "a work of art," the crew staged a minstrel show and what was billed as "a side-splitting farce" in the deckhouse. Violin and accordion airs rose into the Arctic night sky, Boatswain Jack Cole clog-danced to the brink of exhaustion, and Walter Sharvell (presumably freed of all mutinous taint) was the hit of the evening, a maiden alternately coy and droll in beautiful blonde wig, white stockings, and low shoes with blue rosettes. Another performance on New Year's Eve concluded with all hands singing *The Star Spangled Banner*, then De Long stepped forward to display his own forte, that of oratory. The men need have no fear for the future nor cease to harbor pride and hope. "We have confronted danger, suffered injury, been squeezed and jammed, tossed and tumbled, have pumped a leaking ship for a year—but we are not yet daunted, are as ready to dare everything as we ever were."

The *Jeannette* had resumed her northward drift. The new year 1881 opened with shrieking winds that piled snowdrifts up to her rails. On 4 January, after the storm had abated, De Long's attention was caught by "a dazzling Venus, joyfully dancing in the refraction at 3 P.M." He had just been ruminating on the fact that although the *Jeannette*'s position was scarcely more than two hundred miles northwest of where she was first beset, the total length of her convoluted course exceeded thirteen hundred miles, a distance which in a straight line would have carried the ship far beyond the Pole. De Long took the sighting of the fulgent planet as a good omen, and the same night was also exceptional for its auroral splendor, torrents of varicolored fire blazing across the sky.

It was about this time that Jerome Collins, cut off from the instruments he had so zealously procured back home and had so keenly anticipated working with, lingered in his room to compose a tortured letter to the commander.

He declared "the contemptuous disregard for my personal feeling exhibited . . . by yourself and your fellow officers" as unworthy of notice. But as James Gordon Bennett's employee and an official appointee to the expedition recognized by the secretary of the navy, he considered every slight "an infringement on my rights." De Long's remarks to the *Washington Post* at the start of the *Jeannette*'s outfitting had made abundantly clear his disdain for any civilian assigned to the expedition as a scientist, and at that juncture Collins had realized, too late, the trap he had fallen into. "You had and have it in your power to heap . . . any amount of disrespect on me. . . . Under the circumstances I cannot retaliate. I can only resent by silence." He had been relieved of his equipment piecemeal, a cruel process that could only be interpreted as an indictment charging incompetence and neglect. "First the magnetic instruments one by one, then photographic apparatus. . . . Then thermometers, the salinometer, the Damets hygrometer." And no explanation offered, "no more than if I was a lamp-trimmer in the fire room. . . . Don't you suppose I am as sensitive as yourself or Melville or anybody else? . . . You think you can do with me as you please now, and laugh at the future. You are making a mistake common to men of your disposition. . . ."

There is little doubt that De Long received the letter but no evidence of his reaction. Certainly the order barring Collins from duty remained in effect. And the weeks wore on, De Long smarting under his own excruciating sense of injustice. Other explorers beset in the pack had finally drifted to dry land, "but we are jogging about like a modern Flying Dutchman. . . . Thirty-three people wearing out their hearts and souls . . ." But he noted with renewed anticipation the first blush southward of the returning sun. He had postponed a detailed accounting of events for the secretary of the navy until the light improved. In early March, he wrote an extensive rough draft, and its conspicuous omissions were Danenhower's incapacity and the debarment of Jerome Collins as the *Jeannette*'s meteorologist. De Long dealt fully with the latter affair in a separate document that also outlined his dilemma regarding suitable punishment. None could be effectively meted out while the ship was exposed to danger, for "whether inflicted by my order or in pursuance of the sentence of a summary court martial [it] would have necessitated a confinement . . . seriously detrimental to health. I had already suffered anxiety and difficulty in contemplating the possible dragging of one officer on a sled several hundred miles." De Long's charges against Jerome Collins would eventually, as intended, come before the secretary of the navy. A strict disciplinarian, the lieutenant had felt himself equally constrained to follow naval rules and regulations in Master Danenhower's case by composing another separate report. It would never come to light.

THE GREATEST SURGE of hope and excitement on the *Jeannette* since the beginning of her icy entrapment occurred three weeks after Ambler found diatoms—plankton—in the sounding cup and identified them as coming from a river. The doctor's discovery indicated that the *Jeannette* might have drifted into an area containing deposits from the Kolyma River. De Long's bleak comment on 27 April was, "Let us then hope for something from the much lauded velocity of the spring freshets of Siberian rivers, for that is about the only Arctic theory we have not exploded." But his mood radically improved 16 May when Dunbar hailed from the crow's nest, his station several times daily, that he had land in sight on the starboard bow. De Long sent Chipp aloft to confirm and the following day was himself in the crow's nest with binoculars, feasting his eyes upon a distant smudge that he calculated was an island some forty miles off.

Had the North Pole itself come within view it could hardly have glad-
dened De Long more. This was the first land seen since a brief glimpse of
Wrangel Land fourteen months ago. And in these latitudes it had to be
hitherto undiscovered terrain. "Our voyage, thank God, is not a perfect
blank. . . . What this poor desolate island, standing among icy waters, may
have to do in the economy of nature I do not know, nor in fact care. [It] is
to us all in all." The ship drifted toward it with agonizing slowness. De Long
wrote, "Most of us look carefully at our island before we go to bed, to make
sure it has not melted away."

A spell on dry land would do wonders for the crew, especially the sick.
After all this time in the pack, the *Jeannette*'s sick list had lengthened alarm-
ingly. The executive officer, doubled up with stomach cramps, was among
the afflicted. Also Seaman George Lauterbach, ordinarily one of the sturdier
members of the crew, had collapsed under the weight of the umiak (an open
Eskimo wooden boat) he carried from lead to lead on a bird-hunting mission
and had badly wrenched his back. As if Doctor Ambler was not harried
enough by these mishaps, Danenhower's good eye became severely inflamed.
The other eye was, in Ambler's opinion, beyond recovery, short of an operation under ideal conditions. Danenhower was confined to unrelieved darkness again but made aware of the new animation among his shipmates, who
visited him at intervals and described the distant island so vividly that "I
could almost see it through the ship's side."

The men of the *Jeannette* scanned the surrounding ice for favorable openings. From every side came the familiar booming of newborn fissures, some
twenty feet wide, but they failed to connect and form a navigable pathway
to that beckoning nub on the northwest horizon. "I cannot saw through
miles of ice or blast that amount out of my way," the commander bemoaned
on 24 May. But before a steady east-southeast breeze the drift remained more
or less in the right direction. "We will have to trust the wind for our ability
to take possession." The repeated references to "our island" reflect what had
become a pathetic eagerness to salvage something out of what had so far
been a prolonged, soul-destroying term of futility. As the ice and its three-

masted prisoner crawled toward the island, De Long felt his own excitement rise. "Our invalids give me . . . anxiety. Chipp is very weak. Danenhower, of course, will be of no use so long as he is in the ship. But with many things crowding in on me I almost feel that the crucial moment in our voyage is at hand."

CHAPTER TWELVE

RELIEF PLANS

I hope the silly prophecies of outside irresponsible papers about the Jeannette have not frightened you. I am perfectly confident of the absolute safety of the ship and crew. The very fact of her not being heard from yet is to me the best evidence of her success.
James Gordon Bennett to Emma De Long, 2 August 1880

PUBLIC CONCERN IN the United States about the safety of Lieutenant De Long's party was at first subordinate to an alarm in commercial circles over the fate of some valuable whalers. A score of these vessels had left for the north through Bering Strait in the spring of 1879, not long before the *Jeannette* put to sea. Four, tempted by favorable weather, continued hunting in the Arctic until well into fall. This was a risky decision, but whaling had always been risky. During the previous eight years no fewer than thirty-three whalers carrying upwards of six hundred men had drifted northeast from Alaskan waters, had become trapped in the pack, and had never returned. Of the whalers that decided to stay on late, the *Helen Mar* had sighted the *Jeannette*'s disappearing smoke, and within a month the same ice formation that snared the exploring steamer had beset not only the *Helen Mar* but the *Mercury, Vigilant*, and *Mary Wollaston*.

The crew of the *Mercury* had abandoned ship and boarded the *Helen Mar*.

She escaped to clear water after a sixty-mile running fight with the gathering floes and made her way safely back to San Francisco. The *Vigilant* and *Mary Wollaston* had disappeared. The master of the *Mary Wollaston*, Ebenezer Nye, was a widely respected mariner and among a number of whaling veterans De Long had solicited for suggestions on how best to reach the North Pole. Unlike the others, Nye withheld comment until pressed and then replied, "You have a strong vessel? A matchless crew? Sufficient provisions and coal? Then put her in the ice and let her drift. You may get there or go to the devil. The chances are about equal."

Supported by their congressmen, several whaling masters asked the secretary of the navy, Richard Thompson, to send a search vessel after Captain Nye and the other missing whale-hunters. They reinforced their petition with an unanimous opinion that the U.S. Navy's own exploring steamer *Jeannette* must also be in grave danger. The *New York Herald* dismissed such talk as "ridiculous" and ill-advised, inasmuch as its continuance was bound to distress the relatives of the *Jeannette*'s crew. But in June 1880 (the men of the faraway *Jeannette* were just then scouring and repainting in hopes of liberation from the ice) the revenue cutter *Thomas L. Corwin* entered Alaskan waters with search orders added to her routine instructions for enforcing revenue laws and apprehending whisky smugglers.

The *Corwin* called at St. Michaels and then visited St. Lawrence Island, where entire villages were found inhabited only by corpses, victims of starvation evidently brought about by overindulgence in drink, which had rendered the people too befuddled to hunt for sustenance. The revenue cutter next made five runs northward to within sight of Wrangel Land before returning home, her captain convinced that the lost whaling crews must have perished but equally of a belief that the *Jeannette* and her people, whatever their position, were safe and sound.

In the meantime, sufficient apprehension had grown in knowledgeable circles to oblige even the *New York Herald*, habitually looking on the bright side, to belatedly remind the government of its responsibility. The paper had told its readers earlier that the *Jeannette* could be gone three years and still return successfully. "Explorers don't carry telegraph wires." Livingstone, after all, was found alive after a long silence. But at the close of September both Clements Markham and George Nares, British veterans of Arctic travel, stated that if another month passed without news of the *Jeannette* it was the "duty" of the U.S. government to send a ship in search of her. The *Herald* promptly endorsed the proposed deadline, recalling that British relief parties had not gone after the missing Franklin soon enough and declaring that "the blunder of delay should not be repeated on our side of the sea."

Before a packed meeting of the American Geographical Society in Chickering Hall, New York, on 28 October, Isaac Hayes declared that Lieutenant De Long would never turn back unless convinced that success was unattainable. Hayes, who had made three noteworthy Arctic voyages and was among the founders of the "open polar sea" theory, called for a relief expedition should the silence from the North continue. But "I do not anticipate that the *Jeannette* has been either crushed by the ice or hopelessly beset." If the worst happened, De Long could fall back on the Siberian coast where the natives were friendly. "I see the face of Mrs. De Long among us . . . and I want to express my belief that her husband is just as safe tonight, though not as happy, as if he sat by her side."

From such hopes Emma De Long tried to derive comfort. But she felt that the *Corwin* should at least have reached Wrangel Land or Herald Island and have sent a shore party to seek records her husband might have left at either place. As the months passed, neither James Gordon Bennett's reassurances from Europe nor his *New York Herald*'s complacent editorials did much to curb her growing fear. At the same time, Emma's peace of mind was hardly enhanced by a flow of distraught letters from Henrietta Melville, wife of the *Jeannette*'s chief engineer. So laden were they with morbid prognostications and accounts of weird dreams that she grew to dread opening the envelopes with the Sharon Hill, Pa., postmark.

Henrietta was "lonesome . . . unhappy . . . shall never see my husband in this world again." One morning "he came to me as he said he would if he died and he was in pure white." Then Hetty Melville's letters took on a more material character. Her husband, she claimed, had left his family the barest allotment from the navy paymaster, she had the cottage to keep up, two children to tend for. She pleaded for loans, offering her jewelry as security. Emma De Long responded with substantial sums.

In November (fifteen months after the *Jeannette*'s departure and at roughly the eve of De Long's bitter clash with Jerome Collins) the *New York Herald* published a thoughtful letter from George Kennan, a journalist-explorer with more Siberian travel experience than that of any other American. As a young Western Union telegrapher, he had spent two years surveying in that desolate land for a proposed telegraph system crossing Alaska and the Bering Strait to link directly the major metropolises of the United States with those of Imperial Russia. Kennan had returned home to write *Tent Life in Siberia*, a book that Lieutenant De Long ought to have read but probably had not.

Kennan thought that if disaster struck the expedition De Long would probably make with boats and sleds for the northeast Asian mainland. Envisaging such a retreat to the Siberian shore, he urged that the Navy Department lose no time in seeking the good offices of the Russian government. If the secretary wrote an appropriate letter to St. Petersburg, official word could be spread, alerting the inhabitants of the northeastern coastal regions and offering rewards for their providing succor for the American explorers. The Chukchi tribesmen could remain on the lookout for a year to come. Distance and desolation posed no insurmountable barrier. An annual fair and market were held at Nizhnikolymsk, a settlement at the mouth of the Kolyma River which served as a communications hub in the Siberian wilderness. Orders could be telegraphed as far as Irkutsk and, allowing sixty days for a special courier to reach Nizhnikolymsk, the necessary information would still arrive before the natives came in to trade. "The entire expense, including the cost of wires between New York and Irkutsk, would not exceed a few hundred dollars, and in the event of the loss of the *Jeannette* might be the means of saving her crew from weeks of suffering and suspense, if not from a lingering death."

The Navy Department did not consider such representation necessary. In his annual report for 1880, published during the same weeks as Kennan's letter, the secretary cited as an accurate reflection of the department's official view the words of Captain Charles Hooper of the *Corwin*. "I have no fears for the safety of the *Jeannette*. The fact that they have not been heard from seems to indicate that the vessel is safe and that they may consider themselves able to remain [in the Arctic] another year at least." To which the *Corwin*'s ice-pilot added, as confidently quoted in the *New York Herald*, "There is the warm Japanese stream to moderate the climate north of the Pacific. If I had friends on the *Jeannette* I would not worry."

But the silence from the North continued, and at the end of the year a worried note began to creep into pronouncements. Addressing a meeting of the California Academy of Sciences, to whose museum he donated a fossilized mammoth tusk, Captain Hooper reiterated his belief that the *Jeannette* was strong enough to withstand anything short of "mountains of heavy ice" and that she had "hibernated" in the vicinity of Wrangel Land, fully provisioned "and with all hands well, for sickness is scarcely probable among such a healthy set of men." Even so, "inasmuch as Captain De Long and his brave comrades, at the sacrifice of comfort and risk of their lives, have penetrated the Arctic regions in the interests of science," it was the nation's duty to prepare and provide whatever assistance they might need.

Moreover, that "warm Japanese stream" might not be nearly as effective as proponents of the theory had so long and so zealously maintained. Confronted with the U.S. Coast and Geodetic Survey's published findings following its 1880 investigation of Bering Sea currents, the *New York Herald* felt obliged to concede that "a current liable to occasional alteration and reversal by tidal influence and registering only 48 degrees of heat, as . . . demonstrated, cannot after its emergence into the Arctic Ocean be depended upon to cause any extensive, permanent polynia north of Bering Strait or to open an ice-free avenue to the Pole."

Early in the new year interest was heightened by publication of a letter from Judge Charles P. Daly, president of the American Geographical Society, to President Rutherford Hayes. Although bought and fitted out at private expense, the *Jeannette* was a government vessel commanded by "one of the most efficient officers of the Navy." Sixteen months had passed without word from him and as the *Corwin*'s five unsuccessful bids to reach Wrangel Land proved that vessel's unsuitability for the task, the government should send a larger, stronger ship to the Arctic in search of the *Jeannette* and no later than midsummer. Among the published comment stirred by this petition was a tart observation from a sister of Lieutenant Charles Chipp that "it seems strange that a government should allow some of its best young naval officers to go on so dangerous a voyage, and then need urging before sending help."

Anticipating popular pressure, the Navy Department had begun negotiations for the purchase of a steam whaler, the *Mary and Helen*, a 420-ton New Bedford barque of white oak frame and planking, with sides almost three feet thick and solid timber counterbracing. But for all the whaler's well-advertised strength, the opinion of the whaling fraternity in San Francisco at least was that such vessels were inadequate for prolonged ice service and that some sturdy government ship should be detailed and equipped to spend a winter in the pack. The name that most frequently cropped up was that of the man-of-war *Wachusett*. But at a planning conference in the Navy Department the same week that Congress opened hearings on a bill requesting $100,000 for the *Jeannette*'s relief, the now-outgoing Richard Thompson reminded his successor and the assembled bureau chiefs that the *Wachusett* had cost the country a lot of money and too much more would be required to refit her for Arctic service, not to mention the inadvisability of removing her from the Pacific station while war raged between Chile and Bolivia. Thompson's views prevailed, and the *Mary and Helen* remained the department's choice.

Congressional action took up a month. The *Jeannette* Relief Bill was tacked on to a major appropriation bill first debated in the Senate, causing irate House members to argue at great length that for the Senate to originate money bills was constitutionally improper and created a dangerous precedent. Lawmakers who favored the *Jeannette* Relief Bill only out of a humane sense took time to deplore "this constant warfare against the North Pole." In her New York home, Emma De Long read of the Washington proceedings with sinking hopes. But a telegram from Commodore Whiting at the Bureau of Navigation had assured her of the bill's final success. And in this optimistic spirit, finally, in early March the U.S. Congress passed the *Jeannette* Relief Bill.

The new secretary of the navy, William Hunt, convened a seven-member *Jeannette* Relief Board headed by Rear Admiral John Rodgers, who, in his seventieth year, was senior rear admiral on the active list, superintendent of the naval observatory and president of the U.S. Naval Institute. Hunt also asked Mrs. De Long to suggest, from her recollection of the commander's stated views and objectives, the best course the *Mary and Helen* might follow. Emma did her utmost, but, she wrote, "retracing the *Jeannette* is almost like looking for a needle in a haystack." The board turned to experienced Arctic navigators, and in one of the letters she regularly composed to her husband for his reading when and if he ever returned home Emma noted that "it received information from all reliable sources and obtained a great deal of data relating to winds and currents and ice movements north of Bering Strait that would have been useful to you, and I wish you could have had it."

In truth, what the board gathered was of little more substance than that with which De Long had set out. There really was not much to go on. However conscientiously the panel deliberated, it too often found itself awash in conjecture. Broadway may have been newly set ablaze with the electric light, making "night as bright as noonday," as New York newspapers exulted, but sailors and scientists remained in the dark regarding oceanic and atmospheric peculiarities in the Arctic. Late nineteenth-century modernity did not extend north of the seventieth parallel.

Bernard Coglan, a New England whaler who boasted twenty summers in the Arctic, testified to the relief board as to the impossibility of reliable data. Concerning seasonal weather, "there is no law governing the matter. You can never make any calculations on it at all." If calculations were of no use, did you have to wait until you got there to know anything about the weather? "Yes, sir. Sometimes we predict an open season and get there early and find it is the iciest season we have had in years."

There was general agreement on two points: De Long's original intention of reaching Wrangel Land; the other his plan, "in the event of disaster to the ship," to fall back upon the Siberian shore. Regarding the first, ex-Secretary Thompson told the relief board that the lieutenant had determined on a landfall before winter set in and "when spring of 1880 opened to advance into what he hoped would soon turn out to be the open waters of the Arctic Sea." Therefore, the most immediate task of a relief expedition must be to look for cairns on either Wrangel Land or Herald Island. Captain Coglan, the relief board's witness, averred that this would prove a waste of time since the *Jeannette* was last seen steaming more deeply into the pack, and De Long would most likely have refrained from sending people away from the ship as they might not get back again. While agreeing that "it does not seem probable" that cairns would be found, the board felt nevertheless that a search of Wrangel Land and Herald Island should be made. Even if the *Jeannette* had come to grief, "the crew might make their way over the ice to Wrangel Land, where only they can be sought, since the Arctic is too vast to be explored with any rational hope of success in finding the vessel except upon some definite information as to whither they were driven."

With these words the relief board betrayed its anxiety not to endorse any cruise that would subject the expensively overhauled and equipped *Mary and Helen* to the same dangers that may have overtaken the *Jeannette*. Captain Coglan was on one of the whalers that had last sighted the exploring vessel and he reported that she was "in the ice and going along with it. It enclosed her . . ." and the current had begun running northwest at about twenty miles a day, carrying the pack in the same direction. Clearly, the ship was held fast.

It was highly conceivable that the *Jeannette* had been carried on a northwest course beyond Wrangel Land, passing to the south of it—or perhaps north of it if that unexplored mass was an island (as none on earth but the

Jeannette's people now knew for sure). The stretch of Siberian coast to which De Long would have retreated, if forced by disaster, must lie considerably to the westward, as far west as New Siberian Islands and perhaps the mouth of the Lena River. The seven men on the board were acutely aware that if this was the case, De Long's party was beyond recovery by any relief ship from the United States that year. Russian vessels off Siberia might be alerted, and a request that they "keep a friendly lookout" was in fact telegraphed to St. Petersburg late in May, with a response four months later that no trace of the *Jeannette* had been seen.

The U.S. Navy's relief board, obliged to consider only what it deemed prudent, practicable, and affordable, confined its attention to what is today called the Chukchi Sea, the expanse north of Bering Sea and east of Wrangel.

Consequently, in its official report dated 26 March 1881, the board recommended that the steam barque *Mary and Helen*—"the one fit vessel which could be procured in time for the search"—cruise no farther westward along the Siberian shore than Kolyuchin Bay before crossing to Wrangel Land. The ship must not remain more than a single winter in the Arctic, and only then if her captain found a secure harbor. On the way north he would purchase Arctic clothing, dogs, sleds, and supplies from the Russians, using letters of introduction to the governor of the Pacific Coast and the governor-general of East Siberia. These had been requested and readily issued from the Ministry of Foreign Affairs in St. Petersburg. The search vessel would be under the command of Lieutenant Robert M. Berry, a member of the relief board and an officer on the *Tigress* during that ship's hunt for the *Polaris* survivors. It was reported that Berry's crew would take special pyrotechnic bombs "to give sign of their presence in the Arctic" and an observation balloon whose captive ascensions would provide the observer with a view for thirty miles around.

The *New York Herald* thought that the *Mary and Helen*'s name should be changed, as was the *Periwinkle*'s to the more impressive *Polaris*, and the paper suggested *Weyprecht* in honor of the Austrian explorer who, shortly before his recent death, had advocated the internationalization of Arctic research through the establishment of a circumpolar chain of meteorological and magnetic stations. The Navy Department agreed that the former whaler should bear a name more appropriate to her new mission and officially rechristened her *Rodgers*, after the president of the *Jeannette* Relief Board.

Bennett's newspaper, like the Navy Department, continued to publicly eschew alarm or pessimism. The relief board concluded its report with a reminder that "the whole history of Arctic exploration is marked by great dangers . . . wonderful escapes . . . success where appearances forbade any rational hope." Until confronted with proof of disaster, "we will believe that the *Jeannette* and her gallant crew are safe." And the *Herald* thought that "the silence that makes the *Jeannette* seem a thing of the past" would ultimately prove "the darkness from which will dawn a scientific triumph."

The newly named *Rodgers* was in a worse state of disrepair than at first estimated and was unlikely to be ready for departure 1 June as hoped. The revenue cutter *Corwin* was at sea with special search orders again attached to her regular schedule. And a third search vessel, the sloop of war *Alliance*, was undergoing preparation.

Shifting the emphasis which hitherto had been on sea search, the *New York Herald* raised the possibility of De Long's party coming "within reach of the extensive Arctic settlements of Siberia." The U.S. State Department should send a letter to the Russian government. "Russia alone is in a position to push forward a timely search for the *Jeannette* off her Siberian frontier before the gloom of another Polar winter settles down upon the vessel. It is to be hoped our government will lose no time . . ."

What the *Herald* now pressed for so earnestly had been proposed by George Kennan six months earlier. Perhaps the State Department might have taken action on it if the Navy Department had acknowledged that, all things considered, Siberia's nomadic peoples were probably better able to look for De Long than any seagoing vessel from the United States.

There was certainly no reason to doubt Russia's cooperation. U.S. diplomatic relations with St. Petersburg were fairly stable and quite cordial, despite rumblings of revolution in that land and U.S. fears that the state-ordered expulsion of Jews from major Russian cities might jeopardize American nationals. The two governments were participating in the multinational network designed to further Arctic research envisaged by Carl Weyprecht: an American party under Lieutenant Adolphus W. Greely, U.S. Army, was already making for Lady Franklin Bay to set up a meteorological station; and the Russians were expected to establish their meteorology station near the mouth of the Lena River or elsewhere along their vast Arctic shoreline. The St. Petersburg officials had readily furnished letters of introduction to help Lieutenant Berry procure supplies on the Russian side of the Bering Sea, drawing the U.S. Secretary of State's grateful acknowledgment of the "enlightened and humane spirit animating the Russian government." But no steps were initiated in Washington which might have directed that spirit still more usefully toward spreading word of the *Jeannette* among the natives of northern Siberia before summer gave way to fall. Tragedy might have been averted if someone had written a letter.

Stores brought by railroad from New York for the *Rodgers* were delayed two weeks in the middle of the sunbaked Great Plains. They arrived at San Francisco totally spoiled, hundreds of cans of putrid food bursting and maggot-ridden. More time had to be spent replenishing supplies locally. On the other side of the country, work on the *Alliance* had no sooner reached completion when a half-mile-long lumber raft on the Elizabeth River sagged inshore and a section broke off, crashing into the sloop's stern, severely damaging the rudder post. Not until 16 June did the two navy ships put out, the *Alliance*, Commander George H. Wadleigh, bearing northeast into the Atlantic from Hampton roads, the *Rodgers* under Lieutenant Berry clearing the Golden Gate to enter the Pacific. "Nothing appears to remain but to solicit the Russian government," editorialized the *New York Herald*. There was every "probability" that the *Jeannette* had safely wintered, her men gathering information of immense scientific value, but "if cairns are not found on Wrangel Land or Herald Island, what then?" And Bennett's paper at last introduced the heretofore unthinkable, conceding the possibility that "the daring navigators . . . have heroically perished in a great endeavor."

CHAPTER THIRTEEN

THE LAST OF THE *JEANNETTE*

Thursday, June 9. Clear, bright and pleasant weather. At midnight such a snapping and cracking that I concluded we were in for a time.

Journal of Lieutenant De Long

BY THE CLOSE of May, while relief expeditions were being mounted back home with no serious thought of an extended search west of Wrangel Land, the ice-locked *Jeannette* had drifted some five hundred miles west-northwest of Wrangel and to about two hundred miles north-northeast of New Siberian Islands. The ship's company were still agog over the discovery of what De Long called "our island," which he had decided to name "Henrietta" after James Gordon Bennett's mother. The *Jeannette* came to within fifteen miles of Henrietta when, to the commander's delight, a second island appeared far to port. This he would name "Jeannette." As the ship and her ice-prison headed slowly on a course that would take them between the two, he told off a landing party of six men, including the ice-pilot Dunbar, and named a confidently eager George Melville as leader. Fifteen dogs were selected to haul the sled, with a dinghy and a week's provisions. Three animals were found to be worn out and regretfully De Long ordered them shot.

All hands except Danenhower assembled on the ice to cheer Melville's party. De Long took to the crow's nest with binoculars. It was his fervent hope that Henrietta Island would provide a sheltered bay in which to repair the ship's leak, gentle terrain where his sick and weary might rest, and animal or bird life to restore the expedition's food supplies. He watched the receding party until dusk fell and it vanished amid hummocky ice. Above and behind De Long in the crow's nest flew the large black flag at the main truck, which Melville was to keep in view and from which he must take frequent bearings. Should fog envelop the ship her brass gun would be fired every four hours.

Fog seemed unlikely. A fresh breeze blew and De Long seized advantage of it to make the windmill do all the pumping. The state of the crew's health weighed upon his thoughts, grievously so after Ambler reported an unusual number of abdominal-pain cases. They increased, spreading fear that something had crept into the ship's diet to gradually poison her crew.

De Long himself felt the abdominal cramping. So did the doctor as his professional mind wrestled with the problem. The symptoms indicated lead poisoning. At first Ambler suspected the drinking water. The distiller joints were red-leaded to make them tight. Some of the lead might be carried over into the steam and deposited into the receiving tank. This could hardly be avoided, so Ambler "decommissioned" drinking utensils with solder patches and substituted porcelain-lined iron mugs. Then he discovered the real trouble: canned tomatoes. Having higher lead deposits than the drinking water, they were contaminated by broken-off fragments of the solder used to seal the cans. Wrote De Long: "The acid of the tomatoes acts chemically on the solder . . . and a dangerous mixture is formed." The crew had been eating tomatoes daily for a month. Now tomatoes were banished from the galley.

The crew recovered, leaving De Long still worrying over the landing party. The new month began, with no sign of Melville's return. Were the engineer and his five companions stricken by those toxic tomatoes? De Long wondered if he had not sent them off prematurely, the island still too distant for a safe landfall. Might they have lost sight of the *Jeannette*'s black flag? On 3 June he ordered a fire built on the ice, using tar and oakum to send up a thick black smoke.

*   *   *

It was rough going all the way. Outflanking the incessant growth of fissures in the ice had forced Melville's party on an arduous zig-zag course. Lanes split wide under dog teams, and repeatedly the men had to drag their yowling animals clear of frigid water. Time and again the provisions and boat had to be unlashed from the sled and ferried across widening channels. Men and dogs alike were so physically spent by the first nightfall they collapsed as one on a floe-piece. Scarcely enough strength remained to set up a tent. The second day brought no improvement; only laborious cutting and bridging made possible any progress across a chaotic glacial expanse. Faced by a near-impassable barrier of ice ahead, Melville decided to leave the boat and gear on a reasonably stable floe-piece and continue, hauling the sled over hummocks and across leads. Temporarily blinded by fierce sunlight shooting off the restless ice, Dunbar begged to be left behind also, but Melville would not hear of it. The dogs continued to flounder, entangling their traces, dragging each other into one icy breach after another, so that it became Melville's turn to note a shattered preconception: "Dogs dashing in full cry under long whips is a myth."

Not until 5:30 P.M. on 2 June did they make land. Melville strode ashore first, called the others about him, unfurled U.S. colors, and "in the name of the Great Jehovah and the President of the United States" declared the island U.S. territory. Then, at the foot of volcanic slopes that resembled "a vast heap of scoriae discharged from some great blast furnace and streaked with veins of iron," the chief engineer and his muscle-weary men sank to the freezing shingle.

They arose at 4:00 A.M. and conducted a hasty survey. The island was mostly barren rock, black and red, scarred and riven by time and by the action of heat and cold. Five bold headlands reared to from six hundred feet to fourfold that height, each crowned with a permanent ice cap. It was a thoroughly bleak and forbidding vista, without any evidence of a secure anchorage for the *Jeannette*. Melville climbed the most attainable summit and built a cairn to house the copper cylinder he had brought containing De Long's summary of the expedition so far. It included the commander's stated decision to stay with the ship until the end and may have touched on other matters, but the papers were reduced to a pulp, the lettering indecipherable, when Russian scientists discovered the cylinder fifty-seven years and one week from the day of Melville's arrival.

The return from Henrietta Island was even more of an ordeal than the outgoing trip. After recovering the boat and other gear left behind, they had to struggle ceaselessly against gale force blizzards. The men, dragging both the ice-pilot Dunbar, now sightless, and the dogs, shouldered their own equipment. The small party halted repeatedly and were often scattered by suddenly gaping water lanes. Throughout all, Melville maintained his seemingly inexhaustible good humor. He was never at a loss for a joke, even drawing grins from Hans Erikson and Nindemann when those two seamen, in trying to administer brandy and tincture of capsicum to each other (Doctor Ambler's prescription for stomach cramps), clumsily spilled the stuff over their cracked and blistered knuckles.

Melville's flag was sighted from the *Jeannette* early Saturday, 4 June. De Long ordered all colors hoisted and the whale-gun fired. The knowledge that by discovering Henrietta Island his expedition had not, after all, proved a total blank was an intoxication, a delirium even, and rejoicing now over the safe return of the shore party, he rushed blindly up to the bridge, momentarily forgetting the windmill spinning smartly under a 15 m.p.h. breeze. A sweeping wing struck him and he fell. Trailing blood along the quarterdeck he crawled half-stunned back to the cabin, but as soon as Ambler had stitched and plastered the four-inch gash in his temple he was back on deck. He heeded the doctor's orders to rest only after satisfying himself that the returning party did indeed number six and that all save Dunbar were in reasonably good shape.

The principal credit belonged to his chief engineer. Ever proud and charitable whenever one of his command acquitted himself with merit, De Long wrote of Melville: "If his persistence in landing upon this island, in spite of the superhuman difficulties he encountered, is not reckoned a brave and meritorious action, it will not be from any failure on my part to make it known." He issued a general order detailing the names and positions of the two islands and ordered a double ration of whisky served forward. Next morning, bandaged head still throbbing, he read the Articles of War, inspected the ship, and conducted divine service with greater confidence than had buoyed him on many a previous sabbath. "Thank God we have at least landed upon a newly discovered part of this earth. It was a great risk, but has resulted in some advantage. . . . And now where next?"

THE MASSIVE CAKE of ice in which the *Jeannette* lay embedded remained stubbornly solid. The thunderous agitation that had almost destroyed Melville's effort to reach Henrietta Island did not reach within two hundred yards of the ship. Beyond this raged a riot of broken hummocky floes in all directions, clear to Henrietta Island off the starboard beam, Jeannette Island more remotely to port, and the misted horizons beyond both. Water could be glimpsed but in distant and disconnected patches. Occasionally the vessel trembled from the impact of some exceptionally powerful far-off convulsion. The ice-trap bore the *Jeannette* steadily westward, causing hopes of a landfall on either of the islands to fade. The temperature hovered in the twenties. Squalls rose frequently, laden with pulverized ice that struck the ship as storms of shards and needles. In his 6 June 1881 entry De Long wrote: "The changes going on all around, except in our isolated spot, were so kaleidoscopic it would have been impossible to detect . . . a [navigable] lead if one had existed. We were moving along slowly and grandly, a dignified figure in the midst of a howling wilderness."

It was after the newly discovered islands had fallen astern, swallowed up by fog and ice-clouds, that the frozen tumult closed in on De Long's ship. A sense of hope was his immediate reaction. Should the rampage on every side signal a general break-up of the pack, then freedom beckoned. He ordered all necessary gear on the ice brought back on board, and, following some desperate chopping away of ice chunks from the gudgeons, he shipped the rudder. Great pools and tracks of water flashed into view quite close at hand. The *Jeannette* drifted west-southwest now at an accelerating speed. As she moved from the heavy ice, the reduced strain allowed wood ends to come together again, which in turn slowed the ship's leak. For a brief interval De Long believed she would stay afloat after all, rewarding the devotion of her people by carrying them into open waters. The ice cut short this optimism, for by noon of 11 June it had again massed about the ship. This time, it was crushing her with a vengeance.

De Long had the hunters' recall signal hoisted at the main truck. Fireman James Bartlett and Alexey, out since breakfast, obediently hurried back over the ice, dragging a huge seal. By then, floebergs had piled up along the port side, the ship heeling 16 degrees to starboard. The ice pressure mounted on both sides. From deep within the vessel came a dreadful snapping and banging of sprung bolts and parting timbers. Machinist Walter Lee, on distilling duty in the engine room, rushed up on deck to shout that the floes were bursting through the ship's sides into the starboard bunker. De Long growled at him to keep his voice down, and steadying his own he told Melville to check on the situation. As the engineer vanished below De Long ordered the ship's boats lowered away, all but the second whaleboat.

Lantern held aloft, Melville saw a giant crack across the engine room ceiling abaft the boilers. Seams in the planking had opened by as much as an inch. No water poured into the ship yet, but Melville had little doubt that it was only a matter of hours before she broke in half. To the snapping and cracking were added a horrid crunching and groaning, eerily lifelike sounds of torment. From overhead Melville could also hear De Long order the provisions cleared from the deckhouse for lowering over the side and the dogs and sleds hauled off to the more stationary floes.

By suppertime the ice pressure appeared to have relaxed. "We might be able to take care of the ship yet." But an hour later she was angled 22 degrees to starboard and still listing. The freezing air vibrated to an uproar of dismemberment. Dunbar, his snowblindness gone, helped the still-blindfolded

Danenhower find his knapsack. Ambler ducked into the wardroom and reported that the ensign had been hoisted at the mizzen and that the crew was passing necessities over the side because the ship had begun to fill. Danenhower insisted that, as the navigation officer, he be restored to duty at least to the extent of assembling his charts and instruments. Ambler replied doubtfully that he would see what the captain had to say about that. But without waiting for official permission, Danenhower shoved the bandage from his eyes, collected his navigation gear, and carried it up the slanted deck to the ship's port rail where he lowered it to seamen on the ice. When he returned to the poopdeck cabin where he had left his knapsack, the water had risen to halfway up the wardroom hatch. Danenhower aided a still enfeebled Lieutenant Chipp from his room in the cabin and the two officers joined the rest of the people who, quite calmly under De Long's supervision, had organized themselves into little teams throughout the foundering vessel and were unloading it of what equipment, stores, and provisions the commander had determined to save.

At about 8:00 P.M. the *Jeannette* leaned 30 degrees to starboard. Men found it impossible to stand without clutching something. The spar deck buckled. The squeezing ice, besides forcing the *Jeannette* aslant, had raised her forward by five feet or more, exposing the entire port bow. But the ice had also stove in the starboard hull abreast the mainmast. This entire side, including the rail, soon slid beneath the floe-scabbed surface. The waterline reached the hatch coamings. The vessel settled more rapidly now. This was not the eventuality that De Long had had in mind when, a fortnight ago, he felt that the "crucial moment" of the expedition was imminent. But he had come to terms with the inevitability of the command he now gave. In what can be inferred from subsequent testimony were brisk and unemotional tones, he ordered all hands to abandon ship.

She still reared tall though listing, etched against the starred and aurora-ribboned Arctic sky, when her company pitched camp two hundred yards off her port bow for their first night on the ice. The two cutters and the first whaleboat were on the ice lined up with eight sleds, three of which had been specially constructed on board to carry the boats. The second whaleboat still hung from the *Jeannette*'s davits, on the port side well clear of the water, and Carpenter Alfred Sweetman asked Master Danenhower to speak to De Long, standing nearby on the ice, about going back on board and lowering it. Danenhower declined, whereupon Sweetman "turned to the captain who said pleasantly that he already had enough boats on the ice."

In the six tents, few of the men got much sleep despite their fatigue. At 1:00 A.M. the ice opened directly across the middle of their camp. After a lively turn-out, the men hastily shifted the tents and gear to a quieter span of ice. They were piped down again, except for a man on watch, Seaman Albert Kuehne, who at about 4:00 A.M. called his relief, Fireman Bartlett, and quietly announced that the ship was going.

The mizzen mast had already gone by the board. The ship heeled so far over that her lower yardarm rested on ice, her smoke pipe almost awash. But then the *Jeannette* seemed to struggle as if to right herself, and as she came close to attaining an even keel the floes that had crushed her fell back, as if in final respect. With Bartlett and Kuehne the only witnesses, the ship went down in forty fathoms.

Her maintopmast tumbled away to starboard, followed by the foretopmast, then the mainmast crashed leaving the foremast standing alone. The yards had caught across the ice and snapped off, but held by the lifts and braces they were dragged under. Melville wrote long afterwards that the stripped yardarms were broken upwards parallel to the masts so she must have plunged out of sight "like a great gaunt skeleton clapping its hands above its head." From inside his tent Raymond Newcomb heard the ship sink and when he looked out minutes later "she was gone, her only requiem being the howl of a single dog."

The commander's own words on the sinking, written within hours of it, are succinct, devoid of regret or mourning, characterized if anything by yet another surge of optimism and resolve. On 12 June, the first full day on the ice, he called all hands at 9:00 A.M. and arranged for a distribution of clothing, including overshirts and undershirts, drawers and fur coats, trousers and skin parkas. "Set up my work tent. Crew busy getting sleds ready. . . . All cheerful, with plenty to eat and wear. Lauterbach on the harmonica tonight. Kept the silk flag flying." He noted that Chipp, Dunbar, even Danenhower, seemed improved in spirit. His own conduct was level-headed and unhurried. "I have concluded to stay where we are until all preparations are well made. We have provisions to live on for some time without impairing our sixty days' allowance for going south." As for the exploring steamer *Jeannette*, he mustered all hands at the site of the wreck for a farewell salute, but "where the ship sank, nothing is to be seen but a signal chest floating bottom up."

CHAPTER FOURTEEN

RETREAT

Latitude 77° 8' Longitude E 153° 25' We break camp and start southward over the ice tomorrow evening, hoping with God's grace to reach the New Siberian Islands, and from there make our way by boats to the coast of Siberia.

Lieutenant De Long's record, 17 June 1881,

left in a keg on the ice

THEY HAD CARRIED from the ship all the drinking water on board. This was soon gone, whereupon they scraped from the highest ice hummocks what little snow a nascent sun had melted. The snow tasted fresh enough, but Doctor Ambler's silver nitrate tests showed a high degree of salinity. It had, nevertheless, to be used, De Long hoping that their daily ration of lime juice would sustain the one good fortune upon which he could congratulate himself, the expedition's freedom from scurvy. This continued immunity, his innate optimism, and also euphoria after long months of physical confinement and psychological tension on the *Jeannette*, all were enough to cause an exaggerated flourish of his pen. By and large "we are living royally on good things . . . are in glorious health."

In the same self-confident spirit he showed no great haste to break camp and begin the long journey. "Bobbed about until the evening of [June] 17th

166

preparing to go South," noted Jerome Collins caustically. De Long's chief thoughts were on what to take, given the hauling capacity of his men and dogs. They would leave behind piles of belongings, some valuable instruments and weapons, and one of the St. Michaels sleds. The Siberian shore lay at least four hundred miles to the south. The New Siberian Islands, closer but uninhabited, were viewed only as stepping stones to the mainland. Before reaching open water the party would have to drag its sick, its food and gear, its two cutters and a whaleboat, across many miles of pack ice, men and dogs alike hauling everything over a snow cover that steadily changed into cloying slush. The three boats weighed a total of four tons, and the five provision sleds, fully loaded, added another sixty-six hundredweight. With little faith in the pulling power of his dogs, now numbering twenty-three, De Long realized that the chances of his people reaching Siberia depended not upon high resolve alone but on their raw durability as beasts of burden.

The strong sleds made on shipboard to bear the weight of the three boats were each twelve feet long, with ten crosspieces made from whisky-barrel staves, and heavy oak runners shod with whalebone. In addition to the five provision sleds (four were superior McClintocks brought over on the *Jeannette* from England), the two remaining sleds taken on at St. Michaels would carry some of the gear and Doctor Ambler's medicine chest. Two small sleds carried dinghies.

Into the three boats went the camp equipment—six tents, five cooking stoves, iron kettle and stewpot, deerskin sleeping bags (full length and furlined), and thirty-three packed knapsacks each of whose strictly limited contents ranged from mittens, moccasins, and safety matches to soap, skullcaps, tobacco, and twenty rounds of ammunition. Ice-pilot Dunbar had the critical job of advance roadmaker. He would hew out a line of march with his ice axe and mark the route with black flags. The group would travel at night, to avoid noonday glare and to allow the men to dry their soaked clothing in sunlight while they rested. Because the eight-ton deadweight of boats and cargo, provisions and sleds was too much to be dragged all at once, progress would consist of, in the understated words of one survivor, "three steps forward, two back."

Five days after the ship had gone down, De Long read the order of march, invoked heaven's blessing, and the party broke camp. Under Chief Engineer George Melville's direct command, all hands would start by hauling ahead the first cutter. Each member of the drag team wore a harness made of a double-canvas band strapped diagonally across his chest like a baldric. Twelve were hitched to the drag rope, with more men tethered on either side to raise the boat over rough ice and keep it from capsizing. All was ready at 6:20 P.M. when De Long gave the order to get under way, and the men shouted cheers as they strained against their harness, homeward bound at last.

The cheers died quickly. Movement through the gloom of the Arctic night would be more difficult than any could have imagined. Neither could the men have foreseen how disheartening it would become to trudge empty-handed for miles in the wrong direction in order to bring up boats and supplies from the rear.

De Long wrote, a pencil and stout little notebook now his tools of record, that the first cutter "went easily enough . . . slowly, steadily [through] snow kneedeep [that] often had to be shoveled out from under the bow in crossing hollows where the boat would get stuck." After the first hour he detached six men and by "superhuman exertions" they dragged the number one sled about five hundred yards, followed by the second cutter, and then the whaleboat. De Long had continually to be up and down the line of march, urging and encouraging, shifting details, spurring the laggards. But "of course, I could not be everywhere in a road 1½ miles long," and two unexpected developments threw his first-day plans into disorder.

The ice cracked open somewhere short of the second of the black flags Dunbar had planted at about six-hundred-yard intervals, destroying his "road" and cutting the strung-out party in two. Among those left stranded on the wrong side of the fissure were Lieutenant Chipp with fellow invalids Alexey and Seaman Kuehne, who were obliged by the obstinacy of the dogs to drag both the animals and the "hospital sled" themselves. The enforced ferriage was a race against time, the ice still in ominous motion. De Long had the sleds hastily unloaded, their provisions carried across by two small dinghies making several trips. Needing extra manpower, he sent Chipp hobbling on ahead with the hospital sled and instructions to hurry back with some of Melville's force, which he assumed had by now reached the third flag, completing the prearranged first lap.

Melville's people had done that and, unfortunately, more. Meeting the engineer earlier on the ice, Dunbar had informed him that he had planted a fourth flag to mark the end of the day's journey. Melville had accordingly ordered his harnessed men to haul the cutter an additional half mile. Wrote Danenhower, who shared hauling duties despite his infirmity and fought a private resentment against taking Melville's orders, "In our zeal we had gone too far." Melville's party had thus to plod more than a mile back to their comrades stalled at the ferry. On the way a couple of them fell groaning of stomach pains. Chipp, too, fainted in the snow. Everything was finally borne across a watery gap widened to twenty-five yards, and in the dusky glimmer of a midnight sun the process of drawing up to the first cutter was resumed, a haulage now extended by half a mile.

De Long was not the only member of the expedition dismayed by so inauspicious a start. Boats, sleds, and provisions lay scattered along a mile and a half of snow-covered ice, with men floundering among them. Sled runners had snapped off or were badly bent. Once in the privacy of a tent Collins noted: "Started with a rush and broke three sleds. A mess of the worst kind. Men grumbling. . . . Some of the crew thought De Long's journals and logbooks an unnecessary burden." Fueling the meteorologist's disaffection was the fact that his own logbook, an expensive quarto-volume bound in sheepskin, had gone down with the ship. Still officially suspended from duty, Collins had nonetheless buckled to on the first cutter as resolutely as any man.

James Ambler's terse review of that first push southward was, "a general smashup of sleds." He had spent part of the time keeping Chipp upright with regular doses of brandy or crouched in the slush vigorously kneading George Lauterbach's bared abdomen after the seaman collapsed from stomach cramps. The doctor privately thought that, even including his sick, it was Raymond Newcomb who contributed the least to the overall effort, an assessment that failed to take into account the young naturalist's bitterness at having to abandon his precious notes, equipment, and every ornithological specimen except the three prized Ross gulls.

Work was interrupted only by dinner, prepared and served at about 2:30 A.M. Five more hours of toil, then the party halted for supper. "At 8 A.M set the watch and piped down, a weary lot of mortals." But all were still firmly imbued with a will to survive, and if they turned to for the second night's effort without the hurrahs chorused upon departure, their zeal was as strong. Following sled repair and a rearrangement of loads, they pressed on once more, Dunbar ahead with his black flags and ice axe. At times the going was uphill, almost all hands besides eight dogs needed to drag a single sled with its sixteen-hundred-pound load. Sliding downhill frequently ended up with the sled overturned, its cargo half buried in a snowbank, the dogs in a tangle and fighting among themselves.

Although as commanding officer De Long did little of the actual backbreaking haulage (a matter of some criticism later on), he was unquestionably under the most severe mental strain. His sense of responsibility for the safety and well being of the men in his charge, characteristically weighed with self-inquiry, was aggravated now by frustrations. The pressure warped his nature in ways he would ordinarily have abjured, as he more and more vented harsh feelings where before he might have applied tact and self-restraint. Shortly before resuming the struggle on the third night he called Danenhower into his tent and ordered him to remove himself from the main work force. Henceforth he must confine himself to the hospital sled. "You cannot see," De Long told him. "It is evident from the way you stumble in the snow." When Danenhower tried to argue De Long interrupted with, "You are an impediment."

Danenhower afterwards recalled that he returned to his tent "deeply mortified to know that thirty-three men were working for their lives and I was not allowed to help, even though, physically, I was one of the strongest men of the party."

So it went on, the painful process of moving an enormous load portions at a time, having to footslog back for what was left. The road-guide Dunbar always out front, the oldest man in the party and more than ever watchful for openings in the restless pack. Melville following, his hearty curses spurring along two dozen men harnessed like horses and dragging sleds and boats until they sweated and shed their parkas in 20-degree temperatures. Erikson and Herbert Leach running two dogsleds back and forth. De Long giving a hand at loading and occasionally running a sled himself. Ambler and his invalids pretty much on their own with the hospital sled. Again and again the ice cracked wide, and the men would have to manhandle huge floes into position as a bridge. Once all the provision sleds were ahead at the appointed flag, Melville's party would move back for the boats. Hauling those clumsy craft was a particular ordeal as time and again the soft snow banked up against the twelve-foot-long sled runners beneath the overhanging bows.

When the boats were finally up, De Long broke off the cooks to prepare dinner. Provisions included twelve hundred pounds of hard bread, thirty-five hundred pounds of pemmican in canisters of forty-five pounds each, some tea, sugar and coffee, and plenty of Liebig's beef extract. For dinner, the Chinamen and their daily assistant (each man took a turn) shoved the cooking stove in a hole in the snow to preserve heat, and they scraped the tops of the highest hummocks for ice to melt. "The scraping," De Long had cautioned with salt in mind, was "not to go more than one inch below the surface."

After dinner the hauling continued until morning when the furthermost flag was reached. By the time De Long had brought up the rearguard and the dogsleds had arrived with their last load, the first team on the scene had pitched camp—five tents, nine feet by six feet, with a smaller office tent, five or six men to a tent with an officer in charge, a mackintosh covering each floor-space and a firepot in the center for cooking breakfast and supper.

Each haulage period generally worked out as seven forward trips with a load, six faster returns with empty sleds. De Long considered it a good night's work, or outwardly professed to, if his men advanced two miles, having actually covered a total of twenty-six back and forth. On the eighth night of ice travel he discovered something so incredibly cruel his mind at first refused to accept it.

He had only hours earlier written, "We must eventually come to open water by making due south." It was just a question of time. And then, at midnight 25 June, he had obtained a meridian altitude that gave a latitude of N.77° 46'. He went over his figures half a dozen times, getting the same result. He cudgeled his brains for explanation—perhaps some refraction of starlight had affected his sighting? He overhauled the sextant and found nothing wrong with it, plotted a couple of Sumner lines and they checked. Still unwilling to believe what all this pointed to, he decided to wait for a noontime reading with altitudes of the sun.

At daybreak he piped the men down as usual but fought off his own slumber. Lieutenant Chipp in the next tent was also awake but groaned continually. During the morning Ambler reported to his sleepless commander that Chipp's condition had so deteriorated he was unable to dress himself and could scarcely stand, much less walk. He might have to be strapped to a sled and dragged, a necessity De Long had contemplated for his third in command, not his second. Deploring the fact of "my two line officers constantly on the sick list," he consoled himself with the thought that "in Melville I have a strong support as well as substitute for them."

And only Melville and Ambler did he awake after getting an upper meridian at noon that confirmed what he dreaded. As fog crept across the encampment on a freshening west wind he confided the heartbreaking news to the chief engineer and the surgeon. Even as the expedition had dragged its eight-ton load in stages across the hummocky wastes for more than a week, struggling a total of some ninety miles in order to advance southward one-sixth that distance, the icefield it traversed had steadily drifted at a faster rate in the opposite direction. Instead of making any headway at all for

172

Siberia, the men were as much as twenty-eight miles farther north than when they had set out.

"I DODGE CHIPP, Danenhower and Dunbar, lest they should ask me questions," De Long wrote in his office tent on 27 June. It was his turn to keep a grave secret, from his executive officer no less than from Danenhower and the men. Only with Melville and Ambler did he confer on what was now best to do, for "if we go on this way we will never get out."

The pack was actually drifting in a northwesterly direction. De Long felt that to continue south was to waste time and energy. Inclining more to the southwest, in other words at a right angle to the icefield's drift, would more speedily bring them to its edge, where they would take to open water. Melville and Ambler concurred, and De Long ordered the slight shift in course, working with prismatic surveying compasses. The heavier boat compasses had been left on the *Jeannette*.

But try as they might, they rarely exceeded a mile and a half each night. Too often thin ice, undetectable because of snow cover, split open underfoot, hurling men, dogs, and supplies into bone-chilling water. The group regularly had to build flying bridges. "One ice opening yawned sixty feet and to bridge it we had literally to drag an ice island thirty feet wide and hold it in place" while the boats and sleds were hauled across. The men pleaded with Ambler to do something for their sore faces and blistered hands. The doctor was also perturbed by a recurrent inflammation around Danenhower's sightless eye, which was kept bandaged, the other goggled. The navigation officer seemed unbothered by it (the trouble eased when Ambler applied a counterirritant to the eyebrow), and he badgered De Long for permission to do his share. He claimed "he could do a man's work of hauling, etc. Inasmuch as I consider him unfit to perform any duty whatever, and as he would be an impediment and hindrance to anything he attempted to assist, on account of his one eye, I refused positively to assign him to any duty until he was discharged from the sick list."

De Long was adamant, perhaps unreasonably so. An unconscious desire to discipline or punish for what he took as a personal betrayal may have operated upon his feelings. Yet whatever John Danenhower's character flaws, his professional competence was long ago ratified and he gave every appearance of having triumphed over private torment. Likewise his sanity, once a matter for apprehension, had clearly endured. Other than the absence of sight in one eye, he was probably as fit for duty as Melville or any other sturdy member of the party. Doctor Ambler had recorded no other debilitating symptom of the navigator's disease, certainly none since the sinking of the ship.

And De Long knew that vision in only one eye need be no barrier to useful service or even high command. England's naval hero Nelson, besides less illustrious cases, proved that. On 21 June Ambler noted that "Danenhower's eye has so far stood exposure well, fortunately there has been little sun." So at least during sunless periods the *Jeannette*'s navigation officer could have pulled his weight.

There was not much evidence at first that the retreat had benefited from its altered course. "Very likely," the commander noted on 4 July, the third anniversary of the *Jeannette*'s launching, "we are going three miles northwest to every mile we make southwest." Obviously they could not afford to waste an ounce of available manpower. But anyone might have been blinded to the obvious by the brooding despair to which De Long occasionally succumbed. His glorious ambitions were gone with the *Jeannette*. Were it not for his duty to lead the men safely home, "it would have made but little difference if I had gone down with my ship. It will be hard to be known hereafter as a man who undertook a Polar expedition and sunk his ship at the 77th parallel."

He was a commanding officer in extremity. And it was as if the enforcement of discipline, whenever opportunity arose, became through some strange alchemy a reassuring link with a safe and orderly world beyond the icy desolation. Less than a week after setting forth reasons in his journal for not assigning Master Danenhower to duty, De Long summarily robbed his work force of another valuable member.

According to Fireman Bartlett's account of the incident, Jerome Collins was holding a roped floe in position to bridge a thirty-foot-wide crack for the sleds to cross when De Long shouted at him, "Give that rope to Dressler. And, damn you, don't let me see you put your hand to another thing unless I order you." The commander's outburst was all the more startling because he had previously seen Collins working in harness and had said nothing. The meteorologist's version, penciled in his notebook, has De Long reminding him that he was still under suspension. "Had observed that I worked, etc. When he saw the necessity he would order me. Was to do no more duty work until we reached USA. Bien! Spoke doctor next day [about the] depressing effect of inaction forced on me under the circumstances." From Ambler he received only "platitudes" and the doctor's assurance that "no stigma attached to me."

Collins asked that he might be at least allowed to carry and clean his repeating Winchester rifle. Permission was granted, and he promptly shot a young bull walrus. "Handsomely recovered by men in dinghy," wrote Collins. "General rejoicing over fresh meat."

Doctor Ambler's stoical good humor, a trait that long months in Union captivity during the Civil War had failed to destroy, foundered somewhat in present circumstances. He was disgusted with the two line officers on the sick list, having no doubt that in each case the man's own selfishness was responsible. (Lieutenant Chipp's offense had been an obstinate disregard of the doctor's advice to go easy on himself.) The moment Chipp showed signs of recovery Ambler sought relief from his role of nurse. "The sick seemingly convalescent enough to do without Ambler's steady presence," De Long recorded, "I assigned him to the road and bridgemaking in charge of Newcomb and Lee."

This was back-breaking work, in the course of which a sled overturned and swept the doctor into a water lead. After swimming from floe to floe he clambered out shivering, rummaged in the whaleboat for his knapsack and dry clothing, and "stripped and dressed in driving sleet." But he welcomed the change in duty and was congratulating himself on his escape from the hospital sled with its infirm and complaining crew when De Long, at a dinner halt, directed him to bring them up. "I was over the whole road three times pulling a sled . . . over part of it five times working with a pick . . . and when I got back to camp [was] sent back . . . to receive the sneers of our blessed invalids." The doctor made sure that they in turn "heard some pretty plain talk."

On the fourth of July all flags flew in more than just patriotic commemoration. For one thing the date was the third anniversary of the *Jeannette*'s christening at Le Havre. But more important, latest observations with the sun and the sextant showed the party's new position as a thirteen-mile gain over the last figure. They were still about that distance north of where they had started from, but the new readings indicated that the pack had ceased its northerly drift. Moreover, they had just completed a relatively trouble-free stretch across "beautiful hard ice . . . were able to send two sleds ahead at a time." Heavy snow fell the next day, but, as De Long and his people huddled together for dinner under a shelter of rubber blankets rigged between the rails of the sledded boats, he felt sufficiently encouraged by their recent progress to try a stab at humor. Recalling a New Jersey county fair he and Emma had attended, he said cheerfully, "Many people under canvas in Hoboken today would like a little of the coolness we are now having." But the remark "seemed to provoke a desire to exchange places with them, and I said nothing more."

De Long's journal contains suggestions of a darkly subtle humor, an alertness to the lurking presence of absurdity even in their predicament. He appreciated the picture Chipp created when he told him of the means adopted by some of the men, about to go off watch, to arouse their relief without disturbing others in the tent. "While awake the other night [Chipp] saw to his amazement a boat hook slowly coming through the tent door, and pausing a moment over Sharvell, poke him vigorously in the back." De Long added: "This ought to make a good Arctic sketch."

There was the same cracked theatricality about Seaman Ed Starr's discovery of a message stuffed in one of the provision packages. It was signed with initials and bore a New York City post box number. Mumbling aloud in his Slavic accent, Starr read to his stupefied comrades: "My best wishes for your furtherance and success. Hoping when you peruse these lines you will be thinking of the comfortable homes you left behind you for the purpose of aiding science. If you can make it convenient, drop me a line."

CHAPTER FIFTEEN

BENNETT ISLAND

For forty days we have been under way in all kinds of hardships;
but not a murmur, and tonight after nineteen hours work, many of
the men having been overboard, they are cheerful and come up
smiling.

Journal of Surgeon James Ambler, 28 July 1881

BACK MUSCLES THROBBED. Painful welts rose on the men's chests from the repeated wrenching of the hauling belt as their burden lurched into a snow-bank or struck a hummock. Skinned and blistered hands grew numb as they held picks to hammer at the flinty ice. Sudden openings ahead and astern sent the men frantically towing ice-islands to form flying bridges, scrambling back to save the rearmost sleds, struggling forward again to bridge yet more unexpected channels. Bridging and ferrying became the order of the day, four leads to cross within half a mile a common challenge. Wrote De Long after an exhausting mid-July advance, "We take an island as long as a mail-steamer and ten inches thick for a ferryboat. But over we go. . . ." Large mats or tufts of needle ice tore at human and canine feet alike. Between leads, hillocks hindered progress. Ambler, on the road-making team, "cut more than a ton from one cake that was in the way and by the time the boats came up the ice had shifted and I had to come back and cut as much more."

The doctor wrote of "sleeping in wet clothes in a wet bag on wet ice . . . every bone and every separate muscle" aching next morning. Every breath was painful, a pleuritic symptom he noted in his journal but said nothing of to the others.

Eyesight became again a cause for Ambler's professional anxiety, but this time it was the commander's vision. Often De Long would veer off in a different direction from the one which Dunbar's black flags indicated. Once when Ambler pointed out a "perfectly safe passage" a few yards distant, De Long insisted on going the way they had been, with the result that a St. Michaels sled drawn by Erikson and a dogteam plunged into a lead, losing 270 pounds of pemmican. De Long himself ran a sled into an opening and sank to his neck. He was hauled out by Dunbar, who grabbed for the captain's hood, clutched his beard instead, and "almost took my head off." This latter spill may have had nothing to do with De Long's shortsightedness, but Ambler had begun to worry about it, privately "convinced that the captain cannot see with the glasses he uses."

The doctor's own constitution was far from robust after two weeks' "heavy picking [with] the poorest help . . . miserable sled . . . broken down dogs and one man who . . . doesn't intend to do anything and pretends not to understand." Though now in the U.S. Navy, Ambler was a former Confederate cavalryman, and of old and proud Virginian stock. Raymond Newcomb came from Salem, Massachusetts. The doctor's written disdain for the youthful Yankee naturalist owed much to Civil War animosities. That conflict had ended only fourteen years before the *Jeannette* left San Francisco. Sectional prejudice dies hard. In those days so did intraservice pique, a resentment often found between staff officers and officers of the line. Both may account for the derision Ambler privately aimed, now and then, at Chipp as well as Newcomb and even at Lieutenant De Long, not to mention another line officer, John Danenhower. In the doctor's opinion, Danenhower had jeopardized the expedition through his gross indulgence; his bragging of his family's close ties with Ulysses S. Grant hardly elevated him in Ambler's estimation.

Newcomb lost a pick he was using as an ice anchor. Though it had been properly secured, as Ambler's journal testifies, the doctor took advantage of the incident to have him removed from the road gang. Ambler himself had had enough of it by then and looked for deliverance. Lieutenant Chipp's improved condition supplied it. Discharged from the sick list, the executive officer relieved Melville on the hauling party, the engineer was transferred to command of the road-making gang, and Ambler "fell back to my legitimate duty as medical officer."

Lieutenant De Long's invisible burden remained the heaviest. If he shared Surgeon Ambler's anxiety concerning his poor eyesight he neither spoke of it nor betrayed it in his journal. He worried now that food supplies might give out before his party reached the edge of the pack or made landfall in the New Siberian Islands. Some of the men were showing signs of extreme fatigue, although Ambler's sick list had appreciably lightened. Footwear had become a problem. Moccasin soles rotted, stockings were sodden and torn, a few men trudged barefoot through lakes of slush and over ice as sharply notched as sawteeth. De Long authorized the use of leather ripped from oar-looms to repair soles. When this kind of sole proved too slippery on the floes, the men improvised shoes by plaiting rope yarns, manila, and hemp, into mats the shape of their feet. While no longer referring to his people as "my little colony," De Long strove to preserve or revive a sense of entity as an honorable naval expedition. He held divine service every Sunday, though few attended, and read the Articles of War once a month. Given the abnormal circumstances, this insistence on naval routine, along with an apparent inflexibility as a disciplinarian, was to be decried by some as an aberration, a tyranny even, induced by repeated disappointment. Against the twin haunts of frustration and despair, a strict adherence to service propriety and practice may have been the commander's instinctive shield.

On 13 July there occurred what he gravely noted as "the first serious breach of discipline among the crew since our commissioning two years ago." Like that of many a disturbance, its origin was trivial. The haulage team dragging the second cutter had come to a halt near the advance flag, and some were breaking out the sleeping gear while others put up their tents. In the heaving and shaking the boat had undergone, a pair of slippers placed by Melville in the sternsheets had tumbled upon Seaman Starr's sleeping bag. Starr took them off and flung them across the ice. Melville saw him do so and demanded that he pick them up. Starr refused. De Long appeared on the scene, ordered him to be silent and do as he was told. Still the seaman would not move. De Long wrote that "probably everybody in the camp saw the affair." The notation is significant, an appeal for understanding. Three times he ordered Starr to obey, each without response. With all hands looking on, rank defiance of a commanding officer must not be tolerated. Even if it meant depriving the expedition of yet another worker he could not let the insubordinate seaman get away with it. "At the first opportunity," he told him, "I shall have you tried by court-martial. Consider yourself under arrest and off duty."

Self-committed now to a course of unwavering sternness De Long faced the inevitability of a recurring dilemma. Within twenty-four hours of Starr's arrest he was in Danenhower's tent, summoned to hear a charge the half-blind navigator leveled against Raymond Newcomb. The naturalist had complained of inadequate rations and Danenhower had told him to pipe down. "Damned if I will," Newcomb had retorted. "I won't take orders from you." Although on the muster roll as seaman, Newcomb was actually a civilian, a status De Long thought he fairly acknowledged by weighing the incident a day and a night before reaching his decision. Otherwise he showed no discrimination. Newcomb emerged from the office tent after an audience with the captain, handed over his shotgun to Lieutenant Chipp, and took up a marching position at the rear with Starr and Collins.

"Placed Mr. Newcomb under arrest," De Long recorded, "intending to bring him to trial by court-martial for (i) using language tending to produce discontent among the men (ii) when remonstrated by Mr. Danenhower, using insolent and insubordinate language." De Long may have ardently wished that Danenhower had settled the matter in his own tent and not bothered his commanding officer with it. And it was lucky for Danenhower that De

Long could not foresee that a time would come when his erstwhile navigation officer would publicly blame him for the enforced idleness of four strong men and allege, into the bargain, that the captain, Chipp, Melville, and the doctor "added little to the motive power. Eight persons out of 33, or 25 per cent of the whole not working their passage across the ice."

EARLIER THAT JULY the ice-pilot Dunbar had reported land on the far horizon. No one else had seen it, and fog rolled in before anyone could get a second look. By the last week of the month, however, an island was in plain view, bearing west less than five miles. Fog obscured its lower region, but a blue-black tableland, snow-crested, rose above the murk. Hope surged in thirty-three tired hearts. Grudges and conflicts, petty or deep-seated, momentarily faded. As the fog thinned, affording a clearer view, De Long sent word to the rear for Jerome Collins to make a sketch of the island. Lieutenant Chipp conveyed the order with an explanation the commander's procedural mind thought necessary, to the effect that sudden emergency justified his temporarily relieving Collins from suspension. And it was with the inclusion of the others, like Collins, officially under arrest but temporarily pardoned, that all hands bent to the task of dragging sleds and boats across a tumbling wasteland of rotten ice and treacherous waterholes.

For three days and nights they fought to reach dry land, riding floes for ferryboats, groping through dense fog, bridging and road making at a sometimes frenzied rate. The pack played its maddening game with them, veering in the wrong direction. At intervals when the fog lifted, spirits plunged before a view of the island as far away as when conditions had last permitted a glimpse. De Long drove the men to work faster. In addition to its perverse drift the ice split and reared, throwing the men, their boats, and sleds into confusion. Dogs jibbed and had to be dragged or carried.

"The devil to pay generally," wrote Ambler, "the last twenty-four hours mist, rain, fog, coming down and shutting out everything, fog lifts and you have cartwheeled into some other position." Despite the weight of fur clothing and a Remington rifle strapped to his back, Ambler leaped from block to block, profiting from "my old boyhood habit of taking long jumps" and inspired by the sight of the oldest man in the party, Dunbar, still their dogged spearhead, bounding among the floes without even the aid of a pike.

Ice had piled up along the shore, the whole barrier groaning and heaving before a rising gale. Floes rolled and seesawed, surf bursting between them in waterspouts, drenching the men who yearned so fiercely to set foot on solid, unmoving ground. A mad exhilaration characterized that final dash for the shore. "The whole mass alive," as Ambler put it. "Provision sleds with all our grub carried over the breaking cakes of ice too light to float them. The men going like the rush of a whirlwind." They dragged themselves and each other, with their three boats and gear and the dogs, through a breastwork of dirty ice, and staggered across the fringe of shingle to collapse against the bottom of the cliff.

When they regained their strength, they made camp and broke out provisions. After supper De Long mustered all hands, proclaimed the place newly discovered land, and "I therefore take possession of it in the name of the President of the United States and name it Bennett Island." He called for three cheers, upon which someone led the ship's company in three cheers for the captain. They were still remote from the familiar world, had been so long in isolation that none knew, some never to know, who the President of the United States was right then, or that he lay mortally wounded from an assassin's bullet. All they were immediately concerned with was to have firm ground underfoot. De Long turned to Lieutenant Chipp and with mock solemnity if not a broad smile told him to give the crew "all the liberty you can on American soil."

He named the western tip of the island near where they had landed Cape Emma. As on those memorable occasions when he had gazed at auroral displays through the *Jeannette*'s frozen shrouds, he wished that his wife were beside him to share the bleak beauty. Red and yellow-green strata striped the igneous crags, their precipitous faces blotted here and there by black swarms of murres and dovekies. Terraces of traprock flashed with quartz and topaz. Ambler thought the place a geologist's paradise. The doctor, unmarried as were Chipp and Danenhower, had no wife for whom to collect souvenirs but wrote with warmth of a sister, the intended recipient, no doubt, of the amethyst he came across while prowling among the lavatic rocks. De Long, in an expansive mood, gave Collins full freedom to roam with pencil and sketchbook. Newcomb, summoned to the captain's tent, was "informed [that] he found it necessary to restore me to duty under the circumstances. I come on duty as bugs again. What a checkered career!"

Long afterwards, charges and countercharges would fly over the wisdom of tarrying on Bennett Island. Yet at the time a schoolboyish excitement seems to have animated the *Jeannette*'s people, at least in the early hours of their encampment. It resulted largely from the sheer pleasure of being on firm if rocky terrain instead of on undulating ice. The men spent much of the time in raids on the cliff-face rookeries, killing the birds with stones as well as rifles. Novice explorers, they returned from scouting trips to bring the captain moss, scurvy grass, flowers and driftwood, reindeer horn, and what a modestly knowledgeable Iversen, having worked in the Greenland mines, identified as cryolite. De Long and his party could hardly have displayed greater curiosity had they landed on the moon.

Though the boats were badly damaged in that last frantic dash, Nindemann and Sweetman had them repaired within twenty-four hours. As De Long's own words make clear, he did not order an immediate resumption of the southbound journey because he purely and simply wanted his men to rest. He may, in addition, have savored a thrill of geographical discovery and possession. On the last day of the month he sent his executive officer with seven men in the second cutter to explore the coast. Chipp followed the shore through fifteen miles of broken ice and returned next afternoon to report seeing little more than barren slopes with no sign of real game.

They were on Bennett Island nine days. De Long's next objective on his way to the Siberian mainland was one or other of the New Siberian Islands' major components. Faddeyevskiy and Kotel'nyy, each very much larger than Bennett Island, were known to Russian explorers and De Long hoped they would offer bigger game than seafowl. Faddeyevskiy, the closer of the two to Bennett, was still more than a hundred miles distant.

In a message he left in a cairn on the island De Long wrote: "It is my intention to proceed from here at the first opportunity towards New Siberian Islands and thence towards the settlements on the Lena River. We have three boats, thirty days provisions, 23 dogs and sufficient clothing, and are in excellent health. Having rested here a few days, we are now detained by a westerly gale and fog. We cannot say whether or not we can take to our boats . . . or shall be forced to resort again to dragging everything over the ice. The ice travel has been very hard, and two miles a day made good has been our usual distance."

They had consumed half their provisions since leaving the shipwreck. Unless they moved more quickly, their food might run out before they reached the large islands. De Long decided to leave Bennett Island on 4 August but the weather worsened. During this further delay he pondered the folly of keeping "wornout and epileptic" dogs, wasting pemmican on them, and he had the eleven poorest of them shot, with Erikson the reluctant executioner.

On the fifth of the month sunlight broke through the overcast and De Long wrote instructions for Engineer Melville. "We shall leave this island tomorrow." Once water travel became possible, "you are to take command of the whaleboat until such time as I relieve you from that duty. Every person who may be embarked in that boat is under your charge and subject to your orders." Melville was to keep close to the captain's boat, the first cutter, "but if we become separated, you will make the best of your way south to the Siberian coast," shaping course for the Lena. "This river is the destination of our party."

After similar orders were issued to Lieutenant Chipp, in charge of the second cutter, they were on the move again, bent once more to the wearying cycle of sledding and boating. They would strike a promising stretch of water and make a good distance under oars, only to have the ice snap shut again. The sleds would have to be hauled from the boats which in turn were manhandled back onto their sleds. The provision sleds were themselves a burden, and at the first opportunity De Long had all gear and supplies stored in the boats and the provision sleds chopped for firewood. Still the slightest motion brought water sloshing through the rowlocks into the overloaded boats. But they pushed on. Once they made eight miles in a single day, an advance, De Long wrote, "too immense not to glory in." He knew they were in a race against time. When four of seven dogs with Erikson in the dinghy jumped over the side, De Long felt he dare not waste a minute going after them, and their doleful yelps and howls faded into the distance.

During such an icefloe halt Danenhower, in the whaleboat party, protested to De Long about having to take orders from a staff officer. He insisted that he could see and was perfectly able to assume duty. According to De Long's account, he told Danenhower as before that as long as he remained on the sick list he would be permitted no military authority or control. Danenhower then demanded to know why he was not put in a boat with an officer of the line. The tart rejoinder was that officers could not be shifted around to suit his convenience. "Your remonstrance is ill-timed," De Long continued. "You should have thought of all these things long since and they might have been avoided. I have had the anxiety of your care and preservation for two years. Coming to me now is an annoyance."

"I have remonstrated in respectful terms."

"With no effect. I will not assign you to duty until you are fit for it. I will not put the people's lives in jeopardy by committing them to your charge. Your urging me to do so now shows little judgement and is very unofficerlike conduct."

"Am I to take that as a private reprimand?"

"You can take it as anything you please."

Danenhower carried his complaint to Doctor Ambler. According to Danenhower's subsequent testimony, Ambler told him that the sun's glare would collapse both eyes if he were not careful but that once clear of the ice he should be given duty. Ambler's private observations at the time read differently. On Sunday, 21 August, after all hands were called at 5:00 A.M., he treated two seamen for swollen faces then shepherded Danenhower into the medical tent for a closer inspection of what appeared to be fresh inflammation and congestion of the afflicted eye. Danenhower objected to being examined and another argument blew up. After breakfast he was again before De Long, who must have required superhuman strength to keep his temper in check as he told him that "when the doctor represented him as fit for duty he would be assigned to duty and not before; that his position was not a good one . . . that he must act in accordance with the stand I have taken."

It would be charged later that a vengeful Danenhower threatened to use political influence to break Lieutenant De Long from the navy. Ambler wrote privately of overhearing the officer tell Melville of his intention to do something of that sort. "He is very anxious to get on duty, and from his peculiar mind he has, I think, gotten the idea in his head that he is being unjustly treated. Before we started he thought his chances were nil, although I told him I thought he would pull through all right. He was always anxious for me to take the eye out." But now that his condition had stabilized as Ambler had predicted, "he takes the other tack, considers himself a sound man and has given any amount of annoyance in his repeated attempts to get himself placed on duty." He was not fit enough to take charge of a boat, and refusing to face facts had concluded that a conspiracy was afoot to deny him his rights. Ambler founded his diagnosis on his "knowledge of the man after two years experience and after having had frequent opportunities of witnessing the idiosyncracies of his mind."

THE PACK HAD slackened. At times De Long's party accomplished as much as ten or fifteen miles in a day, mostly over open water. The disintegrating ice posed fresh peril: powerful wind gusts drove giant cakes like battering rams across the wavetops. One crashed into Lieutenant Chipp's second cutter, almost capsizing it. The cutter was clinker-built, at sixteen feet long the smallest of the three vessels (the first cutter measured twenty feet, the whaleboat a little over twenty-five feet), and it was not a good sea boat. Stove in at the bows, it was hauled to a floe for repairs and De Long lightened its load by transferring two occupants to the other boats, leaving Chipp with seven men. He also deemed it unwarranted to carry the weight of useless dogs and had three more of the animals shot. Snoozer alone remained as the expedition's mascot.

These measures did little to solve the captain's latest problem, one that affected all three boats. The shipmade sleds that had proved so indispensable when the boats were lumber to be transported over the ice were now slowing progress. If towed astern, they interfered with the steering. If lashed crosswise to the rails, they made the boats top-heavy. The second cutter's sled was secured across the stern, and that vessel, a poor sailer in any event, constantly lagged behind. As their laps under oars and canvas increased, De Long felt more and more tempted to dispense altogether with the three cumbersome boat-sleds.

He had no illusions about the risks. There was no certainty that they had seen the last of the frozen sea. If they abandoned the boat-sleds and an early freeze recemented the pack, they would be trapped in the middle of it to face starvation. The boats could not possibly be dragged long distances over the hummocks without those oaken runners under their keels. Yet, the greater the ice-free passages now opening up ahead, the more suicidal it seemed to hold back the boats by overloading them with freight useless for anything but long-distance ice travel.

For a time, the ice indeed appeared to be coming together again. Strong winds were driving the whole northern pack down upon the New Siberian Islands. After camping all night in a blizzard, De Long contemplated another round of hauling the boats on sleds. But the gale refused to abate, and it kept the ice too slack and convulsed for sled travel. At the same time, the floes were too large and numerous for launching the boats. These conditions completely immobilized the party, and day followed day, the bread giving out, then the coffee. Huddled in their wind-battered tents on an ice-island that never ceased to pitch and roll, the men subsisted on pemmican, beef extract, and tea heated by fires fueled with alcohol. Ambler issued the last of the lime juice. The doctor, like De Long, had found pipe smoking a solace. Now their tobacco vanished also, and they puffed on coffee grounds or tea leaves.

They were under canvas on the heaving floe ten days (another delay fated to stir retrospective argument), during which time De Long took two important steps. One amounted to a gamble and, to a greater extent than he realized, so did the other. He knew that, to compensate for lost time, they would have to attain all the greater speed when movement resumed. So he made up his mind regarding the boat-sleds, ordering them destroyed. Their wood was used as kindling, and when that too was gone alcohol doled out by Doctor Ambler had again to serve for starting a fire. Brief glimpses of land to the southward through rifts in the fog stirred some fear in De Long that he had blundered in ridding his party of the boat-sleds. But the unceasing northeasterly wind seemed bound to sweep their floe past the island, and, in any case, the intervening ice was too active and jumbled for safe passage across it even had the sleds been kept. Neither were any leads visible for the boats.

The second decision, logical under the circumstances, was a gamble inasmuch as it was shaped by the presumptions of the late August Petermann. When his expedition was in the planning stage, De Long had drawn on the professor's theories and recommendations. Now in retreat he had to base his plans on one of the encyclicals that had regularly issued from Gotha—a published article about the New Siberian Islands and the approaches to the Lena River. This was all the information De Long happened to have concerning the region, and it was written in German. On the same day that he waged his latest encounter with Danenhower (it was also the eve of his thirty-seventh birthday), De Long summoned Edward Starr, who spoke German in addition to his native Russian, to the office tent. While Starr translated portions of the text, De Long traced the course that Petermann's words seemed to indicate on a large chart, an old one that reflected the findings of early Russian explorers. The course De Long penciled led down through the channel between New Siberia Island and Faddeyevskiy, thence across the Laptev Sea to the Siberian mainland.

In addition to what he learned from Petermann about alleged native settlements in the Lena delta, De Long had earlier read accounts of how international interest in the Siberian fur trade was opening up Siberia's great rivers. He also remembered that when one of Nordenskjöld's escort vessels detached itself in August 1878 and steamed south to Yakutsk with news of Nordenskjöld's safety and future plans, its course had been along the Lena. (Unlike De Long, the Swede was fortunate enough to have entered the Arctic with three escort ships to share the burden of coal and provisions.) As Danenhower afterwards stated, "It was supposed on our ship, by the captain and by Mr. Chipp, that the Lena delta region had been opened up, and that that was the best objective point to make so that we would be on the route home."

De Long gave Chipp and Melville sailing instructions for the three boats when they made their push for Siberia. Melville's whaleboat and Chipp's second cutter must "in all cases" keep close to the captain in the first cutter. As he explained in his journal, this blanket directive "covers any other point, for if I am always at hand to refer to, they need no orders in advance, and if unfortunately we get separated, things must be left to their judgement. In this latter case they will, without delay, proceed to the Lena and not wait for me or anybody short of a Russian settlement large enough to feed and shelter them." De Long's map of the region was too bulky, so he cut off the portion showing the Lena delta and the river to some two hundred miles inland. He made copies for his executive officer and the engineer and pinned the original to the last page of his notebook for easy reference.

The icefloe maintained a southwestward drift. "Ice closely packed continued to prevent resumption of the voyage." Land was now tantalizingly visible on both beams, that to westward being closer and identified as Faddeyevskiy. This had become De Long's initial objective, but not until noon on 30 August did Dunbar duck into the office tent to report a favorable lead. Hopes restored, the party broke what survivors would recall as the Ten Day

Camp and dragged their boats and provisions to the edge of the floe. "To launch boats in such a hellgate was ticklish, but went ahead." These were Ambler's words the following day. The captain's boat in which he crouched "struck shoal and pounded around for hours." When night fell, fresh gales arose. "Simply awful muddle," wrote Collins, also in the first cutter, "chilled through and sick from the motion of the boat." Melville, long afterward, would remember that in the icy darkness, "our only guides [were] the roar of the surf under our lee and the glare of ice on the other side when the sea surged over."

The three craft whirled down the channel between New Siberia Island and Faddeyevskiy. Dawn found the first cutter bobbing among offshore floes and severely awash, its fourteen occupants shivering in the 20 degree temperature. Soaked to his underclothing, his topcoat frozen like a board, Surgeon Ambler felt "so stiff and numb . . . that at times, except for my brain working, I should not know of my very existence." Everybody else was as badly off if not worse, "but they all stand it without complaints." The first cutter and the whaleboat were still within sight of each other. The second cutter was nowhere to be seen. De Long and Melville tethered their boats to an ice hillock and the captain ordered a black flag hoisted to the whaleboat's masthead as a signal for Chipp.

The executive officer and his seven men had struck the worst weather. They were so exhausted from a day and a night of fighting off the floes with oars and boat-hooks that when the wind subsided and they sought a glacial anchorage only Seaman Starr had the strength to clamber over the gunwale and drag up the boat by its painter. Chipp's men endured another freezing night, clinging to their floe, before they were able to push off again.

On 3 September, with Faddeyevskiy falling astern "while we are still jammed in the ice," De Long sighted the second cutter. It appeared to be wedged to a sandbank by acres of scalloped floes, on which the figures of Lieutenant Chipp and Seaman Kuehne were soon spotted, stumbling toward the main party. All were soon reunited. After greeting his exec with a warm "Glad to see you close to us again," and hearing of his ordeal during the preceding forty-eight hours, De Long announced revised plans. They were drifting more or less westward on a course roughly parallel with the southern shore of Kotel'nyy, the large western body of the island group. De Long now intended a landfall at Kotel'nyy's southeast cape, making next for the lonely islets of Stolbovoy and Semenovskiy, final stepping stones across the remaining two hundred fifty miles to Cape Barkin, on the Lena delta, where, he told his officers, "You will be sure to find natives who will pilot you to the main river."

It grew colder. The floes had welded together into a sprawling hummocky tableland. Water lanes had vanished, so boating to shore was out of the question. That left De Long only one course. He ordered a detail with carpenter's chisels and the sole remaining pick-axe to hack out a road. Any regrets over too premature a destruction of the boat-sleds would have been futile, and none were expressed, at least in writing. All hands bent to the herculean dragging. Each boat's mast lay across the rails, lashed to a thwart, providing a leverage for the men stationed on each side to keep it upright. Even so, the boat often ran out of control, skidding from the hummock peaks into hollows, first scattering the men on the drag ropes then yanking them helplessly in its train. Because there was no protection for the bilges of the boats, razor-sharp edges of ice peeled long oaken strips off the keel. Uphill in the teeth of a snowladen wind the going was especially rough. Each boat inched along behind a harnessed column of befurred automatons whose bodies slanted so far forward their seamed and cracked faces almost scraped the ice.

Sometimes the ice split and a man sank to his neck. Hauled out soaked and shuddering, he immediately went on pulling. This constant danger prevented De Long from attempting to ease the weight, however slightly. "So little food remains, I dare not take it out of the boats and carry it by hand. . . . If a man falls in he loses a can of pemmican—a day's ration for all hands."

He had always considered it an impossibility to haul heavy boats over ice without the benefit of sleds. And indeed, more than eight hours nonstop would probably have exhausted his men beyond further motion or have injured the boats beyond repair. But at that time they reached a navigable stretch of water. The boats were refloated, to sail ahead before northeasterly squalls. Although the bottoms of all three boats were ripped, none foundered, but they now ran a risk of staving on the ice floes.

The men fought on until the ice grew too packed for their boats to penetrate. Wearily they debarked and waited for it to slacken, and when it did not they had to unload and once more portage the boats. Dunbar collapsed. After examining him, Doctor Ambler told De Long that the icepilot's heart had weakened and that strain or excitement might kill him at any moment.

De Long removed Dunbar from all heavy work, saying he must do nothing henceforth but steer the second cutter through water. When water travel again became possible, the party reloaded and launched, braving a blizzard to make a full ten miles before pitching camp on a reef within reach of firmer shore and where driftwood abounded.

"I am thankful we have a sandspit to live on though I don't know where we are," wrote De Long on 4 September. It was the first Sunday in the month, routinely the day when he read his company the Articles of War, but this time "I postponed them to a more favorable occasion." Other rituals he clung to. "Standing by the fire, with my congregation holding wet stockings and other gear to dry, I read divine service."

They were still off Kotel'nyy, the southwest portion. Those who managed to go inshore found a few long-abandoned huts and some moldering tusks but no good evidence of game. De Long himself hardly ventured from his tent. He had chilblains and several toes were cracked and bleeding. Of the officers, Chipp and Ambler did most of the exploring, and it was after an unproductive five-mile survey along the shoreline that the doctor returned to find Machinist Walter Lee swaying and mumbling in front of the medicine chest. He had evidently got at the alcohol. Ordered to his tent, he kept babbling curses far into the night, refusing to cease even when De Long sent word for him to "get out of my hearing." Lee was not, like previous offenders, removed from duty. But when circumstances permitted, "I shall try him by

court-martial for intoxication and for abstracting alcoholic stimulants from
the public store."

If any of the seamen kept private journals, none survived. It is only from
much later testimony that an impression can be formed of a growing disenchantment among the seamen with De Long's command. There even appears to have been talk of deposing him as officer in charge and transferring
allegiance to Lieutenant Chipp. James Bartlett, First-Class Fireman, for example, recalled how he and a shipmate, chafing against the "unnecessary"
delay on the Kotel'nyy sandspit, plotted to steal a can of pemmican, a rifle,
and ammunition, and desert. "If De Long had not moved, we would have
left him . . . probably to our sorrow and death, but we had that idea."

Early on 7 September the pack opened up and they got away again,
bearing southwest for Stolbovoy Island. The freshening wind raised the sea,
and the boats took in water at every roll. Broken ice surrounded them; waterspouts shot twenty feet in the air from huge honeycombed floes. Drenched
and half blinded by freezing spray, each boat's oarsmen pulled manfully,
some with bare hands or makeshift cotton mittens, as their fur gloves had
long since rotted or vanished. Others furiously pumped and bailed. The first
cutter and the whaleboat managed to cling together, but, as usual, the second
cutter struggled in the rear. In De Long's boat the dog howled incessantly.

The whaleboat sprang a leak, and water poured in faster than the pumps
or bucket brigade could eject it. Melville ran the boat to a floe, where the
men hauled it out and overturned it for a bilge inspection. Prolonged car-
oming through the ice had dislodged a drain plug. Melville hammered it
back into place and sawed off a protruding portion likely to cause the same
trouble. The crew righted the boat, and under lugsail and oars they plunged
off again. Chipp meanwhile had fallen farther astern. De Long and Melville
had to double reef their sails or they once more would have lost the second
cutter. Night fell. The sea increased. Wrote Ambler when all hands were
camped on a solitary floe after thirty-three wild hours, "We took in water
everywhere, bow, beam and stern. I was as usual in a particularly forward
spot, sea after sea taking me from the shoulders down."

Next morning, 9 September, they took to their boats again. They had swept past Stolbovoy, and continuing northeast squalls now carried them over a lumpy ice-flecked sea in which cakes large enough to drag their half-paralyzed limbs upon grew fewer and fewer. But after darkness fell Melville's men, far ahead of their shipmates in the other two boats, heard the welcome roar of surf. Daybreak brought sunshine and spent winds. The waves subsided. Above the southern horizon loomed mud-brown cliffs and by nightfall all three boat crews were encamped on tiny Semenovskiy Island. The travelers scooped fresh water from muddy pools. A hunting party brought in a 120-pound doe. Venison steak and hot tea were greedily consumed, and "for the first time in months [we] enjoyed the almost forgotten sensation of feeling replete and distended with palatable food."

They crept into newly dried sleeping bags. Warmth combined with full stomachs brought a peaceful sleep, but the sense of security was deceptive. De Long felt that his men needed the halt to rest and recover their stamina, and the boats needed repairs. The final push for Siberia would test men and equipment anew.

There had been, since the beginning of the retreat from the lost *Jeannette*, longer stays than the halt at Semenovskiy. More spleen than true observation may have inspired Jerome Collins's private reference to "some grumbling among the men at the delay on this island, as we have a fair wind and open sea and are only 96 miles from Barkin. This is our 90th day from the ship, and for the sake of a feed of meat we are delaying or losing two good days." But George Melville also seems to have felt misgivings, for he later admitted that "when we killed the deer and De Long said now we would have a good meal, I said 'Captain, miles would be better than meals.' "

Under Melville's direction, Cole and Bartlett cut the canvas boatcover from the stern of the whaleboat and tacked it around the rail at both bows, raising it on sixteen-inch wooden stanchions lashed to the gunwale on each side. The result was a rough cockpit to shelter the men. Weathercloth was similarly improvised for the other craft. While this work proceeded, hunters once more swept the island and Surgeon Ambler's scientific curiosity led him into what he described as a field of tumuli, from which he dug a portion of a mastodon's tooth.

The party had been on Semenovskiy Island some forty-eight hours when De Long composed a terse record which he sealed in a can and buried, marking the spot with a tentpole, "in case of any search for us before we can place ourselves in communication with home." All hands were in good health, "have had no scurvy. . . . We have yet about seven days provisions—full rations." 11 September was a Sunday. He conducted the formality postponed a week ago, mustering the crew and reading them the Articles of War. Divine service followed in his tent. It was destined to be the last attended by the *Jeannette*'s complete brotherhood of commissioned officers.

CHAPTER SIXTEEN

THE BOAT DASH

*We are all well, have had no scurvy, and hope with God's aid to
reach the settlements on the Lena River during the coming week.*
Lieutenant De Long's report left on Semenovskiy Island,
11 September 1881

AN OVERNIGHT SNOWFALL half buried the tents. On the morning of the
twelfth the temperature stood at freezing. Whitecaps ran before a fresh east
wind, but there was little floating ice. De Long's people, as he had noted in
his sealed report, were in generally good condition. For this, Surgeon Ambler
could award himself credit. Seaman Erikson's frostbitten feet were no worse,
and the commander's were improving. Danenhower's defective left eye had
grown discolored and more congested, but, even wearing a dark glass over
the other, he managed to move about with little or no aid.

At breakfast De Long reminded Chipp and Melville of their instructions
as commanders of the second cutter and the whaleboat. He intended to make
southwest across a hundred miles of open sea to Cape Barkin and with native
guidance enter the Lena River at its northern mouth, marked "light tower"
on his chart. On the passage to Barkin the whaleboat and second cutter must
endeavor to keep within hail of the captain, in the first cutter, but once at
the delta they need not wait for him but should instead "proceed up the river
to safety."

Melville was not quite in harmony with this plan. The Lena delta consisted of a baffling number of mouths, what the engineer would call a "perplexity of entrances." He would have preferred a landing at either the mouth of the Yana or even that of the Indigurka, respectively two hundred miles and five hundred miles east of the Lena. Because the expedition was now too far westward to consider either course, Melville proposed that they at least make for the eastern side of the Lena delta, where Nordenskjöld's escort steamer *Lena* had gained entrance after vain attempts in the northern approaches. De Long, with Chipp's support, argued that small boats might succeed where the larger steamer had failed. No further objection coming from the chief engineer, the conference in De Long's tent ended, the party broke camp, and by 9:00 A.M. all three boats were under way.

Except for an interlude of repair to Melville's whaleboat on a floe, the forenoon hours brought smooth sailing. After lunch on the floe, which was well scraped of snow to fill iron stewpots and kettles, the boats sped on again, their dipping lugsails drawing full under an increasingly brisk northeast breeze. When the wind rose, Melville took one reef in the sail and continued on this way until late afternoon, the first cutter slightly ahead and off his starboard bow. Then the wind began to blow so hard that the first cutter and the whaleboat, if not Chipp's lagging vessel as well, were obliged to sail close-reefed. By 5:00 P.M. the whaleboat, faster than the others, had veered out of formation and was bouncing along five hundred yards off the first cutter's weather quarter. She looked as though she would shoot right past.

De Long took a barometer reading. Even as he noted its rapid fall, the storm struck. "We shipped one sea that nearly swamped us, filling our boat to the thwarts." Men began pumping and bailing for dear life. "Taking seas over our stern and quarter, two right after each other. Part of one reef shaken out, attempting to stay ahead. Did no good." The words are Ambler's, and, while his firsthand account portrays the whaleboat drawing up and passing, he says nothing of De Long trying to communicate with it by waving. Neither do the other diarists in the first cutter, Jerome Collins nor the captain himself.

Others were heard from much later. Danenhower, in the whaleboat with Melville, testified that the chief engineer had sought his advice about how to get back into position near the first cutter. He replied that this could be done by jibbing twice and lowering the sail. "He then told me to take charge. So I jibbed carefully, ran down to the captain's wake, then jibbed her again, each time having lowered the sail and gotten out two oars to keep up the headway before the sea while shifting the sail." With Seaman Herbert Leach at the helm "we ranged along the weather side of the first cutter. . . . At dusk the captain stood up in the boat and waved his hand as if for us to separate. This is what the men say. I did not see it."

What the men said varied. Will Nindemann was in the first cutter, and his stated recollection was that De Long's purpose in waving was to bring Melville alongside so that he could tell him to keep close. Fireman Bartlett, seated aft in the whaleboat, described its position as ahead and to windward of the first cutter, which Chief Engineer Melville could not see unless he turned around. Bartlett called out that he believed De Long was signaling. "Melville said, 'To go ahead or come back?' I think I said, 'To go ahead.' 'Well,' says he, 'don't look back again.' "

Melville maintained in testimony that the boats were taking in so much water it was absolutely necessary that each look out for itself. He remembered his whaleboat as "a little ahead of and on the weather bow of the first cutter." When someone in the whaleboat shouted that De Long was making signals, he looked about him and "saw [De Long] waving his arm." To get the whaleboat closer to the captain's boat he lowered his sail (Melville's account gives Danenhower none of the credit in this operation) and gathered in the foot of it. But slackening speed in this manner brought huge waves piling over the stern. "It was with difficulty that [the whaleboat] could be kept afloat. Lieutenant De Long seeing the position I was in shook his head and waved me on with his arm." In an amplified version Melville wrote of shouting down the wind to De Long that he must run or swamp, that De Long's response was "lost in the noise of the gale." But while noise and poor visibility (the vessels were at least four hundred yards apart) ruled out positive communication, "I felt we understood each other; that if I would save my boat and crew I must run for it; that to lay alongside of De Long meant quick destruction; and that if either of the open and overladen boats should swamp or roll over, the other could not possibly rescue the unfortunate crew." So when one of Melville's men said he thought De Long was waving to the whaleboat, "I told him he must be wrong and further directed that no one should see any signals now that we were cast upon our own resources." The captain had signaled "permission to leave him." That was enough. Melville hoisted sail, shook out a reef, and the whaleboat leaped forward. Trying to keep position near the first cutter, as ordained, had invited disaster, but "now that we were separated I resolved to concern myself with the safety of my boat."

As to the anguish and terror of that last sea dash, there could be no dispute. Any of the fourteen occupants of the first cutter and the eleven men in the whaleboat who glanced back through the spray-blurred twilight saw their shipmates in the second cutter fall farther and farther behind. By the time dusk had dropped over the sea, Charles Chipp and his company had vanished. Of the imperturbable lieutenant, the stubborn old ice-pilot Dunbar, the carpenter Sweetman, whose fortitude in the frigid bowels of the flooding *Jeannette* had earned him his captain's nomination for the Congressional Medal of Honor, of the seamen Kuehne, Starr, Warren, Johnson and Sharvell, no trace was ever to be found.

THE OTHER TWO craft drove on, now in utter blackness and along diverging courses. Melville strove to keep his whaleboat ahead of the racing sea. Running dead before the northeast gale, the boat had been in danger of broaching to. He had hoisted sail, shaken out a reef, and hauled about more to the southward, bringing the wind hard against his port quarter. Swathed in spume from every wave that combed over the whaleboat's stern, Seaman Leach stood braced at the tiller, steering admirably, while others in the boat scooped at each incoming torrent with fingers nearly frozen to the pots and pails they clutched. Melville's improvised weather screen, a canvas awning half resting on the backs and shoulders of the men, gave scant protection. As the boat soared and plunged with each successive wave, some clung to the thwarts in sheer terror of hurtling overboard.

As the gale raged on, there grew a certainty among all hands that the boat must fill, roll over like a log, and sink. Melville knew he had somehow to swing its bows full into the wavecrests and heave to, riding out the storm head-on. The only practical means (proposed by Danenhower, or so the half-blind navigator alone would claim) was through employment of a drag-anchor. Properly fashioned and launched from the bow, it would act like a parachute, cleaving water instead of air, and keep the vessel's head to sea. Still clinging to the sheet with hands cracked and stung by icy saltwater, Melville detailed Seaman Frank Mansen and Boatswain Jack Cole to make the drag, and under Danenhower's immediate direction they lashed three tentpoles together, forming a triangle with eight-foot sides. The drag itself was a section of tent cloth laced to the three-cornered frame; the anchor cable was a length of manila line, attached to the corners of the drag by a three-legged manila bridle.

All this took up two hours, working in the dark with waves constantly crashing into the boat. The weathercloth was taken down to clear space, the drag placed forward of the mast ready for use, the anchor line coiled and clear for running. Melville chiefly worried whether the drag would be heavy enough to submerge while not so heavy that it sank altogether and hung vertically beneath the bows, compounding the danger of the boat foundering. Both he and Danenhower hoped that the iron straps, hooks, and brass tips of the hickory poles would be of sufficient weight. Another concern was bringing the boat about in such heavy weather. Danenhower asked Melville, beside him in the sternsheets, for permission to direct the operation. The chief engineer hesitated, then assented "since Danenhower was a professional sailor and perhaps aware of special points in seamanship that I was ignorant of." The exchange was necessarily brief in a boat shipping water every minute, and Danenhower lost no further time. He ordered Mansen and Henry

Wilson to the oars, placed Boatswain Cole at the halyards for lowering the sail, and moved Aniguin and Charley Tang Sing to gather in the canvas as it came down. Bartlett, in the bow, would launch the drag. Melville still tended the sheet. Lauterbach and Raymond Newcomb strenuously bailed, and the tiller remained in the hands of Seaman Leach, who stood in the stern—an awesomely stalwart figure streaming with water. His position was crucial to the success of the maneuver.

In less harrowing circumstances John Danenhower might have relished the satisfaction of command restored, however momentarily, and of challenge and responsibility, long deferred. But the job to be done dominated all thought. The lives of all hands, himself included, depended on his snapping forth an order at precisely the right split-second. His begoggled eye narrowed against the freezing spray, he watched for a chance, gauging the rhythm of the seas, timing the boat's rise to a crest and plunge into a trough. At the first opportunity he shouted, "Lower away." Out shot the oars, port and starboard, and down came the sail, but the lull was deceptive, too fleeting, the sea cresting again before the whaleboat could fully come about. The fresh wave struck broadside, almost capsizing the boat. Danenhower met the crisis expertly, setting half the men back to bailing, slackening off one oarsman, and spurring the other to fiercer effort. Around came the boat, and the instant it was head to wind Danenhower ordered oars eased and the drag launched.

Bartlett flung the drag from the bow, and the effort combined with the whaleboat's forward pitch almost sent him flying after it into the sea. He saved himself by grabbing the halyards. The boat rising to meet another wave threw him back against the mast. Dismayed shouts that the drag had not submerged, was too light, brought further quick commands from either Melville or Danenhower. Jack Cole, standing by with a heavy copper firepot (and laughing insanely, his shipmates would recall) promptly slid it out over the bow and down the anchor line to the sea.

The drag fell obediently beneath the surface. The sail was furled, the oars brought in. The canvas weathercloth was once more raised to its stanchions along the gunwales and off the men's soaked and aching shoulders.

The half-decked forecastle instead of the open stern now bore the brunt of a storm that refused to abate. The whaleboat bucked and tossed like a tethered beast gone berserk, but the drag performed as it was supposed to and kept the vessel's bows to the sea. Leach had at last abandoned the tiller; a steering oar astern would suffice to aid the drag at the bow. Shouting above the thunder of waves and wind, Melville divided the men into two watches. Cole and Bartlett would have charge of the forward part of the boat, Leach, Wilson and Mansen taking two-hour shifts at the steering oar. Melville was suddenly aware that his legs had swelled, his feet were bereft of feeling. He slumped against the mast, "leaving me in command," Danenhower would say. In the more memorable words of the chief engineer, "Thus we passed the night, an incubus of horrors."

WHEN THE WHALEBOAT broke formation and surged ahead, passing him off the port quarter, Lieutenant De Long had just put a reef in his sail. He wanted to slow his cutter's speed so his executive officer struggling astern might catch up. But now the storm had reached full fury. At dusk De Long could see neither whaleboat nor second cutter, and it was touch and go whether his own craft would endure. He shook out the reef and endeavored to pick up headway, the cutter shipping heavy seas that drenched Hans Erikson at the tiller and his frantically bailing shipmates. The boat was overloaded, carrying not only fourteen men and a dog but an assortment of cargo, most of it wedged beneath the thwarts, which included tents and poles, navigation instruments, rifles and shotguns, the doctor's medicine chest, cooking pots and cans of pemmican, and two or three tin boxes containing ship's logs and other records.

After darkness fell, a particularly violent wave slammed the boat into a bad yaw and heeled it over. For seconds it hovered almost horizontally to port, the men hanging on to whatever their numbed hands could grasp, Snoozer the dog half-drowned and clawing wildly at the thwarts, Seaman Erikson all but submerged yet still wrestling with the tiller. The mast came away at the step and tumbled into the foam, dragging sail and yards with it. The heavy load jammed under the thwarts acted as ballast and rolled the cutter back upright, and on it plunged again, dead before the wind, its dazed men once more bailing hard. The sheered-off mast and billowing sail trailed by the halyards, an unintentional sea anchor. In the sternsheets, with water swirling about his waist, De Long fought to maintain control. He ordered the oars out to steady the boat, drove the bailers into redoubled effort, and had the impromptu sea anchor hauled in before its dragging weight capsized the boat.

Even so, a sea anchor was necessary, to hold the cutter's bow on to the waves. De Long had one made of an old boatcover and an alcohol keg. The boat rode under its lee no more than an hour before it broke away, but another drag was hastily fashioned out of a pickaxe, two oars, and a sled cover. Launched from a reeling bow this latest contraption shot sideways instead of ahead, to ride the length of its taut line off the cutter's beam, holding the vessel in the wave troughs, where it wallowed all night and into the next day. "Utter misery," wrote Jerome Collins when he was able to. "Hopeless except in the mercy of Almighty God we sat jammed together for nearly 72 hours. Surgeon served out small brandy doses. . . . All the hair washed off my parka as I sat under every sea that came over."

The weather finally moderated. In the afternoon of the second day at sea a damage party led by Nindemann had hauled in the toppled mast and lashed it upright again, with a jury sail rigged of sodden canvas spread at the yard. The bailers kept going all the time and were able to relax their aching muscles only toward midnight when the seas fell and departing clouds gave way to stars, a bright moon, and auroral flashes.

On the fourteenth the barometer continued to rise. De Long scanned the waves but saw nothing of the second cutter or the whaleboat. His own vessel continued to run westward, losing speed as the wind dropped. For some days, De Long was in no condition to command. His feet and hands were swollen and blue, and he had what Ambler described as "a nervous chuckle in the throat." The doctor gave him a double dose of brandy. Two of the men worked his benumbed limbs into a sleeping bag, where he remained until Saturday, the seventeenth—the day of their landfall in the Lena delta.

De Long's company had made way steadily westward, creeping along under their little jury rig, until low patches of land appeared on the southern horizon. De Long, huddled with bandaged hands in his sleeping bag, ordered an attempt to make shore. It proved a prolonged and discouraging experience. The cutter soon encountered young ice through which, with six men straining at the oars, it buffeted its way, only to ground while still two or three miles offshore. High tide increased the water's depth by only a few inches. But De Long had concluded that it would be folly to remain on the ocean. Aware that he had drifted some distance west of Cape Barkin, the appointed rendezvous for his separated people, he also knew that to pursue it as his destination meant struggling back eastward under oars with an exhausted crew and diminishing food, an alternative he felt was no more prudent or practicable than continuing westward into the unknown. Moreover, new ice steadily formed an ever-widening coastal barrier that would make landfall increasingly difficult. So he ordered the cutter partly unloaded and sent those who could walk and shoulder gear wading waist-deep through ice-encrusted surf. Once their loads were deposited at the water's edge, they sloshed back to the lightened boat and hauled it bodily over the hidden shoals, all hands bending to the work except those crippled by frostbite.

Thoroughly soaked and often stumbling over submerged rock, the men dragged the cutter fully a mile before it stuck fast with a thousand yards still to go. At that point the unloading was completed, and the boat abandoned. Three more floundering trips each way, the last one in a snowstorm, brought the entire party, with its invalids, the dog Snoozer, its still-considerable baggage, and a single sled, assembled on a strip of frozen shingle bestrewn, fortunately, with plenty of driftwood for their campfire.

CHAPTER SEVENTEEN

A Fatal Delay

*I did all I could in the circumstances to get my people up the river
and relief to De Long.*

Chief Engineer Melville

SIBERIA IS ENORMOUS. The Autonomous Republic of Yakutsk, which is the
name today of the region in which De Long landed, has a half-dozen great
rivers, all flowing into the Arctic Ocean. Of these rivers, the mightiest is the
Lena. Almost three thousand miles long, it drains a million square miles of
Yakutsk's central plain, nourishing a basin rich in gold and mica. Histori-
cally, the Lena is a route from the polar seas to the southern steppes over
which have traveled Russian explorers, Cossack freebooters, tsarist legions,
Bolshevik revolutionaries, the enduring aborigines of the north such as the
Yakut, Chukchi, Tungus, and Yukagir, and chance intruders from distant
lands, among these Lieutenant George De Long.

He had to look for the river. More than any similar confluent system,
the Lena delta is an estuarial maze, a bewildering mesh of streams and inlets,
two hundred sixty miles along its coastline and covering an area almost as
large as New England. On detailed maps, its configuration suggests a fully
spread fan, the left half more or less plain, the right half minutely filigreed.
That eastern section is not so much a land mass veined by streams as a huge

cluster of bog-like islands, ice-covered for eight months of the year and interlaced with countless twisting channels. The first voyagers up the Lena from the Arctic Ocean, seventeenth-century Cossack plunderers, soon learned to enter the river along either the southeastern or the western side of the delta, in preference to the more baffling northern approaches. Eighteenth-century expeditions thus confirmed that it was possible to avoid entrapment in the delta, sure disaster during winter when, as Chief Engineer Melville was to pronounce for the benefit of future travelers in the region, "the whole of the north and east part of the archipelago lies in the silence of death."

The men of the *Jeannette* reached the Lena delta as summer gave way to winter. But after their stormy crossing of the Laptev Sea from Semenovskiy Island, De Long's group and Melville's group, neither certain of the other's survival, landed at widely different points.

De Long was well beyond Cape Barkin, that much he knew. His chart told him little more. De Long's focus on Barkin as a rendezvous, the site of a native settlement, had derived from Petermann's exaggerated notice of it, which was in turn based on notes made in 1822 by Lieutenant Peter Feodor Anjou during his survey of Siberia's Arctic coastline. All that Cape Barkin could have offered, had any of the *Jeannette*'s company landed there, was a handful of empty huts used in summer months by Tungus fishermen and reindeer-hunters. Sagastyr was another possible objective, and here De Long's party might have met with better luck. The "light tower" on the chart that had caught his attention was a beacon Anjou's explorers were supposed to have erected sixty years before to mark the mouth of the river's northern branch. (Captain Hans Christian Johannesen of the *Lena*, seeking a northern entrance in 1878, had looked for a "signal tower" and found none.) At Sagastyr, only a few half-ruined huts or *baligans* remained of what was once a village, but within a few miles stood at least two settlements, Kitach and especially North Bulun, with about one hundred inhabitants. Had De Long allowed himself just another six or eight miles westerly passage in the first cutter, gone ashore at Sagastyr and struck south, he would have quickly found shelter and assistance.

Adding to his disorientation, however, was the fact that Sagastyr was marked twice on his chart, properly on the northern shore and misleadingly to the south, near the head of the delta. The chart did not show North Bulun, of whose existence he was unaware. There being no sign of life in the vicinity of his landing place, he set his new goal as Kumakh-Surt, a settlement on the main river south of the delta. He guessed the distance to it from his present camp as about equal to the voyage just completed from Semenovskiy, about a hundred miles. The chart showed deceptively few of the delta's multitudinous branches. With each spring flood, so many new streams and islets appeared, and old ones vanished or took new direction, that no permanent, reliable chart of the delta was possible.

Betokening an abundance of game in the delta, a gull swooped over the beach and Alexey downed it with the Winchester. With bird soup a welcome change from their pemmican, De Long gave his people a Sunday's rest. Ambler took the opportunity to treat the frostbite cases, the worst of whom was Hans Erikson, whose foot blisters had to be drained of their bloody serum and the blackened toes dressed with carbolized vaseline and cotton batting. Pain still throbbed in the captain's own feet and hands, but he kept his thoughts on the task of leading his men safely home. He outlined his latest plans in a brief message that he buried in a cache near the beach, marked by an embedded tentpole. His last such record, left on Semenovskiy Island, had expressed a hope that his party would "reach the settlements on the Lena River during the coming week." That was eight days ago. His latest one concluded: "We must now try with God's help to walk to a settlement, the nearest of which I believe to be 95 miles distant. We are all well—have four days provisions—arms and ammunition, and are carrying with us only ship's books and papers, with blankets, tents and some medicines, therefore our chances of getting through seem pretty good."

Thick snow fell upon the two tents that evening as De Long prepared to read divine service. He found his bible too sodden and read instead from a prayer book. Calculating the day to be the fifteenth Sunday after Trinity, he afterwards noted that the ordained text was "peculiarly apt to our situation." It was Matthew VI, 34. "Take therefore no thought for the morrow . . . sufficient unto the day is the evil thereof."

The following noon, all stood to for departure. Among the material left on the beach were De Long's sextant and the artificial horizon, a stove, one of the tents, and the remains of sleeping bags rendered useless through saturation and cut up to make footnips. With two cases of ship's records lashed to a sled hauled by four men, De Long took the lead, shouldering a flagstaff from which flew the blue silk ensign his wife had sewn. With Snoozer trotting alongside the column, they began their long march south by trudging directly into the delta.

No trees obscured the view. The Lena delta is a vast tundra sliced into sandbanks and swampy islands by the river's ramifications. No more than a few hundred yards could be traveled in a straight line. By nightfall the party had covered only four miles. Shortly after the dinner halt, Nindemann shouted from the rear and when De Long and Doctor Ambler turned back to investigate they found Erikson on his knees in the slushy moss pleading to be left there. De Long would not hear of it. With the doctor's aid, he hauled Erikson upright and assigned two of his shipmates to help him along. Nindemann carved a crutch out of driftwood for him. Geared to his hobbling pace, though, they could make little more than a mile each hour. "Reaching anywhere with him disabled is out of the question," De Long wrote gloomily. He began to think of sending two of the most able-bodied of his party ahead for assistance, but his immediate decision was to further lighten the load.

His selections for sacrifice rankled some of the men and would spark future debate. The single remaining tent had been cut in half, the two sections rigged on a crude wood frame to form a dual shelter. (Beds were logs and blankets.) Jerome Collins thought it would have been wiser to retain the other tent or the navigation instruments, and leave cached the expedition's voluminous records, "a lot of truck, logbooks, etc., etc., what weighed the men down beyond their strength." Collins had not forgotten the loss of his own prized log, and his by now almost pathological scorn for the leader excited him to wildly cryptic observation: "The general plan of running the machine that has been our bane so long, still holds like a horse-leech and sucks our chances of escape away." But however indicative of a tortured mind, words more pitiable than convincing, they were to some degree in line with the view of the meteorologist's less embittered colleagues. "Our outlook at this rate is a poor one," wrote James Ambler, and it was probably at his urging that De Long sent Nindemann back to stow in the cache at the beach the *Jeannette*'s logbooks covering two years.

Keeping to the east bank of a sluggish stream assumed to be an outfall of the main river, they made five more miles on the third day of travel. Blinding snow hampered them all the way, and at the dinner halt they huddled in silence waiting for matches and wood to dry before the fire could be built. Then they tried to sleep, two knots of seven men, each covered by half a tent, in De Long's words "like tarpaulins over merchandise." The next afternoon, they reached a bend in the stream and found two vacant huts, one run-down, the other more inviting. De Long took this to be all there was of what his chart signified with a barely pronounceable name: "Is this Tschol-bogoje? If this is a 'settlement' our chances of keeping on are very slim. According to my account we are 35 miles from the next *station* and 87 from a probable settlement." De Long's "account" was his chart, which named the second Sagastyr and further below it, Kumakh-Surt. "We have two days rations after breakfast tomorrow, and we have three lame men who cannot move more than five or six miles."

Again he pondered the question of sending two strong men ahead, with Ambler a likely candidate, while "we . . . stay here and eke out," he wrote in one of the huts. "Though loth to do anything that looks like abandoning us [the doctor] is willing to try anything." In his own notebook Ambler explained his lack of "compunction about leaving [De Long]" as due to a belief that "the chance of surviving the winter here was as good as making 100 miles over unknown country without food and shelter."

The anxious cogitation of both men was interrupted by a knock at the hut door, and there stood a gleeful Alexey back from a hunt, brandishing the hindquarters of a reindeer and two tongues as evidence of his kill. The two animals were so large it took six men led by Nindemann to bring them in. "This changes plans. We can remain here a day or two and let our sick catch up," De Long wrote. The most severe frostbite cases were Erikson, Boyd, and Ah Sam. "They cannot move now, and we are so well off for deer meat (100 pounds probably) that the necessity for separating our party seems not a pressing matter."

Few reprieves could have been more reveled in. De Long's old good humor began to creep back as he watched his men gorge themselves on fried steaks, liver, and hearts. For several meals to come the cooking pot would steam with bones boiling for soup. Collins lost some of his grouchiness; his private journal shows that he "made sketches of scenes en route for C.O." Among the others, resigned discontent with De Long's leadership momentarily gave way to sympathy and devotion. Seaman Carl Görtz, for example, made the captain a pair of mittens and greased his painful feet. "Our three lame men can walk," wrote De Long on 24 September as they prepared to leave the huts. Two days ration of deer meat remained, perhaps to be replenished if Alexey's good luck and marksmanship held, and the two days supply of pemmican was sealed in its can for reserves.

Strength regained, morale fortified—now was the ideal time for De Long to have crossed the stream and struck due west. It would not be easy going, but they would have had to build a raft eventually, regardless of what direction they took through the delta. Some streams were patched with ice, not yet thick enough to bear weight but no barrier either to poling across. Three or four days westward travel would have brought his party within sight of North Bulun. But De Long had no means of knowing this. He wrote another summary of events, stating as before that "each officer in charge of a boat had written orders to proceed in case of separation to the Lena River and not wait for anyone short of a settlement." He shoved the paper into a tinderbox and tied it to a post in the hut. Because one of the Winchesters had a broken stock, he left that in the hut as well, and imagining the reaction of natives who might come upon it he called it "a surprise for the next visitor." He could not have divined that the huts in which his men had fed and rested two nights were indeed to receive visitors within forty-eight hours, an eastbound pair of Tungus huntsmen from that not-so-distant settlement. By then the Americans were several miles south, still on the lookout for the main river while plunging deeper into the maze.

MELVILLE'S BOAT HAD parted company with the others at about one-third the distance from Semenovskiy Island to the Lena delta, the second cutter falling astern and out of sight, De Long's vessel running before the wind, the whaleboat riding out the storm bows on to the sea. Next morning Melville roused himself and reassumed command, to the extent that he had lost it to Danenhower during the long night. Frozen and exhausted, Melville's people monotonously bailed. As soon as the wind had calmed sufficiently for the whaleboat to get under way again, Melville tried to make south for Cape Barkin but repeatedly shoaled with the land not yet in sight. Melville then obeyed instincts that had told him all along, since before the departure from Semenovskiy, that the southeastern edge of the delta afforded the safest means of reaching the river proper. Carrying reefed sail, with Fireman Bartlett sounding with a tentpole and Danenhower "at the coxswain's feet conning the boat," they worked southeastward under oars towards the unseen coast, constantly avoiding sandbars, until the night of 15 September found them entering the Bay of Buorkhaya. It was now so cold that the bailers had to work fast, casting out the sea before the water froze to the thwarts. Some of the men wept from the agony of frostbite.

During these hours, with neither De Long nor Doctor Ambler at hand to declare him unfit for duty, and eager to compensate for his mortifying period of idleness, Danenhower had sought every chance to assert his seniority. That Melville foiled him each time, or tried to, was enough to put the half-blind officer in a simmering mood, but it was Raymond Newcomb, an old irritant and technically still under arrest, who touched off his rage. Danenhower ordered Newcomb at 4:00 A.M. to get a sounding. Newcomb's first response was to enquire where the lead line was. Danenhower told him it was at his feet in the dark, and then "he asked me how, but he had bragged often enough about being a practical yachtsman and I said, 'Stop mumbling, get that sounding.' He said, 'I have as much right to talk as you.' Instantly I choked him, threw him to the bottom of the boat and told him that if he didn't obey I would kill him." So Danenhower testified later, an account which the naturalist never denied. (Both Danenhower and Melville appear to have kept journals, but neither record has come to light. The following chronicle of events is pieced together on the basis of their testimony.)

On the sixteenth, eight oarsmen steadily pulling, the whaleboat crept into one of the river's many mouths and at nightfall, having sighted a hut, Melville led his men ashore. Cape Barkin was now an unknown distance up the coast (subsequently established as about forty miles), and Melville had no intention of spending any more time in search of it. The people were fatigued and half frozen. They "had had enough of Arctic seas for the present," Melville recognized, and they rested in the hut with aching limbs outstretched, the frostbite sufferers quickly discovering that baring feet to the fire only replaced the familiar numbness with an excruciating tingle. Next morning they were under way again, holding course westward, constantly on the lookout for one of the settlements which Melville, no less than De Long, believed to be scattered across the delta. Instead the engineer could see only "a desolate maze of shoal, swamps and muddy islands. . . . Bitterly we cursed Petermann and all his works which had led us astray." They pressed on, "working always towards the headwaters of the delta as long as we could swing oars."

But at that instant, Melville and his party were surer of their position than the crew of the first cutter ever was of theirs. The whaleboat had entered the delta at its southeast edge and had cut across the lower right-hand corner of the open fan. They followed the stream under oars or closely reefed sail, and, despite the twists and turns and shallows that kept Bartlett ever watchful at the sounding pole, Melville correctly determined that his party had arrived at the Lena's main southeast outlet. Thus he had outflanked the labyrinth in which his captain and thirteen shipmates were steadily losing themselves.

On 19 September, weaving in and around sandspits and ice-caked mud-flats, the whaleboat made a convoluted thirty miles. With fresh hope, its crew glimpsed huts on high ground to the south. During a meal break, the first natives appeared, three Tungus huntsmen in dugout canoes. Following an initial wariness on both sides, each group gave way to a mutual display of belongings—"they showed their hunting gear, we our compass, watches, rifles"—and a friendly interchange of victuals, pemmican, and hot tea for fish, goose, and venison. The settlement to which the seamen were escorted, afterwards designated Little Borkhia, consisted of four huts, several store-houses, and a graveyard. It overlooked a bight in which fishermen were casting nets. Here Melville's party stayed overnight, lodging together be-neath the same roof. It was now that a series of attempts began, probed later in a swirl of controversy, to get to a place called Bulun.

The valleys and plains south of the Lena delta are today a target for mineral prospectors, professors from the Yakutsk Permafrost Institute, and graduates of such political education centers as the Institute for Northern Peoples in Leningrad, whose mission is to keep remote school systems briefed on the latest advances in Communist learning and culture. Yet, despite a withering away of tribal traditions, most inhabitants of the northern tundra and taiga (subarctic coniferous forest) still depend on fishing and the fur trade, as their forebears did at the time of the *Jeannette* and for generations preceding. From Bulun today, almost in the shadow of the Lower Lena Hy-droelectric Plant, fishermen still ship their catch fifteen hundred miles south to Yakutsk. Bulun (not to be confused with North Bulun) lies less than one hundred miles south of the Lena delta (about fifty miles upriver from Kumakh-Surt, De Long's objective after abandoning the first cutter), and in the late nineteenth century was the region's point of departure for the city of Yakutsk, which linked Siberia with the rest of the world by special courier to the telegraph station at Irkutsk.

Melville's stated purpose in settling on Bulun as his goal was that he could communicate with the Russian authorities and arrange a search for his missing shipmates. Not that he had much hope of finding any alive, he recalled, and the rest of his party felt the same way. On the evening of his first meeting with the natives at Little Borkhia, the chief engineer strove through pantomime, pencil sketches, and by shuffling three sticks, to convey his story of the *Jeannette* and her three separated boatloads, and to impress upon the natives the necessity of getting word to Bulun. The people responded with negative signs which the Americans took to mean that anyone who tried to make the journey would most likely perish.

The whaleboat party nevertheless pushed off next morning, without native escort. Danenhower took the helm until the snow fell so thickly it smothered the glass over his good eye. Melville ordered the boat anchored to a shoal with three tentpoles, brass tips rammed deep into the mud, and his party rode out the night whipped by snow squalls and unable to sleep. When dawn broke, Danenhower recommended going back to Little Borkhia and forcing the natives into service. "We had two Remingtons and a shotgun and I knew it would be easy to carry our point." They did go back, with four frozen men including Melville, "my legs a mass of blisters and sores from the knees down." But Danenhower's proposal to enlist native help at gunpoint went no further.

Their next departure from Little Borkhia was in a different direction, more southeastward, and they went at the persuasion of the natives, who led them to Cape Bykovskiy, at the upper end of an anvil-shaped peninsula jutting into the Bay of Buorkhaya. That journey took about five days, almost as long as it would have taken had they instead continued their original westward thrust along the branch then south upriver to Bulun. The Tunguses wanted Melville to visit their main village, Zemovialach, one of a cluster of little islands opposite the cape, and meet its starista, or head man. The starista, Nicolai Shagra, greeted the eleven strangers in a friendly fashion and offered them food and shelter, but he too emphasized that it was a bad time of year to think of heading for Bulun. Winter, too close for ice-free river navigation, was not yet close enough for sled travel.

The next morning, however, he had his servants put sixty fish in the whaleboat with nets for catching more and provided three pilots, each with a canoe. Again the whaleboat pushed off but had not gone far under oars or sail when ice formed among the shoals. The natives made signs that they should proceed no further. By then, more of Melville's party were in a bad way from frostbite. That evening the starista reiterated his warning against too early an attempt to make Bulun. If they waited fifteen days, when sled travel became possible, he would furnish every assistance. Meanwhile they would be properly quartered, and the sick men given a chance to recuperate. Melville recalled his reaction to this advice in words that reflected common-sense if not quite his usual breezy self-assurance. It was "imperative for me to be cautious and not risk the lives of those entrusted to my care." If they ventured on the river and the ice caught them between Zemovialach and Bulun, it would mean probable death. So he had the whaleboat hauled high and dry, saw that the men were comfortably installed in the two huts placed at their disposal, and bade them rest and stay cheerful during the fortnight's wait.

The starista's pessimistic assessment of the odds against a safe journey to Bulun applied to Zemovialach on the twenty-eighth of the month, not to the fishing camp at Little Borkhia from which Melville had made an abortive attempt on the twenty-first. In this narrow subseason, neither summer nor winter, the passage of six days and a fifty-mile relocation southeast could make quite a difference. From Little Borkhia, the whaleboat party might have reached the head of the Lena delta in two days and thereafter made good progress southward, the broad river still open. Bulun was not nearly as far away as Melville afterwards claimed to have thought. He could have been there within five days, or at least the strongest men in his party could have been, the sick remaining behind at the fishing camp. All in all, hindsight tells us that an earlier effort from Little Borkhia was Melville's last real opportunity to reach Bulun in time to have done De Long's party any good.

Even from Zemovialach some chance still existed, despite the starista's pessimism. But just how much hope, if pursued with zeal and competence, was a riddle that reams of opposing testimony made difficult to clarify. Ze-movialach stood at the mouth of the main eastern branch of the Lena—it was here that Captain Johannesen and his steamer *Lena* had entered for a trouble-free passage up the river to Yakutsk. That had been in late August not, as now, late September. Melville was to insist that between the middle of September and the middle of October lengthy travel in these parts was ruled out. Other evidence indicates that the ice about Cape Bykovskiy ex-tended only as far as the shoals, that had Melville managed to push over the bar from Zemovialach at any time during the first week in October he would have found ice-free water as far as Bulun.

Not fifteen but thirty-three days were to elapse before he set out for Bulun. On various occasions afterwards he would blame a prevalence of ice and an absence of ice, uncooperative natives and language difficulties, the poor condition of his men and a shortage of dogs. The delay of Chief Engineer Melville and the whaleboat party at Zemovialach, so fatal to their shipmates, was not easily accounted for. That they were on Cape Bykovskiy at all, so far out of their course to Bulun, was subsequently explained by Melville as in compliance with the wishes of the Tungus fishermen who wanted him to meet their head man, an act of courtesy he had felt it of advantage, indeed a duty, to go ahead with. For his part, John Danenhower would disclaim all responsibility, ready to point out that Melville, after all, had been placed in command, while saying of the natives only that "the reason they did not take us to Bulun, as they promised, is not very clear, even to me."

CHAPTER EIGHTEEN

DEATH IN THE DELTA

And where are we? I think at the beginning of the Lena River at last. My chart is simply useless. I must go on plodding to the south-ward, trusting in God to guide me to a settlement.

Journal of Lieutenant De Long, 1 October 1881

THE SAME DAY on which the whaleboat party under Melville reached Ze-movialach, some seventy miles northwest in the Lena delta a frustrated De Long, truly not knowing which way to turn, felt compelled to stage another show of discipline. The blow-up had been brewing for days, Nindemann "short and surly with me, has a bad habit of answering me as he would a shipmate." De Long valued the carpenter as a mainstay of the party, a quarter-master no less, but curt familiarity from an inferior was not to be counte-nanced, especially before the others.

Through no fault of Will Nindemann's, an earlier attempt to build a raft had failed. On the second attempt, working with rotten driftwood, in-sufficient lashings, and only a dull hatchet, he kept "growling and mutter-ing." When the raft was built and had taken its first load of three men across, De Long thought that Nindemann wasted time looking for shoal enough to avoid wading ashore. He shouted for him to hurry up, only to receive a sarcastic response. Returning for another load, Nindemann waited until the captain's back was turned then shook his fist at him and growled, "By Jesus Christ, I would sooner be with the devil in hell than along here with you." De Long overheard, spun around and told Nindemann to consider himself under arrest pending court-martial. But the futility of ritual in harsh circumstances may have become apparent to the commander, who also could not have forgotten that he had recommended Nindemann for the Congressional Medal of Honor. And after all, "our crazy raft," as Doctor Ambler called it "answered the purpose quite well." Four hours of hard paddling got the party and its gear to the other side, and before then De Long had ordered Nindemann to collect his traps and go to work again.

They camped at the foot of a bluff, conveniently situated so that they were able to rig a more satisfactory shelter, tricing up the sections of tent as a lee and bedding down around the campfire. Uncertainty weighed on De Long's mind. He believed himself to have struck the main branch of the Lena and to be no more than twelve miles from the head of the delta, but "it is hard to tell whether we stopped on the river or not. . . . We took a frozen stream, south-southwest, for the sake of walking, then cut 'across lots' to what I thought was *the* river. We will see in the morning." But next day he was no surer of his position. The spectre of starvation loomed distinctly. Twice in his journal he had mentioned, half in joking, that they might have to eat the dog. Now he touched on the possibility again, perhaps acknowledging to himself that it was the principal reason why they continued to take the animal along.

They had long eaten the last of Alexey's deer and were back on pemmican. All that remained on 27 September was enough for a single meal per man. But Alexey and Nindemann brought in another sizable buck. "Saved again," De Long wrote, with not only the human members of his party in mind, for had Alexey not proved himself once more quick on the trigger, firing when the mainspring broke on Nindemann's Winchester, "our provisions would consist of poor Snoozer."

They came across a line of moccasin prints which Alexey estimated were only two days old. This stirred speculation that a search party might be in the delta looking for them, a hope chilled by practical second thoughts. De Long was unaware of a more ironic possibility, that in their zig-zagging and occasional backtracking his men had crossed the path of two hunters who, it later transpired, had been quietly following them for two days. These were the natives who had called at the hut where he had left the other Winchester. Collecting that weapon, the hunters had trailed De Long's party until giving up for unknown reasons and reverting to their own course southeastward across the delta. Their destination was said long afterwards to have been Zemovialach.

Food ran short again. De Long's hunting detail sighted nothing but a few ptarmigan. Still he kept all hands pushing on, cutting across river beds by raft, tramping over swampy tundra, and sometimes sinking knee-deep in ponds thinly coated with ice and hidden under snow or moss. Frozen slush encased their improvised boots and De Long wrote of footwear heavily balled, "large and unwieldy, as if walking in sandbags." Erikson's every forward step had become an agony, his right foot shedding blackened lumps of flesh, exposing bone and tendons. "So far he has been able to keep up," Ambler recorded, "but God knows how long this will continue." Once they reached a settlement, his feet might be saved, his very life. Otherwise "the whole party would be sacrificed, for no man will be left alone."

When driftwood was plentiful they built bigger fires than they needed for just warmth or cooking. "God grant that our smoke may be seen by some party [bringing] assistance." Görtz lashed poles together into a twenty-foot flagstaff on which he raised a black blanket as a signal flag. At least it attracted a gull, which Alexey shot, providing soup for the fourteen. The birdgut served as bait on a fishline the Alaskan carefully lowered through a hole in the ice, but he caught nothing.

De Long had hopes of reaching the second Sagastyr on his chart. He had decided that it must be near the head of the delta and on the west bank of the channel they followed. But driftwood had become scarce, and they had chopped their last raft for firewood. "Though I think we have reached the edge of the delta, I am not sure of it and I don't like the idea of standing still. No boat, no material for building even a funny raft. One does not like to feel he is caught in a trap."

When next they found a hut Ambler examined Erikson's feet. The toes of his right foot were unrecognizable as toes; they were black, grossly smelling stubs. The doctor told De Long that moving on and forcing Erikson to carry on with them would most likely shorten his life. To stay where they were might prolong his life but at the risk of everyone starving to death. "I can do no more," De Long wrote. "We cannot cross water until it freezes or we are ferried over. I may be mistaken in our position and we may still be twelve miles from the delta end. This river making to the east may be the one I thought we had rafted some days ago, we may be that much out."

He sent men out searching for wood, enough to build a sturdier raft than before, for the water confronting them was five hundred yards wide and deep in midstream. More timber meant more lashings. But all that the men had to secure enough planks on which to float themselves were the ends of lanyards from their bundles of personal belongings.

The last day of the month dawned with a temperature of 16 degrees and the wide stream covered with ice. Collins and Alexey were off seeking reindeer, while some others looked for wood. Yet others remained in the hut, trying to comfort a shipmate as Doctor Ambler sawed four toes from his right foot and one from the left. Erikson bore the amputation without great pain, for by now the forward part of his feet had lost all feeling. But, as Collins noted when he and Alexey returned from the hunt empty-handed, "it cripples a big, able man and puts an end to his calling as a seaman." To De Long it was "a heartrending sight . . . the cutting away of bones and flesh of a man I hoped to return sound and whole to his friends. May God pity us."

Nindemann had found a four-foot plank and scraps of driftwood, from which he improvised a sled. They placed Erikson on it, and two men took up the drag line. Then all hands crossed the river, carrying their gear and the dog, dragging Erikson, and keeping themselves widely spaced so that the ice would not break under their concentrated weight.

In the hut, De Long had left his customary report, brought up to date: "We have two days provisions, but having been fortunate enough so far to get game in our pressing needs, we have no fear for the future." Confiding in his journal he was less sanguine. Winter had begun. From both sides of the frozen river, if river it was, stretched the endless patchwork of bare tundra and intersecting streams. Burning fires to attract attention was all very well, "but the attraction of whom?" One thing at least he felt he could be confident of. "If Chipp or Melville got through, they would naturally send back to look for us."

Once on the west bank they swung south again, advancing in spurts seldom longer than a hour, with fifteen-minute rests. One halt was longer because Ambler had to cut away more of Erikson's toes, leaving him finally with one, on his left foot. Nightly the man's delirious babble wrecked the others' sleep. Often the "river" narrowed to a small artery of ice which rambled this way and that, leaving De Long "much bewildered." Carefully, he rationed out the dwindling deer meat. "There is no denying it, we are pretty weak. Our food is not enough to keep up our strength." Sudden winds across the tundra swept the ice of efflorescence, leaving glassy spots, and De Long took his share of bad falls, "slip, slide, and down you are on your back."

De Long had crossed the river to find Sagastyr. He felt it had to be near the head of the delta. At one point he figured it as only four and a half miles away. "Tomorrow will show if I am right, and if Sagastyr is a settlement." Following a night too cold for sleep, they resumed the march, reaching a promontory where the "river" turned sharply south then forked east and west, each channel four hundred yards wide. "I am inclined to think we have reached the end of the Delta." He had revised his calculations. "Sagastyr, if there is such a place, is five miles southwest of us." They proceeded in that direction. Three days later, twelve more miles behind them, he wrote off Sagastyr as "a myth. We saw two old huts at a distance and that was all."

He had begun to note the passing days in relation to the date of their departure from the *Jeannette*. October 3 was "the 113th day . . . 5 A.M. . . . ate our last deer meat . . . Our remaining food now consists of four-

fourteenths pounds of pemmican each and a half-starved dog." By midday they had covered five miles, but the afternoon was a maddening waste of effort. Alexey twice reported seeing a hut on the eastern shore. "My desire was to get to it as quickly as possible." The party accordingly took to the ice again, crossing diagonally, resting on a sandbank while Alexey and Nindemann climbed a knoll for a better view. Alexey returned to announce that he could see not one but two huts. Nindemann was not so sure, but the Alaskan had seemed quite positive. De Long wrote, "not seeing very well myself, I unfortunately took his eyes as best and ordered an advance." They had made half a mile when De Long fell through the ice, sinking to his chin before the knapsack on his shoulders brought him up. "While I was crawling out, in went Görtz behind me to his neck, and behind him Collins to the waist. The moment we came out of the water we were each one sheet of ice." With no means of thawing themselves, they staggered on until it was apparent that their objective was nothing but a mound of earth, "a hut in shape only. Sick at heart, I ordered a camp to be made in a hole by the bluff face and soon, before a roaring fire, we were drying (and burning) our clothes while the cold wind ate into our backs."

They had nothing to cook for supper but Snoozer. De Long wrote of what he had prayed would never become necessary in a matter-of-fact tone, concealing his sorrow. "I ordered him killed and dressed by Iversen." Stew was made at once of the viscera. The remainder, to be carried, weighed twenty-seven pounds. Snoozer had been no better nourished than the men.

By daybreak the wind had risen higher, the temperature dropping fast. De Long could not accurately measure the cold for the last thermometer had smashed in a fall on the ice. In the night Erikson had worked his gloves off. Some of the company rubbed circulation back into his frozen hands but when they lashed him to his sled he was still unconscious. The party at last found a hut, just in time, for by then the southwesterly wind was blowing a full gale and snow fell heavily. In the hut, when they had a fire going, Doctor Ambler felt Erikson's pulse and told the captain that the man was dying.

De Long read prayers for the sick, "though I fear my broken utterances made little of the service audible."

Each man's food ration was a half-pound of fried dogmeat and a cup of tea from old leaves. Hardly a banquet, De Long thought, noting with relief that none voiced any complaint. Evidently they were grateful for shelter from the driving snow and the wind pounding on the walls of the hut. Racking his brains to figure out just where they were, he told himself they must have reached the island of Tit Ary, at the extreme southerly tip of the delta and would therefore be only twenty-five miles from Kumakh-Surt. "This is a last hope, for our Sagastyr has long since faded away. The hut we are in is quite new, and clearly not the astronomical station marked on my chart." It was however a hut that might at any moment be visited by natives. "Upon this last chance and one other seem to rest all our hopes of escape."

The "one other" derived from his plans to send two of the strongest on ahead while the main party labored along with Erikson and the other bad frostbite cases, Machinist Walter Lee, Fireman George Boyd, and the Chinese Ah Sam. This advance pair should make Kumakh-Surt more speedily and be able to bring back relief. In this connection De Long was consulting with Nindemann, the storm still howling about the hut, when they were twice interrupted, first by Alexey returning from an attempted hunt to report that the snow fell too thickly for even him to grope through. Then the doctor, who had been attending to the prostrate Erikson in a corner, reached over to close the man's eyes, turning to announce that he had died.

"I addressed a few words of cheer and comfort to the men." Little else could be done beyond the practical necessity of disposing of Erikson's body. Sewed up in flaps of tent and partly covered by De Long's blue ensign, it lay in the hut while his clothing and effects were reverently distributed, a bible and hymn book, a lock of hair, some personal photographs going to Kaak and Iversen, his closest messmates. The ground was too hard and snow-packed for grave digging, even had there been more tools at hand than Nindemann's hatchet. De Long ordered a hole chopped in the ice. After he had read the service for the dead and the men had drunk a little warm water with alcohol, they carried Erikson to the frozen river. Brick-hard sods hacked from the bank were thrust into the canvas shroud about the dead man's feet as weight. Iversen fired three shots with a Remington into the snowladen air, and Erikson's body was slipped through the ice. Nindemann hammered a board into the river bank, inscribed with: "In Memory H. H. Erikson. Oct. 6, 1881, USS *Jeannette*" and Doctor Ambler entered in his notebook, "Peace to his soul."

Next morning, each man ate his last half-pound of dogmeat, the copper kettle boiling the last grains of tea. The snowstorm had abated. "Now about to undertake our journey of 25 miles with some old tealeaves and two quarts of alcohol. However, I trust in God, and I believe that he who has fed us thus far will not suffer us to die of want now." They were three days in the hut. He left another record, this one reporting Erikson's death, and the party's continued determination to "make a forced march to Kumakh-Surt or some other settlement on the Lena River." He left the unusable Winchester. Their remaining weapons were a pistol and two Remingtons, with 243 rounds of ammunition. Nindemann thought the two heavy cases of ship's papers, De Long's journals and meteorological records that Lieutenant Chipp had assembled, should also be left behind and he said as much, "but the captain replied, 'Nindemann, as long as I can get along on my feet these records will go with me.' "

At noon, De Long likened their latest three miles' trek over barren ground between sinuous streams to "wandering in a labyrinth." He was back on the west bank (Kumakh-Surt and the settlements south including Bulun were all to the west of the river). But the region was more deceptive than he could possibly have thought and misled by his charts he had repeatedly overestimated direct distances covered. He was not on Tit Ary Island but some fifty miles still north of it, and instead of twenty-five miles to Kumakh-Surt the distance was more like eighty.

Alcohol was now the only nourishment. It appeared to Doctor Ambler that the three-ounce ration per man reduced the craving for food and kept up strength. This too proved an illusion. Feet frostbitten and eyesight failing, the captain himself could hardly drag his limbs forward. It had become an effort even to maintain his notebook entries. He felt he could no longer keep up with the men, much less lead them, and on 8 October he proposed to Doctor Ambler that they be given the option of staying at his side or making their own way south. Ambler's response was firm. If De Long gave up then he (the doctor) took command, in which case, "no one should leave him as long as I was alive."

But there could be no further delay in sending two men on ahead for relief. The stalwart Nindemann was an obvious choice. De Long was willing to let the doctor go as well. "But," wrote Ambler, "I thought my duty required me with him and the main body for the present." Louis Noros was selected. Early on the ninth all hands were mustered to wish their two shipmates godspeed. De Long gave them final instructions. They must keep to the west bank of the river, avoid wading, make for the other side only upon evidence there of natives or game. If Kumakh-Surt turned out to be another Sagastyr they must push on forty-five miles farther to Ajakit. A large Russian chart De Long carried showed Bulun as the next stop beyond that. Bulun was the ultimate objective. De Long gave them a copy of the small map he was working by, and pointed out Tit Ary, where he now supposed himself to be. He also issued them two ounces of alcohol, a rifle and ammunition. If they shot reindeer within the first two or three days travel, they must return to let De Long know. A blanket and a lightly packed knapsack made up the rest of their gear. Because it was Sunday, De Long read divine service, then he bade the pair adieu and they set forth. Long after the eleven men behind them had left from view, Nindemann and Noros thought they could still hear their faint cheers.

WHEN NINDEMANN AND Noros left De Long's party, seventy-five miles southeast across the delta at Zemovialach the whaleboat people were enjoying the benefits of an eleven days' rest. All but Seaman Leach had regained vitality. Bartlett attended to Leach's blackened feet, paring the rotted flesh

226

away with a jack-knife. Melville's legs were improved. Danenhower was generally fit and had picked up some of the local language. The men little fraternized with the natives, keeping mostly to their huts. They had fashioned a checkerboard and playing cards with which to pass the time. (Aniguin was reported to have found a sweetheart in the village.) They also speculated over the fate of the other two boats, some of them favoring a forced march to Bulun even without native help. Melville forbade such a move.

Bartlett was to recall that their Tungus hosts would have shown greater cooperation if the chief engineer had toned down his bullying and swearing at them. Melville had vehemently protested against having to eat so much putrid geese. (The Americans were unaware that it was Tungus practice to kill geese during molting time and leave the birds strung up undrawn for an entire summer before cooking.) Bartlett was also the principal source of charges that any hopes of reaching Bulun and organizing a search expedition to go after Lieutenant De Long were undermined by jealousy between the staff officer and the officer of the line.

In the second week of October a Russian named Kusmah Germayeff visited Zemovialach. He was a convicted thief originally banished to Irkutsk, then to Yakutsk, and finally to the still more remote Lena delta. Exiles had been sent into Siberia since the sixteenth century and, in the latter half of the nineteenth, there were probably twenty thousand of them, criminal or political, scattered throughout the bleak land. Kusmah now lived at Tamoos, a settlement on the Bykovskiy peninsula about five miles across the frozen bay from Zemovialach, to which he had come over by dogsled. Danenhower was in touch with him at once and accompanied him back to Tamoos, where he met his wife, who had a smattering of education and may have spoken a little English. They talked of ways to get to Bulun. On promise of payment, Kusmah offered to make the journey there and back in five days, leaving the following weekend, and he added that it made no difference who if anyone went with him.

Danenhower brought this information, with some of Kusmah's tobacco and provender, before Melville the next morning, as well as Kusmah's promise to come himself the following day and discuss matters further. Danenhower was to say that from the time of their arrival at Zemovialach, everyone in the whaleboat party had expected him, by virtue of his rank and superior physical condition, to go to Bulun when the time came. "I was to bring back food, deer and sleds for the whole party and take the dispatches." Upon hearing Kusmah's offer, however, Melville declared that if anyone should go to Bulun with the Russian it was himself. Melville felt he was "in a quandary. Captain De Long had ordered me not to permit Danenhower to do any duty, and although we were now independent of De Long, I did not feel like disobeying."

Bartlett for one, however, thought the engineering officer was afraid that if Danenhower got to Bulun first he would send off his own dispatches for telegraphic transmission to Washington and to James Gordon Bennett of the *New York Herald* portraying himself, in the absence of De Long and Chipp, as rightful commander of the expedition. It was evidence of this kind that would lead a judicial investigator to describe Melville's attitude as "a kind of cat in the manger business, in not going [to Bulun] himself and not allowing other people to go." According to Danenhower, when Kusmah appeared Melville told him that it was best he should go on his own, that he would then make better speed. Melville's story took the opposite tack, describing Kusmah as refusing to go unless he went alone. The officers' versions coincided only insofar as they both reported being surprised when they learned that Kusmah, because he was forbidden to leave his zone of banishment without official escort, had as a traveling companion the starista Nicolai Shagra.

Engineer Melville was to insist that he could not have left Zemovialach for Bulun before 12 October, sixteen days after his arrival. The reasons he volunteered ranged from his fellow officer's limited vision and Seaman Leach's frostbitten legs to lack of proper clothing, native guides, and dogs. "There were a few over at Tamoose . . . miserable, low cur dogs." By that October date boat travel was impractical. Too late for a journey under oars or sail, it was time for sleds. Yet neither George Melville nor any other member of his party accompanied the Russian exile and the Tungus chieftain when they left Zemovialach on 14 October. Apparently it was enough that those two carry news of the shipwrecked Americans to Bulun—and without supportive documents. Melville had written long letters for the secretary of the navy in Washington and the U.S. minister in St. Petersburg, but they were not taken along because, as Melville afterwards explained, he did not trust them in Kusmah's hands. Yet he apparently trusted Kusmah enough to expect him to return in five days as promised, bearing all that Melville would need to get to Bulun himself.

Danenhower recalled telling Melville that the emissaries should be directed to spread word of the missing sailors along their route, offering rewards. According to Melville, it was nobody's idea but his to have Kusmah offer a thousand rubles "in my name" for useful information and that Danenhower had merely reminded him when he forgot to tell the Russian about it.

Danenhower had formed an impression (from misinformation supplied by Kusmah) that Cape Barkin lay only fifty versts, about thirty-five miles, to the northeast. Since that was the original rendezvous on the Siberian shore there was a possibility that some of the *Jeannette*'s missing might be found in the area. Danenhower asked Melville's permission to make a search. With unconcealed skepticism the chief engineer gave his assent. Danenhower secured a sled and a sturdy dog team. Unfortunately the native guides were unreliable or unable to comprehend, and they took him on a three-day roundabout journey that extended no more than a dozen miles from the point of departure. When Danenhower spoke of his foray much later he conceded that it was "fruitless . . . did not amount to much, but it shows our hearts were in the right place." According to Bartlett, during Danenhower's absence Melville had growled that he ought to be brought back "dead or alive. He is insane." Melville himself derided Danenhower in the book he was to publish much later. Danenhower had returned to Zemovialach "a doleful would-be hero" who had been "fooled [by] a villainous-looking Tungus. Thus ended the first organized search for our lost companions." The men, recalled Melville, had indulged in "plenty of hilarity" over this "joke . . . on Danenhower."

The date of Kusmah's anticipated return from Bulun had come and gone. Unknown to Melville or his comrades, Kusmah had not even reached Bulun. He owned a summer hut on the banks of the Lena, thirty miles north of Bulun, and there he had halted, sending Nicolai Shagra on ahead. He remained in the summer hut, waiting for the starista to return, and was still there five days after he was supposed to have reappeared in Zemovialach.

Meanwhile, Melville would not budge. Danenhower's attempted search, which he so heartily ridiculed, had at least proved the availability of dogs for a sled journey. But now "cold weather had set in. Inaction was worse than death by the roadside . . . and I almost yielded to the tempting arguments of the men, some of whom, Bartlett leading, volunteered to haul Leach on a sled . . . if I would only give the order to start. . . . But where was the guide? . . . Looking around at the miserable objects about me, the scant and tattered clothing, crippled feet and legs, I finally and resolutely determined the risk too great and profitless." Why incur such danger, revived hardships? Was not Kusmah, their messenger, due hourly? When he wrote this, Melville may have forgotten his stated distrust of the exile, also that other testimony, his own included, pictured the men as by that time in good condition, able to laugh, sing and play games. Melville argued he had stayed where he was, in Zemovialach, because to march his party off in search of their shipmates would have been to play another game, a fatal one of "mock heroics."

Not until 29 October did he bound into action. On that day Kusmah finally showed up, full of excuses for his delay but also bearing news of two half-dead wanderers brought into Kumakh-Surt by Tungus nomads. One of the two men had scribbled a note for telegraphing to St. Petersburg but Kusmah had seized it and brought it back for Melville to read; "Note— Arctic Steamer lost June 11. Landed on Siberia 25 September or thereabouts. Want assistance to go for the Captain and Doctor and 9 other men. Wm. T. C. Nindemann, Louis P. Noros. Reply in haste. Want food and clothing."

*   *   *

THE DAY AFTER Nindemann and Noros left them, De Long and his party had swallowed their last half-ounce rations of alcohol and were ravenously chewing on scraps of deerskin footwear. "All hands weak and feeble, but cheerful," De Long wrote on 10 October. "God help us." Ambler doled out glycerine, a spoonful of the syrupy liquid to each man. When the glycerine was gone they "tried a couple of handfuls of Arctic Willow." The only substantial growth in an otherwise barren tundra, the lichen started to appear as the party moved southward closer to the head of the delta. The men boiled the shoots in a pot and "drank the infusion." It was of little use. They grew weaker by the hour and on 13 October another powerful gale had stopped them in their tracks.

Straining eyes that he knew were steadily deteriorating, De Long peered southward for some sign of Nindemann returning with a felled deer. He saw none. "We are in the hands of God and unless he intervenes we are lost. We cannot move against the wind." Alexey was an exception. Despite his own obviously failing strength he had staggered forth daily in quest of game. When the wind slackened a bit, De Long led his men a further mile, crossing yet another river branch or a bend in the one they had been following, then discovered that Machinist Walter Lee had fallen behind. He tramped back for him. Crumpled in the snow, Lee pleaded to be left alone to die. Alexey had also wandered off from the party, but with his Remington at the ready, and he returned with a ptarmigan, which meant soup for supper and a resuscitated Machinist Lee.

That, however, was the Alaskan's final success. Doggedly he continued to hunt, but would return practically crawling. He had once plunged through ice into freezing water without losing hold of the rifle. But on the fifteenth De Long noted, "Alexey and Lee broke down." That same day, from their camp on a flatboat found jammed in the ice and overgrown with frozen fungi, De Long had thought he saw a smudge of smoke in the twilight sky to the south. Probably Nindemann's campfire, he decided, but he had also begun to wonder why, if either of the other boat parties had survived, none had come out to look for him. "We cannot move against the wind, and staying here means starvation." They had boiled and eaten the last strips from their moccasins and on 17 October, as they huddled on the flatboat beneath a crude shelter of loudly flapping portions of canvas lashed to three tentpoles, it was obvious that Alexey was going.

"Doctor baptized him. Read prayers for the sick." (In this same entry De Long again made cryptic reference, as he had in 1879, to that member of his party once a particular thorn in his side. "Mr. Collins' birthday—forty years old.") Before night fell, they were mourning the death of the faithful hunter from St. Michaels, who more than once, in the nick of time and celebrated by his own delighted laughter, had saved his companions from starvation.

Doctor Ambler dutifully certified the Alaskan's death as caused by "exhaustion from hunger and exposure." De Long accorded him the same naval honors as rendered for Erikson when he died. He placed the blue ensign across Alexey's chest and read the funeral service over him. Mustering their frail strength the men then carried his body out on the frozen river, where they covered it with slabs of ice. The following morning they left the scene for a new campsite three hundred yards away, dragging each other and what remained of their gear including De Long's rolled-up charts of the *Jeannette's* cruise and the two metal cases of personal logs and papers. Their shelter was more threadbare than ever, most of the tent having been cut up to make footwear for those who would otherwise have struggled over the tundra barefoot.

They had advanced about twelve miles from the spot where Nindemann and Noros had left them when Doctor Ambler rested his leatherbound notebook on the mahogany medicine case whose contents had so long assuaged pain and sustained life and wrote a final letter to his family:

On The Lena
Thursday, Oct. 20, 1881

To Edward Ambler, Esq.,
Markham P. O., Fauquier Co., Va.

My Dear Brother:

I write these lines in the faint hope that by God's merciful providence they may reach you at home. I have myself very little hope of surviving. We have been without food for nearly two weeks, with the exception of four ptarmigans amongst eleven of us. We are growing weaker, and for more than a week have had no food. We can barely manage to get wood enough now to keep warm, and in a day or two that will be passed. I write to you all, my mother, sister, brother Cary and his wife and family, to assure you of the deep love I now and have always borne you. If it had been God's will for me to have seen you all again I had hoped to have enjoyed the peace of home-living once more. My mother knows how my heart has been bound to hers since my earliest years. God bless her on earth and prolong her life in peace and comfort. May His blessing rest upon you all. As for myself, I am resigned, and bow my head in submission to the Divine will. My love to my sister and brother Cary; God's blessing on them and you. To all my friends and relatives a long farewell. Let the Howards know I thought of them to the last, and let Mrs. Pegram also know that she and her nieces were continually in my thought.

God in His infinite mercy grant that these lines may reach you. I write them in full faith and confidence in help of our Lord Jesus Christ.

Your loving brother,
J. M. Ambler

Too feeble to write any more he thrust the notebook deep into the folds of a long woolen muffler which, to ease the pangs of hunger, he had wedged under his waistband.

The ten men tried to sleep pressed close to one another but what warmth this provided was of little avail against the harsh wind and temperatures now well below zero. De Long wore his uniform coat beneath a sodden ulster. Most of the men were ill-clad, wrapped in tatters of fur, and when Walter Lee and Heinrich Kaak died within hours of each other on 21 October (Kaak in the night as he lay between De Long and the doctor) some of them carefully stripped the bodies for their own warmth.

Only De Long, James Ambler, and Collins could summon enough strength to carry the two bodies from the tent, "around the corner out of sight." It was then, De Long recorded, that "my eye closed up," but he managed to read divine service on the twenty-third. That same Sunday he wrote of "suffering in our feet. No footgear." And then "Thursday, October 27th. 137th day. Iveson broken down. Friday, October 28th. 138th day. Iveson died during early morning. Saturday, Oct. 29. 139th day. Dressler died during night."

De Long realized by now that he had not been traversing Tit Ary Island, that he had overestimated the distances traveled. Tit Ary was thirty-five miles south of his position, which was actually at what today's maps show as Baran-Kel Island. Tit Ary is on the Lena proper. De Long's men were still in the delta, but close enough to the apex for him to have detected, even with his fading sight, Stolboi Island rising high and rocky above the bleak mosaic of snow and ice. Stolboi, in Yakut legend, was the haunt of three witches who exacted tribute from passing boatmen. A disgusted De Long had relegated Stolboi to the status of myth as he had Sagastyr when that feature of his chart had failed to come into view where he thought it should have. But now his party could have seen Stolboi, twelve or fifteen miles to the south, dominating the headlands and guarding the entrance to the main river.

"Sunday, Oct. 30. 140th day. Boyd & Görtz died during the night— Mr. Collins dying." They had hauled themselves to the foot of a bluff and lighted a fire. Jerome Collins may have died muttering some holy words while he fingered the rosary that would be found on him. Carl Görtz and Nelsk Iversen lay dead in the snow a couple of yards away. Boyd had taken Iversen's psalm book with the inked inscription "Presented by the California Evangelical Society for Foreigners," and he crawled nearest the fire, so close his scraps of clothing burned through to the skin as he breathed his last, but Iversen's psalm book was safe, tucked under his body.

De Long, to the end, was concerned for the safety of the expedition's records. If left alongside the river and no one found them in time they might be swept away by the first spring floods. With the aid of Doctor Ambler and Ah Sam he managed to get the five-foot-long roll of charts, the medicine case, the hatchet and teakettle, up some thirty feet near the top of the rise. The second load would have included the Remington, a tin cup, the blue silk ensign, and the cases of De Long's private logs and papers. But the men were too weak for any more climbing in the deep snow. Ah Sam was probably the first of the three to die. He lay face upwards, arms folded across his chest as if someone arranged them this way. Ambler most likely died last, his diary still with him, also a pair of scissors, a magnifying glass, and green goggles with one eyepiece missing (John Danenhower had worn it). Ambler sprawled face down with his feet almost touching Ah Sam's head. The doctor's right hand held De Long's Colt navy pistol. His left hand was pressed against his mouth, which was bloodied. But the cartridges were all loaded, he had not shot himself. The eventual conclusion was that he had taken the captain's pistol to kill any bird or beast that approached the bodies, and in the throes of death he had bitten at his left thumb and forefinger.

Up there on the slope they had lighted a fire, its curling smoke visible to anyone within a dozen miles. Standing as erect as he was able to and facing south, De Long would have had a good view of the Stolboi, the distant rock in the middle of the river, the head of the delta that had defeated him. Watched no doubt by the dying Ambler he sank into the snow, very close to the fire, on his right side, right hand under his cheek and his head pointing north. A chronometer was slung about his neck and among the contents of his pockets were two pairs of spectacles, a silver watch, a policeman's whistle, and the blue sealskin pouch Emma had given him at Havre in 1868. It still carried the original contents, a lock of Emma's hair and a gold cross set with three pearls, to which had since been added another family memento, a tiny china doll.

De Long had also kept the notebook with him until the end. No one would know his final thoughts, however, he had apparently written no last letter to his wife, to Bennett, or anyone else, unless he had penciled something on the page, torn off and never found, next to that which carried the 30 October entry. The notebook was found about six inches from his shoulder, as if he had stretched his left arm aloft and let the book fall in the snow behind him, away from the fire. This was the commander's last gesture. He died with the arm upraised, and so it would remain, petrified by death and another long Arctic night.

CHAPTER NINETEEN

MELVILLE'S SEARCH

I have a pretty good chart to search for the missing. If time and weather permit I will go to the north coast for ship's papers, chronometer, etc. I may be gone a month. Fear not for my safety. I will see the natives take care of me.

Engineer Melville to John Danenhower, 5 November 1881

THE LONGER HE remained at Zemovialach, the surer the *Jeannette*'s engineering officer felt that Lieutenant De Long and the rest of the first cutter's company had perished in the Laptev Sea, that Chipp's party had drowned as well, and that to subject his own weakened number to further risk and hardship in a futile search would be wrong. But upon the exile Kusmah's return with a note signed by Nindemann and Noros, he knew that De Long had come ashore safely, was alive during at least the first weeks of the whaleboat crew's prolonged inaction, and might yet be in the delta awaiting some sign of relief procured by the two men sent on ahead. Melville then sprang into action. He prepared at once to leave for Bulun where, according to the Russian, the two survivors would have arrived under native care. Ordered to put everything back on the sled, Kusmah protested that his dog team needed rest. But fresh animals were quickly obtained from nearby Tamoos. "I would not brook delay," Melville afterwards claimed. And the following morning (the date of De Long's final diary entry) he at last set out for Bulun.

Except for two Tungus dog-drivers Melville traveled alone. He had left Danenhower with instructions to organize the rest of the whaleboat crew and to follow on to Bulun and proceed thence to Yakutsk. But Melville's immediate purpose, according to his subsequent testimony, was to intercept Gregory Byeshoff, the Cossack *ispravnik* (regional commandant), who Kusmah had told him would soon be at Zemovialach, and turn him back to Bulun where his authority would be needed in mounting a search expedition. The two failed to meet, passing each other on the frozen tundra because the Cossack commandant had taken the reindeer route while the American headed in the opposite direction along the dogsled road. It was never explained why Melville might not have learned of this eventuality from Kusmah before setting out.

He reached Bulun in three days and found Nindemann and Noros emaciated but slowly recovering. They told their own tale of ordeal in the delta, of Erikson's death, of De Long's decision to send them forward for food or native help, their initial destination being Kumakh-Surt. They had staggered from hut to empty hut, keeping themselves alive with moldered scraps and fish-heads, the offal left by natives heating and pulverizing their catch to extract oil for lamps. When this was not available they sliced and ate strips of Nindemann's sealskin breeches and then the soles of their moccasins. After ten days on such diet and floundering through snowstorms they finally collapsed in a hut and were near death when found three days later by Yakut nomads. The natives were at first scared off by the strangers' spectral appearance, then induced by their pleading, alternated with feeble flourishes of their rifle, to give them food and clothing. Nindemann and Noros could not, however, make the Yakuts understand that help was needed without delay for ten comrades stalled to the north. Even when Kusmah had shown up at Kumakh-Surt he misunderstood their signs and pantomime, presuming them to indicate Melville's party at Zemovialach where he had just come from.

The two men told Melville what they knew of De Long's position, helped him rough out a chart, and stressed the importance of Stolboi, the big rock in the river, as a landmark. After leaving the captain, they had taken so long to travel because of their physical condition and ignorance of directions. They estimated that properly equipped and with knowledgeable guides, a search party from Bulun might make the distance in two or three days. Noros wanted to go with Melville and point out the way. The engineer refused him. Neither he nor Nindemann was fit for additional hard travel and besides, "both of them believed that their companions had long since been dead when they themselves were found."

Melville sent off three identical messages: to the U.S. minister at St. Petersburg; to the London office of the *New York Herald*; and to the secretary of the navy in Washington, telling of the *Jeannette's* sinking and events thereafter. His whaleboat party had found a native village and were safe and sound. "As soon as the river closed I put myself in communication with the commandant at Bulun," where Nindemann and Noros had arrived with word that the captain's people had landed at the northern mouth of the Lena and were stranded in the delta, frozen and without food. Promising a "vigorous and constant search" Melville asked that money be telegraphed to sustain it. The messages left Bulun by native courier, but with more than three thousand miles of icy desolation to travel before reaching the telegraph station at Irkutsk in southern Siberia, this first official report of the loss of the *Jeannette* would not be flashed to the outside world for another six weeks.

Melville at Bulun was "becalmed, as it were, unable to move until the return of Byeshoff who alone had the authority to furnish me with necessary outfit." He was not becalmed long. On arriving at Zemovialach and discovering that Melville had passed him en route, the commandant drafted instructions for his subordinate at Bulun to equip the American with two dogsleds and direct him to Barulach, on the east bank of the Lena almost opposite Kumakh-Surt. Fireman Bartlett carried these instructions to Bulun, enabling Melville to head north, again without one or more of his shipmates, who could have assisted in the search. He had ordered Bartlett to remain at Bulun and come after him only if he, too, got lost in the Lena delta. Meanwhile Danenhower and the rest of the whaleboat party had reached Bulun and there found Melville's orders to continue the long journey to Yakutsk.

Melville had not fully recovered from frostbite. At Barulach he allowed an old woman to massage his legs with goose grease, while he took note of how the natives managed their "internal household economics." The Cossack *ispravnik* Byeshoff arrived, spurred action, and with provisions and two dog teams Melville left for the delta. This was 5 November. Four days later he reached the first hut where Nindemann and Noros had sheltered after separating from De Long. Another forty-eight hours sledding brought Melville to an abandoned hut on a small point or island the natives called Mat Vay. He had just passed the Stolboi prominence, and was hardly more than eight or ten miles from De Long's last camp, eastward across the ice.

Had he now searched this area, following the chart based on Nindemann's information (and most certainly had he allowed either of the first cutter's two survivors to accompany him) Melville would have come across his lost shipmates. Not that De Long or Ambler was likely to have lingered all that time, ten or twelve days after the commander's last diary entry. But while aware of how close he probably was to De Long's last camp Melville was unable to make a search, having discovered, to his surprise, that his provisions were running low. This was to be his sworn testimony. Someone at Barulach had played him false, loaded his sled with less food than he had thought. As a result, the mood of his dog-drivers turned ugly and disobedient, even though he struck one "a staggering blow with the native's own staff" and fired his rifle over their heads. Finally, after stopping at a handful of huts called Cas Carta he forced them on to North Bulun for fresh supplies and dogs. He had become badly lame, unable to stand without assistance.

The halt at North Bulun enabled Melville to recover strength and once more observe Tungus family life. He stayed with relatives and neighbors of one of his drivers, sharing a cramped hut with some fifty souls, boards over the chimneys keeping heat in and fresh air out. His host's son had just married a girl "pretty after her kind, plump and round," who never tired of teasing her mate, to the point of pulling off his clothes whereupon, "rolling the blushing youth into his little bed, she finally let fall the greasy calico curtain, which shielded their love from our vulgar gaze." Melville's absorption with primitive ways was short-lived. Natives brought him two of the reports De Long had left at intervals on the retreat after coming ashore, then one of North Bulun's womenfolk drew a third paper "from the depths of her bosom." Next morning Melville had yet another of the captain's reports in his hands and also one of the broken Winchesters. This report, dated 22 September, told him precisely where, on the northern shore of the delta, the first cutter's party had buried the logbooks, navigation instruments, and other gear they had been unable to carry.

Melville may have determined on recovering this material when Nindemann told him of it. It had certainly become his objective now. He found the cache hidden beneath snow but marked by the tall flagstaff. Why had he gone out of his way to retrieve these things, increasing his sled loads, when he had every reason to believe De Long would be found in the opposite direction? His explanation was that he had considered it "important" to secure the ship's records, whereas "commonsense and my own judgement" had convinced him beyond a shadow of doubt that the people had perished. "I was morally certain."

Nevertheless, he resolved to labor on "until I found them dead or alive." But food ran short again and he had to suppress another native mutiny with blows and warning shots. He returned to North Bulun, commandeered what supplies he could from villagers themselves facing winter famine, and resumed the search, "confident that if I could strike De Long's trail I would find him and his party, doubtless dead." But even with three native dog-drivers the going was rough and baffling. "The whole delta is nothing but a congregation of frozen islands." Snow fell continuously. He made for the relative security of the known route southward through Cas Carta. Approaching the hut at Mat Vay to within sight of the Stolboi rock, Melville kept his frostbitten feet firmly on the trail for Kumakh-Surt and beyond it Bulun, once more avoiding the short swing eastward that would probably have brought him to De Long's last camp. It was late November. "I had done all possible in the season. Corpses I could find in safety in the spring."

ENGINEER MELVILLE EMERGED from his twenty-three days solitary search in the delta to find waiting at Bulun, besides Bartlett, five members of Danenhower's party: Nindemann, Noros, Lauterbach, Mansen, and Aniguin. Transport to Yakutsk had been available for only six and Danenhower had selected the five weakest to accompany him, those being Newcomb, Cole (whose sanity had snapped), Leach, Wilson, and Charlie Tang Sing. Melville now followed on with the others, striking southeastward from the Lena. In winter the most favorable route to Yakutsk was not along the valley of the Lena but eastward, through the valley of the Jana, approaching Yakutsk over the Verkhoyanski Mountains. Melville reached the settlement of Verkhoyansk, about halfway to Yakutsk, early in December and stayed two weeks, served and befriended by an exiled nihilist student named S. Leeon, who acted as interpreter and helped him compose a letter to the *ispravniks* at Verkhoyansk and Bulun. With an intellectual's scorn for tsarist bureaucracy, Leeon believed a peremptory tone the best means of achieving results. Melville's instincts were in accord, and the dispatches read more like directives than civil requests, instructing the Russian officials to carry out "a diligent and constant search for my missing comrades be they dead or alive." The search was to be conducted regardless of whether American officers were on the ground to assist, and, should the explorers be found dead, all documents were to be taken from their bodies and forwarded to Melville, if still in Siberia, or to the American minister at St. Petersburg.

Traveling by reindeer and horse-drawn sled as had Danenhower before him, though with fewer overturnings, Melville crossed south of the Arctic Circle for the first time in more than two years. He completed the eight-hundred-mile journey from the head of the Lena delta to the fur-trading outpost of Yakutsk. Danenhower's men had already arrived and were sheltered in one of the town's clustered low-roofed loghouses. For a brief period all thirteen survivors of the *Jeannette* were reunited, their needs attended to by General George Tcherniaeff, the regional governor. Pens were busy. In a letter home Danenhower made terse mention of his eye trouble, adding, "I always hope for the best and am disposed to look on the bright side. That sort of philosophy has carried me through very trying experiences in the past three years."

Melville's purpose was to lead the party to Irkutsk, his movements thereafter subject to Navy Department orders. But on 6 January 1882, while still at Yakutsk, he received Secretary Hunt's response to his original word out of Bulun reporting on the *Jeannette*'s fate. He was to "omit no effort, spare no expense," in trying to succor the missing men and in the meantime "the sick and frozen of those already rescued" should be moved to a milder climate. James Gordon Bennett had also acted, specifically upon estimates from his Paris correspondent in touch with St. Petersburg and Irkutsk that a sum of 6000 rubles was needed to defray the costs of further search in Siberia and the transportation of survivors. Bennett did the necessary through Messrs. Rothschild, his continental bankers, and before the end of the month Melville had formed new plans for a return to the Lena delta. Bartlett and Nindemann would accompany him, and with General Tcherniaeff's assistance he engaged the services of two Russian interpreters and Joachim Grönbeck, a Swede who had once served on the river steamer *Lena* and had been a member of Professor Nordenskjöld's party on the *Vega*. Grönbeck spoke Russian and English.

In the middle of February, with his newly organized party, Melville was at Verkhoyansk on his way back to Bulun. Danenhower and the other survivors had by then completed another twenty-five-hundred-mile journey homeward, had reached the Angara valley beyond the headwaters of the Lena, and were resting in the caravan crossroads city of Irkutsk.

A commercial metropolis in the making, Irkutsk profited equally from its two-centuries-old trade routes through neighboring Mongolia into China and its modern telegraphic links with Europe. At the same time it preserved a picture-postcard aspect with its weathered loghouses ornamented by gin-

gerbread eaves, pedimented windows, and doorways of chocolate-colored fret-
work. Irkutsk's attitude to its American visitors was inquisitive but
hospitable. Some of the townsfolk bought them new clothing and entertained
them. The *ispravnik* had told Danenhower to consider himself a guest of the
Russian government. Seaman Cole, still deranged, was placed in the care of
a Cossack guard. Danenhower himself, with a declared anxiety to mount a
spring search for his missing shipmates, was advised otherwise by a local
oculist. During the journey from Yakutsk in temperatures of 70 degrees
below zero, when human breath can freeze with an audible crackle, the single
green goggle over his right, good, eye had repeatedly frosted over, blinding
him. Although the other eye was bandaged, he had dispensed with the glass
and as a result overtaxed that good eye, which had to be shielded from light.
And now, once more in the dark and having released Raymond Newcomb
from "arrest" to write the letters he dictated, John Danenhower began the
long battle in defense of his honor.

Newspapers were read to him daily as he sat blindfolded in a city official's
suburban home which commanded, had Danenhower his full sight, a splendid view of Irkutsk across the frozen Angara. The first innuendoes circulated
in Paris but had their origin in sentiments expressed at home by the noted
traveler and lecturer George Kennan. Following news that the whaleboat
party, with its two officers, were assembled at Yakutsk and presumably
homeward bound, Kennan's remarks, published in the *New York Herald*,
struck a distinctly sour note amid general expressions of relief that at least
one-third of the expedition had survived and that the Russians could be
counted on to seek the rest. Kennan feared that the missing men had "wandered into a labyrinth. It is unnecessary at present to discuss whether Master
Danenhower and Engineer Melville, when they reached a place of safety,
should have gone personally with the natives in search of the missing
boats. . . . There may have been circumstances which rendered it impracticable or inexpedient and harsh criticism at this time would be unjust. . . .
There can, however, be no question that it was the duty of these officers to

at least stay at the mouth of the river until the fate of Lieutenant De Long and his party should be decided."

Secretary of the Navy Hunt had already cabled orders to the American minister at St. Petersburg for relay to Melville and Danenhower. They were not to leave the ground until the remainder of the expedition was found. "Help search by every means in your power," they were told. Sensing deep trouble ahead and feeling "censured from Paris," Danenhower sent an extraordinary letter to Wickham Hoffman, the American envoy in St. Petersburg, bidding him make clear to the secretary of the navy that Melville was the officer in charge of the whaleboat because he, Danenhower, had been kept on the sick list "against my will and protest." Even so, it was his seamanship that had saved the whaleboat from disaster, and he also noted that "I was the first man to start in search of my comrades." His left eye was ruined but "I have not backed out and would lose my right eye to find De Long."

The following week he addressed the secretary directly. When his left eye first became inflamed "from a cold," he had continued working until it began to suppurate. Fifteen operations were performed on it in nine months and for most of the time he was a prisoner below deck. When the ship sank and they were thrown on the ice he had "begged to go in harness with the men but the captain would not allow it." In further communications Danenhower informed the secretary, and James Gordon Bennett, that according to the Irkutsk oculist he might lose the sight of both eyes unless he remained in the city another fortnight, blindfolded or in a darkened room. He was soon in receipt of Navy Department orders forbidding him to go back north.

Transcontinental and transatlantic cables now hummed with intelligence concerning the *Jeannette*. Bennett, whose whereabouts alternated among London, Paris, and the Mediterranean in rounds of business and pleasure, felt there might be something about his late expedition that he had better know of before the rest of the world. He assigned John P. Jackson, probably the *Herald*'s most perceptive and energetic European correspondent, to get the facts while the *Jeannette* survivors were still in Siberia. Accompanied by M. A.

Larsen, an artist for British and American journals, Jackson was in St. Petersburg collecting travel passes for the east even before Danenhower had reached Irkutsk. Filing colorful travel stories for the *New York Herald* and the *Illustrated London News* at every convenient stop, Jackson and Larsen rode an overheated train from Moscow to Orenburg, Russia's easternmost railhead, and traveled three more weeks by sled across the steppes to reach their destination, the newspaperman by then under telegraphed orders from his publisher "not to air soiled linen." At Irkutsk, thanks to Bennett's influence with the U.S. Navy Department, another significant telegram awaited Jackson, this one from the secretary authorizing him to "open De Long's and Collins's papers, if found, and forward any matter for Bennett or the *Herald*."

Jackson immediately closeted himself with the blindfolded Danenhower for the first of seven or eight interviews, at the villa overlooking the ice-covered Angara or in the newsman's quarters at the Hotel Deko. Jackson had brought family correspondence for the *Jeannette*'s men, magazines, issues of the *Herald*, and also notice of Danenhower's promotion to lieutenant. (During the expedition's absence Melville's rank was raised to chief engineer and De Long's to lieutenant commander.) Danenhower volunteered a complete account of the voyage which he wished reported "in my own words." Off the record he stated "what I thought of particular people . . . that I would fight to the bitter end with De Long over the propriety of putting me in a boat with the engineering officer in charge." Mindful of Bennett's warning about "soiled linen" Jackson withheld some of the new lieutenant's sharpest confidences. But what the *Herald* eventually published over his byline was more than enough back home to touch off an uproar.

IN THE SAME wintry weeks while Danenhower and Jackson made separately for Irkutsk and Melville mounted his second search expedition from Yakutsk, Emma De Long had composed an exasperated letter to her husband. Sustaining an impression of his continued presence, she had written to him regularly. Now she refused to believe him lost. "Three times we have heard from the Lena river." First it was of Danenhower with five men reaching Yakutsk "and you not yet found." Then Melville had returned to the Arctic Ocean, "found your logs, instruments, but not you." Sending Danenhower and the others off homeward the engineer had anticipated a renewed search in March. "How does he suppose you are going to live until then in such a country?" She wrote each letter in triplicate, providing it three chances of reaching De Long by different routes. For possible delivery she had entrusted at least one copy to Lieutenant Adolphus Greely, U.S. Army, before his departure north with twenty-five men to establish a base as America's contribution to the planned circumpolar chain of scientific observation posts.

Emma De Long prided herself on the dispassionate manner with which she could mask emotion, a talent under severe stress as passing months had brought only a flurry of conflicting reports. She was not convinced that the relief expeditions of the preceding year had been competently managed. The *Alliance* had returned from the fringe of the polar pack in the vicinity of Spitzbergen, the revenue cutter *Corwin* from no further north of Bering Strait than Wrangel Land. Neither vessel had brought back any news of the *Jeannette*. The *Rodgers* had simply not been heard from since last summer. (Of that ship's experiences along the north Siberian coast, of conscientious efforts by Captain Berry's search parties costing the life of a valued officer, of the *Rodgers*'s destruction by fire in St. Lawrence Bay, nothing would be known in the United States until the following spring.) It had seemed almost a seasonal gift when the *New York Herald*, on 21 December, ran an item supposedly from sources in Siberia to the effect that the *Jeannette* was found, her crew saved. Emma, staying at Burlington, Iowa, with her sister, had simultaneously received a telegram from James Gordon Bennett reporting the ship as crushed "but Commander De Long has reached the mouth of the Lena safely and is now well and looking after the sick members of the expedition." But in these same hours Melville's first dispatches from far-off Bulun had arrived at the Navy Department saying that while De Long had made a safe landfall he was still in the delta, confronting death.

This was the news, with endless comment and theorizing, which filled press columns that holiday week, a happy Christmas, it was said, for Chief Engineer Melville's wife who, her raven hair "in the old-fashioned style of high puffs and rolls at each side above the forehead and [who] has other charming oddities," was only too willing to accommodate Philadelphia newshounds competing with their New York and Chicago counterparts in the fashionable forage for sensation. Relieved that her husband was safe, she recalled his last words as that the *Jeannette* would never come back, was "utterly unfit for the service intended." And she talked of Emma De Long— without mentioning the loans she had received from her. Before it was known that Melville had survived, Mrs. De Long had tried to cheer her out of a fixed belief in his death "but now the positions are reversed and it is De Long who is in peril and my husband safe."

Relayed to Emma in Iowa, Henrietta Melville's prattle aroused feelings of which she would leave no more than a hint as record. Perhaps they were beyond words. Writing to Bennett however, she urged his influence in getting her a passage to that remote land in which her husband was lost so that she might be at hand, if need be, to nurse him back to health. "I know there are great difficulties in traveling to Siberia . . . but I would have the courage."

Bennett termed this notion impracticable, and, while apologizing for the earlier telegram that had "raised false hopes," he continued to profess confidence in De Long's safety, especially after the news that Melville had found the commander's records in cairns and huts. "Polar milestones," said one paper, "such as all Arctic explorers have erected along the way." Bennett told Emma that if the commander was "leaving letters behind him" it could only mean that he was alive and aware that people were out looking for him. Such fallacious reasoning was unlikely to have impressed Emma, but she continued to indulge in a brave make-believe, writing her husband on New Year's Eve that someone was getting up an expedition to the North Pole by balloon. "He told me he would look out for you on the way. No more undertakings like this for my husband or I will get a divorce. It is evening, I am writing this in the library. Little Sylvie [the De Longs' daughter] is in bed fast asleep, having said her prayers for her father's health and safety. There is a blazing fire in the grate, the two dogs are stretched out on the fur rug in front of it. How would you like to spend the evening with me? Or is it pleasanter where you are? I suppose I must not tease you."

As the winter snows accumulated around the home in Burlington, Iowa, the daily papers Emma read reflected deepening pessimism. On 24 February George Kennan had reminded fellow members of the American Geographical Society in New York that logbooks and instruments were the last things an exhausted and retreating party abandoned. De Long's men must have waged a final desperate struggle for life, one they had by now surely lost. In response, the *New York Herald* took Kennan to task for his "haste to inflict premature sorrow." Emma De Long betrayed a desperation of her own in the last letter she was to write the commander before resigning herself to the knowledge that he was never to read her words. "I cannot show you my love, my sympathy, my sorrow for your great sufferings. I pray God constantly . . . my own darling husband, struggle, fight, live! Come back to me!"

CHIEF ENGINEER MELVILLE was then in Zemovialach, the scene of his five weeks sojourn the preceding year. With Nindemann, Bartlett, Captain Grönbeck, the two interpreters, and the dog-drivers, he had stopped at Bulun long enough to buy reindeer for the plunge back into the delta. Dogs too were needed and best procured at Zemovialach, a mission Melville undertook himself. At this now-familiar settlement off Cape Bykovskiy he also stocked up with eight or ten thousand dried fish. Neither native haggling nor language difficulties hampered Melville now, for besides interpreters he had also equipped himself with contracts and letters of authority from Russian officials.

He journeyed through worsening weather across the head of the delta to Cas Carta, which was to serve as his forward base. Taking advantage of a delay forced on him by heavy snowstorms, he composed a letter which prefigured the sort of defense that time and again would be demanded of him. It was addressed to James Gordon Bennett and explained last year's halt at

Zemovialach as due to the condition of his men and "ice thick enough to stop any boat, yet not strong enough to walk on." Long before he had reached Bulun, "I fear[ed] my comrades' troubles were over."

When the weather cleared at Cas Carta he sent Bartlett with an interpreter scouting to the east while he took the rest of his party northward. Storms had so changed the face of the tundra that Nindemann was at first unable to find his old trail, and they trudged fruitlessly in all directions until after two weeks, and rejoined by Bartlett, they neared the hut at Mat Vay. Nindemann sighted the derelict flatboat where he and Noros had first halted after leaving De Long. Then appeared four poles lashed together and jutting from the drifted snow. Melville immediately ordered the four native drivers to dig, and they soon had to be restrained from bolting in panic when they uncovered the bodies of Seaman George Boyd and Seaman Carl Görtz. At the same time Melville had ascended the bank above the ice level for a clearer survey and was making across the snow toward a half-buried cooking pot when he almost stumbled over George De Long's rigidly protruding left hand.

The doctor was discovered, Ah Sam, Iversen, Dressler, Jerome Collins, the natives prising them one by one from the grip of densely packed snow and rolling them alongside each other. Fresh digging produced De Long's pocket diary, his pencil, the silken flag folded in its oilskin case, the two tin boxes Machinist Walter Lee had made on the *Jeannette* for De Long's main journal and ship's charts and papers. Lee was found beside Kaak, both stripped of their last shreds of fur by freezing shipmates. Melville had his people bring the bodies in next day while he remained at the hut, drying and repacking the contents of the tin boxes, and drafting telegrams to James Gordon Bennett and the secretary of the navy. "At Lena delta, March 24, 1882, we found De Long and party, all dead." He made a copy of the diary's October entries and attached it to his dispatches, which he sent off south with one of the interpreters.

He designed a tomb, selecting for its site the crest of a hill southwest of Mat Vay rising four hundred feet above the junction of the Lena's countless branches. This necessitated hauling the dead fifteen miles, a strange funeral procession of nine fur-muffled men with four dog teams, ten bodies lashed to sleds, toiling across frozen streams and tundra and on up the snowclad slope. At the top, which constant winds kept almost clear of snow, Melville managed to pry out broken rock to a depth of three feet. This would be the foundation for a cross he had Nindemann rig by joggling a tent's ridgepole into a driftwood spar. With Grönbeck's assistance Melville chiseled an in-scription on the cross: "In Memory of 12 of the Officers and Men of the Arctic Steamer 'Jeannette' who died in the Lena Delta, October 1881," the names (including those of the undiscovered Alexey and Erikson) following in a vertical list down the shaft.

The derelict flatboat had also been dragged to the burial site, and from its planks Melville had an oversized coffin made, seven feet wide, twenty-two feet long, two feet deep. He had ordered the bodies searched upon discovery, clothing examined and pockets emptied, all articles tied separately in handkerchiefs or, as were the notebook and wadded papers taken from Jerome Collins, sealed in one of the provision boxes. Melville told Nindemann to "overhaul the bodies" once more before interment, especially De Long's, "as there was one leaf torn out of the notebook." Nothing additional was found except a bronze crucifix around Collins's neck. Bartlett detached it but Melville, after some hesitation, ordered it replaced, to be buried with him. Once all ten men were in the giant casket, the remnants of their last tent spread over them, timbers were laid diagonally across it and weighed with stones, to form a base for a pyramidal cairn of logs and rocks rolled in at the sides. All work was done with mittened hands, and the tall cross swayed in the freezing wind gusts as the men hoisted it into position. Once fully raised it was chocked in place with large stones. Standing twenty feet above the cone of the pyramid it was visible for about as many miles in every direction.

The task of transporting the dead and building the crude mausoleum had taken more than a week. Everyone was exhausted but anxious to leave the scene. No services were read. The party made for Cas Carta, where Melville would divide his team and proceed on a final search for Chipp. The cross-crowned tumulus on the hilltop at the head of the Lena delta was left to the Siberian winds and driving snow, but it was not to remain undisturbed very long.

CHAPTER TWENTY

THE SURVIVORS COME HOME

Perhaps the detailed story of the search and discovery will clear up the mystery . . . until that happens it must seem inexplicable that the fate of two boats' crews which landed on the Delta at the same season and within a few hours of each other should prove so different.

New York Herald *editorial, 6 May 1882*

THE LAST OFFICIAL word from Siberia as released by the Navy Department was that Chief Engineer Melville had gone back to the Arctic fully equipped, with Russian assistance, determined to continue the search until his comrades were found. Meanwhile, Melville's wife spoke of receiving a letter from him dated 1 January, ten weeks earlier, in which he discussed plans "to search for De Long and the others who perished at the mouth of the Lena River." As usual Henrietta elaborated, describing her husband as a plain-spoken man who always chose his words carefully. "I wish Mrs. M. could have spared me this until the question is solved," Emma De Long wrote Bennett. "I am too reasonable a woman not to see how overwhelming are the chances against me, but I cannot give up." Bennett must, however, set wheels in motion "in case the worst has happened. If Mr. Melville's opinion is correct and he finds only the remains, I want my husband brought back to me."

She had no sooner sent this off when the appearance of a second letter Mrs. Melville "consented" to be published drove her to write with still greater urgency to the far-off chief engineer himself. This latest alleged Melville missive, appearing in the *New York Times*, 15 March, seemed to document what Henrietta had previously made public about her husband's private misgivings over the *Jeannette*'s fitness for polar exploration. Purportedly his last letter from San Francisco, it reiterated his belief, from the moment he had laid eyes on the ship, that "she would never do." Unable to honorably withdraw from the enterprise, "I have left nothing undone to provide against what I see is ahead of us. Some of us may weather it . . . but I am sure the *Jeannette* will never come back." The following week brought a curious sequel. Henrietta Melville made a partial retraction, implicitly under anonymous pressure, saying the now-famous letter was a distortion of what she had quoted from memory, the letter itself having been destroyed. Melville had merely a presentiment that the *Jeannette* would be lost, and his criticism was confined to the vessel's light build. This latest affirmation appeared to satisfy at least the *Brooklyn Eagle* for "If the chief engineer *had* discovered the *Jeannette*'s unsuitability . . . he was guilty for not signifying so to his superiors."

Four months would pass before Emma De Long's letter questioning Melville about his wife's statements to the press caught up with him across the sea. His reply that "for cheap notoriety or possible profit the unfortunate woman I married did publish a letter or fraction . . . without my knowledge or sanction" was hardly a clearcut denial of the letter's meaning. About this time, an official forum was about to be arranged, at which Chief Engineer Melville could refute its existence or intention. That controversial letter could not alone have brought about an investigation, especially after the damage inflicted by then on Henrietta Melville's credibility. What started the train of events towards formal inquiry was publication of John P. Jackson's interviews with Lieutenant Danenhower at Irkutsk, the first of which appeared in the *New York Herald* at the close of April.

Accompanied by a sketch from Raymond Newcomb of "The *Jeannette* Caught in Hummocky Ice," the article detailed the ship's first year in the pack, affording the *Herald*'s readers a feast of vicarious thrills seasoned with generous praise for the skill and indomitability of all hands, including Melville, with whom Danenhower had "constantly discussed the [polar] question, and [we] both felt assured that if the ship could remain intact long enough she would eventually drift out between Spitzbergen and Bear Island to Atlantic waters." Those early articles appeared at home while Danenhower and his party (he was also in charge of the logbooks and relics found on Melville's first search mission) had finally reached the east Russian railhead at Orenburg and were on the train for St. Petersburg where Tsar Alexander himself was to honor the *Jeannette* men at a grand reception. Melville was still in Siberia. It would be some time before the chief engineer read with fury of Danenhower's self-portrayal, under Jackson's prompting, as savior of the whaleboat crew during the storm in the Laptev Sea.

But from Melville's standpoint, not to mention those of Emma De Long, the Navy Department, and the *Herald*'s own publisher, the most ominous charges emerged during the final interviews, published on the 3rd and 5th of May. "Six splendid Ritchie boat compasses were left behind on the sinking ship, much to our detriment at a later period." "I was not allowed to help even at the cooking, although physically I was one of the strongest men of the party." The party had trudged along, "the well handicapped by the six or seven who furnished no motive power at all." Gone was the esprit de corps which had characterized the first Danenhower interviews. Now all his fellow officers, Melville included, were said to have added little: "Twenty-five per cent of the whole not working their passage." As for the delay at Zemovialach, the lieutenant conceded that it was "not clear, even to me," why the natives had not somehow helped them to Bulun. But the prime responsibility was Melville's. He was under De Long's orders to get the party to a place of safety and communicate with Russian authorities. He knew that Bulun was De Long's intended destination, with or without native help. Nindemann and Noros would almost certainly have been met, to serve as guides for the succor of their shipmates, "had someone gone to Bulun with Kusmah and started an expedition north immediately."

On the evening following publication of that final interview, the secretary of the navy received Melville's telegram reporting the discovery of De Long's party "all dead." Next day's *Herald* ran the sad announcement with biographies and words of sympathy in columns bordered black, a format not used since the death of President Garfield. But controversy had stirred: "Somebody Blundered," declared the *Chicago Tribune* which followed with a charge that traditional intraservice rivalry had fore-doomed the expedition. Even the *New York Herald* headlined an editorial on the delay at Zemovialach as recounted by the *Jeannette's* navigation officer "Mystery of Obstacles in Danenhower's Path." George Kennan opined that Melville lost his remaining chance of saving De Long when he and his natives "gave up the search in November." Kennan pictured De Long as cursed with bad luck—in his choice of landing places, his movements in the delta, the fact that the one man in the expedition who spoke Russian and might thus have accelerated Melville's efforts to reach Bulun and organize a search was in De Long's first cutter, not the whaleboat. "The fates seemed to fight hard against him."

Emma De Long's reaction was, typically, more stern resolve than grief. She promptly dispatched letters to Bennett and the Navy Department insisting that the cooperation between private enterprise and the federal establishment that had led to the launching of the *Jeannette* expedition be revived to bring home its dead. And at Sharon Hill, at the "picturesque little cottage embowered amid twining honeysuckle and fragrant blossoming lilies," the Melvilles' flag flew at half-staff and their eight-year-old daughter, at the piano, played *Melville's March to De Long* which the child had composed under the coaching of her mother, who only last week had sent a copy of the music to the commander's now-sorrowing widow.

JOHN P. JACKSON, whose few weeks at Irkutsk had gained him more than enough copy to ignite a furor in America, considered Louis Noros a true-blue mariner and, moreover, acquainted with De Long's route in the delta. It was imperative that Jackson get to and secure any papers of the De Long expedition that were intended for the publisher's eyes only. Again through James Gordon Bennett's influence in Washington, the news reporter obtained Navy Department authority for Danenhower to assign the seaman to him as a guide. Bennett seemed still attracted to the Stanley-Livingstone leitmotif and doubtless had relished the possibility of his man in Siberia finding the lost explorers alive. But even if they were dead, his telegram to the secretary of the navy requesting Noros's enlistment in Jackson's search implied that finding the papers was very important. "Harber will get there too late." Lieutenant Giles Harbor and Lieutenant William Schuetze, also under the secretary's orders, had arrived in Siberia to take over the search for survivors. But Harber reached Irkutsk at the close of March, his force augmented by five *Jeannette* men from Danenhower's party, only to encounter difficulty in chartering a steamer for the passage down the Lena. Jackson meanwhile, with Noros and the illustrator Larsen, had set out north and was resting at a deer station after a grueling climb over the Verkhoyanski Mountains when informed by a southbound Cossack *estafette* (mounted express courier) that he was not the only *New York Herald* man roaming the Siberian wastes.

William Henry Gilder had helped boost the *New York Herald*'s circulation through his lively dispatches while with Lieutenant Frederick Schwatka's 1878 expedition in search of the long-lost Franklin party. He was Bennett's natural choice, which meant active participant, on the *Jeannette* relief expedition sent out under Lieutenant Robert M. Berry in 1881. Berry and Gilder were on the north coast of the Chukchi Peninsula seeking traces of De Long when news overtook them that their ship, the *Rodgers*, had caught fire in St. Lawrence Bay, the crew had slipped her chains and run her aground. Berry had told Gilder to sled as fast as he could across northeast Siberia and hasten word of the disaster to a telegraph station. Reaching Verkhoyansk, Gilder learned from the helpful exile Leeon of the *Jeannette*'s destruction and Melville's search for survivors, then intercepted the Cossack courier carrying

Melville's dispatches, which he got him to hand over. Gilder used them to draft the first full story of the *Jeannette* tragedy, returned the documents with his own copy (including the *Rodgers* account) to the *estafette* and sent him on his way. Gilder then altered his own course for a personal interview with Melville in the Lena delta.

In this strange convergence upon that region, Gilder's fellow-journalist Jackson trailed him by hundreds of miles, himself anticipating a scoop for he carried Navy Department authority to search the *Jeannette's* dead, if found, for papers. Many miles still further astern, also delta-bound, Lieutenants Harber and Schuetze were temporarily stalled at Irkutsk while sorting out travel and supply arrangements. And Captain Berry, with thirty-six men from the fire-wrecked relief ship, themselves now in need of relief, were stranded in Siberia's extreme northeast corner. "Americans, Americans, again! This was the cry today," Leeon had written of the reaction in Verkhoyansk to news of Gilder's approach and that "many other Americans had landed." Never before and seldom thereafter were more Americans to be found somewhere or other amid the tundra and taiga of the Siberian frontier.

Jackson was at Verkhoyansk on 8 April. The exile Leeon, serving as conduit for Melville's messages south, told him that De Long's party had been discovered dead. This made Jackson all the more anxious not to miss the chief engineer. At first uncertain which part of the delta he should make for, he decided on the ice-locked little island of Zemovialach and after sledding across the Bay of Buorkhaya, Noros, Larsen, and Jackson landed at Cape Bykovskiy. Gilder was there, having crossed the head of the delta from Bulun. So was Fireman Bartlett, who had completed a coastal descent from Cape Barkin without learning anything of Chipp's fate. Bartlett told Jackson that Jerome Collins had indeed written private letters for Bennett, but that at Mat Vay everything taken off Collins's body had been handed over to Melville.

Melville and Nindemann, with Captain Grönbeck, had also returned to Zemovialach about twenty-four hours after Jackson's arrival from the opposite direction. Melville's search for Chipp had taken him northwestward from Cas Carta, then down the fan-shaped coastline as far as the Olenek River before he had swung back east. Nindemann's assignment in the central part of the delta was equally unproductive. He had rejoined Melville at Cas Carta, continuing east with him to the rendezvous at Cape Bykovskiy, where the engineer, upon hearing that two newspapermen were on the scene, "directed Nindemann and Bartlett to keep quiet, avoid useless talk." Melville also explained why. "Men might talk too much . . . say things they were not prepared to swear to."

After an unsuccessful bid to attach Nindemann and Bartlett to his party ("He seemed to imagine he only had to order in the name of his master," recalled Melville), Jackson got directions to the cairn mausoleum, which Larsen wanted to sketch, and obtained fresh dog teams from the Yakut villagers. The two groups went their separate ways, Melville's party with Gilder crossing the bay, intent on beating the melting of the snows. More dangerously courting the same risk of floods cutting him off from the south, Jackson pressed on deeper into the delta. Once at the snow-draped sepulchre, a reluctant Noros assisting and the dog-drivers too terrified to lift a finger, Jackson took down the cross, opened the tomb, and removed the bodies. Larsen sketched. Writing to his publisher Jackson was to deny charges of ghoulish acquiescence in the illustrator's wish to draw the dead men. The exhumation had nothing to do with art, "I had to clear up [Bartlett's story] that Collins had letters addressed to you. As he said they had not been found I thought it best to convince myself." Jackson discovered no papers but found the bronze cross, which he pocketed for Collins's relatives. The dead reinterred, the tomb was resealed. Before replacing the tall cross Jackson told Noros to cut "Mr" before Collins's name on the upright, to distinguish him from the seamen.

Jackson next hastened to Bulun, with two good reasons for speed. The snow was steadily melting, but he had also determined to catch up with Melville and, flourishing the authority of the Navy Department telegram, examine the papers Melville had removed from the bodies. Jackson's dogs gave out at Bulun, and no reindeer were available. "The best deer had taken from the tundra to the mountains, and the thaw had already begun," Jackson wrote. He reached Verkhoyansk on horseback, Melville still five days' journey ahead of him. But snow still blocked the mountain passes, and Melville had halted. Not until the end of May was he able to proceed again, and by that time Jackson had overtaken him. So, too, had Lieutenant Berry and Ensign Henry Hunt of the *Rodgers*, anxious to reach a telegraph station and hurry up relief measures for their shipwrecked crew. A floundering passage with reindeer and horses over ice-scabbed marshland brought the almost all-American caravan to the banks of the Lena and into Yakutsk. From here on 10 June the navy men and the two journalists embarked aboard a small steamer for the twenty-five-hundred-mile journey upstream to Lake Baikal and Irkutsk.

BY THEN JOHN Danenhower had been home fourteen days. He arrived with his small party on the White Star *Celtic* from Liverpool and was met in New York Harbor by a Brooklyn navy yard tug and another tug the *New York Herald* had chartered for friends and relatives of the homecoming men. Boatswain Cole's welcome was especially pitiful as he peered about him for his wife, unaware that she had died during his long absence. (Cole was kept in ignorance of her death until his own after two years in the Government Hospital for the Insane.) Tang Sing and Cole were ushered off under naval escort; Newcomb caught the first train for Salem. Danenhower, apprised before stepping off the boat of the displeasure wrought by those Irkutsk interviews, issued a statement to reporters glorifying Melville and looking to a "very searching" inquiry that would affirm the chief engineer's spotlessness.

Thus far no investigation had been scheduled. But having "vindicated" Melville in an attempt to kill one persistent rumor—that of a fatal jealousy between the officers in the whaleboat—Danenhower ratified another later in the day toward the end of a reception held for him at the Fifth Avenue Hotel. Doctor Daniel Collins of Minneapolis and Bernard Collins of Brooklyn had pushed through the guests to introduce themselves as Jerome Collins's brothers and to ask Danenhower if there was anything to stories that the meteorologist was not allowed to carry out his scientific tasks. Danenhower had led them into a private room. Stretched on a sofa with a compress over his eyes, he told them that their brother's life was "merely a hell in the Arctic region for three years," that had he been in Collins's shoes "I would have gone over the side."

The Minneapolis physician returned home determined to work up a congressional investigation. Congressman William Washburn of Minnesota advised him that while this was impracticable he had secured the secretary of the navy's agreement to a naval court of inquiry and was prepared to introduce the necessary resolution. Doctor Collins gave reluctant assent. Congress approved Washburn's resolution early in August and Emma De Long, questioned uneasily even by Bennett as to whether the commander was ever considered a martinet, entered a privileged liaison with the Navy Department as the first move in a campaign to protect her husband's reputation.

Appointed U.S. minister at St. Petersburg (ensuring his continued involvement with *Jeannette* matters), William Hunt had earlier in the year been succeeded as secretary by William Eaton Chandler, nicknamed the "stormy petrel" of New Hampshire politics. Controversial, cunning, and rambunctious, Chandler was at least consistent in his advocacy of a strong naval force. Hunt, before him, had broken a pattern of bureaucratic inertia by reviving active interest in new ship construction. In the fifteen years between Gideon Welles's Civil War tenure and Hunt's bold stewardship, one secretary after another had presided over the atrophy of the fleet. Hunt's innovative program for a revitalized navy was interrupted by his sudden assignment to Russia, but Chandler took it up with zeal, bluntly stating in his first report to Congress that as a fighting force the U.S. Navy was extinct. It was Chandler's dream that America would greet the new century, less than two decades away, boasting a naval strength equal to that of any European power, and he pushed aggressively for steam-driven warships with steel hulls to replace the wooden-walled relics under canvas so cherished by the diehard foes of naval modernization.

Shipyard scandals had occurred in previous administrations. Even in Chandler's case, coupled with his patriotism was the less sublime expectation of political or monetary rewards for favoring private shipbuilders with government contracts. But at this particular time the Navy Department could afford no unsavory publicity of whatever nature. Three days before Congress approved the appointment of a naval court to look into the *Jeannette* affair, it had given Chandler authority to prepare plans for building two steel cruisers. The voting on appropriations for their construction would come in the next session, by which time he intended to ask for more steel warships. For the prospects of a rebuilt navy, the intervening months would be a period of touch and go. Alert though he was to a growing national consensus in support of naval expansion Chandler knew only too well that another scandal in the service or the department would serve as fresh ammunition to the antinaval forces in Congress and the press.

Scandal was certainly brewing over Bennett's ill-fated expedition. Detecting "something hidden in the *Jeannette* story," newspapers were having a field day with rumors concerning the conduct of the officers, the alleged persecution of Jerome Collins, and Melville's misgivings about the ship as recounted earlier by his garrulous wife. The 13 May issue of *The Saturday Review*, a British publication popular on both sides of the Atlantic, had expounded on "Mr. Gordon Bennett's vicarious enterprise" and in the process cast not only the press baron but De Long and the U.S. Navy Department in a most unflattering light. The *Jeannette* had been too small to withstand the pack, De Long should have abandoned her before the second winter. After the ordeals of the first "it must have been evident to any experienced Arctic traveler that the game was up." Staying in the ice a second year could only be explained by "the fatal Micawberish hope" that luck would turn. The disaster had left a lesson. "These private adventure explorations in circumstances so dangerous . . . are mistakes unless the adventurer goes himself. When a private person, presumably interested only in the chance of having a great discovery somehow tacked on to his name, equips explorers for an adventure of such risk . . . the position of the commander is a very unpleasant one. He feels himself bound to give his owner a run for his money; he is reluctant to quit the quest without something solid and sounding. . . ."

Chandler had instinctively preferred a naval court of inquiry to a congressional probe. The navy would take care of its own. Visiting New York, he called on Emma De Long, who had returned from Iowa to her parents' residence, and asked her to frame questions she wanted put to witnesses. Virtually at Emma's insistence the secretary had also convened a board of two captains and the surgeon general of the navy to study the feasibility of bringing home the *Jeannette*'s dead. They would have to be hauled nearly five thousand miles before even reaching a railroad. The task was possible only while the ground permitted sled travel. Chandler's board estimated the overall cost, including thawing and embalming in St. Petersburg, as $25,000. He sent the board's report to the House Committee on Appropriations, action was approved, and the department accepted an offer by the Metallic Burial Case Company of New York of ten hermetically sealed steel caskets. Via telegraph and native courier, orders were issued to Lieutenant Harber, somewhere in Siberia, assigning him supervision of the harrowing logistics. Harber had, by that late summer, solved his own transportation problems and with Ensign Henry Hunt of the *Rodgers* and Fireman Bartlett, detached from the homeward-bound Melville party, formed the latest team of Americans to invade the Lena delta.

ON THE MORNING of 13 September George Melville jumped nimbly from the side-port of the ocean liner *Parthia* to the deck of a beflagged tug that had come alongside. As he embraced his waiting sisters the chief engineer heard a member of the civic welcoming committee observe how well he looked and nodding back he added, with what a *New York Times* reporter called "strange emphasis," that there was nothing wrong with his eyes.

As everybody knew, there was something wrong with Danenhower's, and that was the stated reason the lieutenant failed to attend the grand reception given Melville at New York City Hall and the banquet that followed at Delmonico's. Newspapermen were impressed by Melville's appearance, his bullish shoulders, the bald dome-like pate with brown hair matted behind it, his cold blue eyes, the profuse sandy beard gleaming red in Delmonico's gaslight. He parried their questions about Danenhower and himself but his formal address, praising shipmates who had done their full duty, contained the cryptic assertion that "those who did less were not men at all."

A special railroad car took Melville to Philadelphia for another reception at the Continental Hotel, where he stayed overnight. Next morning he arranged for the two metal cases of the expedition's records that had accompanied him throughout the long journey from Siberia to be deposited in the vaults of the Farmers and Merchants Bank pending shipment under close guard to the Navy Department in Washington. That afternoon he left for Sharon Hill. His own personal papers included Emma De Long's letter about his wife's published statement that he had told her the *Jeannette* was unsuited for the Arctic, a doomed ship. In his reply to Emma the chief engineer had said that he never would have permitted any letter of his to be made public and he denounced Henrietta in emotional terms. "I have had a miserable existence for seventeen years and there seems to be no relief until death clears the obstruction."

At Sharon Hill that Saturday dusk when the train drew in, crowds lined the rise above the station. After a greeting from local dignitaries the Arctic hero and his Philadelphia entourage boarded carriages for a drive through streets illuminated by colored lanterns and here and there a locomotive's headlamp. An arch of laurel and evergreens with the words "Welcome Home" spanned the approach to the Melvilles', an attractive cottage with bright flowers in the garden, Old Glory above the roof, and an ornamented anchor in the window. Three girls waited on the porch, and after they had embraced their father the door closed on him. As someone wrote in the melancholy aftermath, "no mortal eye saw the meeting" with his wife, but to some of the neighbors, naval officers, and visiting Philadelphians who filed in later she appeared tense and tearful. The reception lasted two hours, with a good supply of wine and brandies on hand. Outside on the lawn a brass band from nearby Darby played patriotic selections. Henrietta, at the piano with the girls, sang a ballad she had composed called *Tired Hearts*.

In the middle of the night, long after the guests had gone and Sharon Hill was quiet again, tensions broke in the Melvilles' bedroom. He refused to sleep with her, took a pillow, and stormed downstairs to the parlor. She followed, imploring or threatening, whereupon he donned his jacket and slammed from the house. He walked two miles along the Chester Pike to a friend's home in Darby, consulted others, and before dawn on Sunday had begun arrangements to have his wife locked up. The Melvilles' family doctor called in a second physician and they paid Mrs. Melville a fifteen-minute visit that afternoon which he referred to in a subsequent deposition. He had never actually seen her intoxicated so it was "not from any previous knowledge of the case but from the emergency of the moment" that he and his colleague signed a paper certifying that her mind was "deranged by chronic alcoholism." This he delivered to Melville, who earlier had sent off two telegrams, one to Emma De Long in New York, "Mrs. Melville requires restraint . . ." and the other to the secretary of the navy in Washington, where further receptions had been planned for him: "My wife is insane. Request a delay until secured."

On Monday morning Melville entered his wife's room with a magistrate's order for her commitment. She was in bed. He sprang to the pillow before she could extract the pistol hidden under it and told her to get dressed, that if need be she would be carried off in her quilt. The children came in weeping and Henrietta begged that they be allowed to accompany her. A carriage waited outside. The gathering crowd included newspapermen whose briefing on the situation was well under way. Most of the Melvilles' neighbors were quietly sympathetic but several described Henrietta as mentally ill, liquor the cause. Some said that she claimed to have seen apparitions, visions of snakes, comets, feathers, a throne, and that she had lately taken to wheeling an empty perambulator along the sidewalk, inviting passers-by to peer within at her new baby. In other press accounts she was dangerous, a dead-shot with firearms, had been known to descend on the Navy Department and physically harass the secretary. When Melville refused to share her bed that night she had threatened to shoot the children and burn down the house. (Henrietta was to countercharge that he had once fired point-blank into a closet where she stood and almost killed her.) According to a naval colleague of Melville's acting as his spokesman, her wild spending habits, squandering her husband's generous allotment, were but another symptom of the woman's unfortunate condition.

Lanterns and flags still festooned the trees. Neighbors who had listened to Henrietta Melville at the piano on Saturday watched as the magistrate's constable brought her cloaked and bonneted and crying from the house with the anchor in the window. Melville was supposed to have consented to the children riding with her but near the carriage she seemed to have a sudden premonition that they were about to be snatched away. Clutching them, she shrieked and spun back for the porch. Hands grasped her. She fell struggling and sobbing to the flower-bordered lawn where the band had played for the chief engineer, who now stood some distance off with his head bowed.

Three hours later at Norristown the gates of the Pennsylvania State Asy-lum for the Insane closed on her. Separated from their mother, the girls were placed in the care of Sharon Hill citizens or one of Melville's sisters. The *Philadelphia Press* retracted a charge that Melville had abandoned his family and fell in with the general drift that alcohol had driven his wife crazy, that at the height of thanksgiving for his safe return from a long ordeal in polar regions he was obliged to have her lawfully put away. Henrietta Melville was still behind bedlam walls three weeks later when the naval court ap-pointed to "diligently and thoroughly investigate" all aspects of the *Jeannette* expedition began by examining the ship's fitness for Arctic exploration.

CHAPTER TWENTY-ONE

THE NAVAL INQUIRY

The condition of the Jeannette on departure from San Francisco
was good. The general conduct of the personnel of the expedition
seems to have been a marvel of cheerfulness, good fellowship, and
mutual forbearance.

From the findings of the court of inquiry on the loss
of the exploring steamer Jeannette

SECRETARY CHANDLER'S OFFICE was formerly a library and probably the most beautiful room in the east wing of the State, War, and Navy Building where the department was located. The walls were inlaid with marble panels and a slab of lapis lazuli from Pompeii surmounted the doorway. The floor was also a checker-board of inlaid tiles, with bronze sea emblems dominating each corner. In this ornate setting Chandler had installed a battered old standup desk, from behind which he extended a ready welcome to visitors. Waiting in anterooms had been done away with and, it was said, his office door remained always open. This was not quite the case, however, on the eve of the *Jeannette* inquiry when the secretary held private strategy meetings with Melville, Danenhower, and Emma De Long.

The naval court consisted of Commodore Frederick W. McNair, Captain Joseph N. Miller, its sixty-year-old president Commodore William G. Temple, and a neophyte judge-advocate, Master Samuel C. Lemly. It met at the beginning of October and heard the first witness, Commodore Edmund Colhoun of the Mare Island navy yard, testify that while the *Jeannette* may have proved a sturdy ship, he would not have chosen her for an Arctic cruise. But at that time, the commodore's hesitancy to appear critical of a naval project sponsored by James Gordon Bennett had evidently outweighed his personal reservations for he had not then addressed them to the department. This same curious reluctance was admitted to by Captain Philip Johnson, senior officer of Mare Island's second board of examiners. To have made the *Jeannette* fully suitable for the task ahead would have meant rebuilding the ship. She was too lightly constructed, "very logy, heavy seas would, I should think, strain her so as to leak badly." Johnson's testimony was reaffirmed by a deposition from Mare Island's chief naval constructor, George Much. After alleging that Lieutenant De Long had himself agreed with the board's "every recommendation" but was afraid that they would prove too expensive and cause Bennett to abandon the expedition, Much described the board's misgivings in technical detail. And why was this not done in its formal report? Because, in Captain Johnson's words, the expedition was "a private enterprise [and] it was rather a delicate thing to express an unfavorable opinion of it in our official capacity."

For those with an interest in confirming the fitness of the *Jeannette* upon departure, such testimony was too authoritative an endorsement of the doubts attributed to the ship's own engineering officer by his wife, now out of reach of the press. Emma De Long wrote to Sir Allen Young in London citing his confidence in the vessel, "I might say love for her," and requesting his aid in quashing the "unpleasant rumors." She had asked Secretary Chandler to frame questions and wanted Young to "answer them as favorably as you can. . . . My husband's reputation is at stake." The British baronet's reply left nothing to be desired in praise of his former *Pandora*, but in the meantime John Danenhower had begun testifying. When asked his opinion of the *Jeannette* he said that in retrospect he would have preferred a less wedge-shaped model, "a kettle-bottom vessel with flare-out sides, because the ice would shore under her and lift her quicker."

Danenhower just then was a lionized success on the lecture circuit. At the Brooklyn Academy of Music he had cut a striking figure in evening dress, a gold chain across his vest, muttonchop whiskers above a high collar with white satin necktie, eyes shaded by dark goggles. He was a confident talker, it was said, who spoke without transcript. At one of his lecture engagements he met the daughter of an Oswego, N.Y., businessman and shortly thereafter he married her. Before the court of inquiry Danenhower displayed the same ease of manner as he did on the podium. Melville wrote privately that instead of posing as a hero he should be exposed for what he really was, "put back on the sick list." But a "compact" was in force, discretion the order of the day, and compromises were essential no matter how sorely they might go against the grain.

After a narrative account in which he blamed his eye trouble on long hours of work by lamp and candlelight, Danenhower faced questions. Were he in command, would he have pushed deeper into the pack to reach Wrangel Land? "I would have tried to get out." The prospects of so doing? "Good." And those delays at Bennett Island and Semenovskiy were not, as had been claimed, justified by a need for respite or boat repair. The work could have been done on the ice, and the people were in better shape on arrival at Bennett than when they left. But these were the only instances of Danenhower straying from the script and although they were enough to cause a few jitters, Melville assured Emma that the lieutenant had more or less played it safe. And "if we keep Danenhower muzzled I have no fear for the rest."

Melville's turn came the first week in November, when right at the outset he was provided a chance to undo the damage caused by Henrietta's hapless dalliance with the press. During the ship's fitting out, had he expressed himself to anybody as dissatisfied with the *Jeannette*? "I expressed myself as fully satisfied with all her fittings and strength." He was then permitted, as Danenhower had been, to give his own version of events. In part he testified under Emma De Long's privately solicited guidance. "Let me know how you want that put," he had asked her on the matter of the commander's signaling him from the first cutter. "I think De Long saw a separation was inevitable." The widow's feelings directly influenced the court itself whose president, Commodore Temple, had confidentially assured her that she need not worry; the Navy Department would resist any attempt to besmirch her husband's name. "Be patient, and firmly convinced that De Long's memory is in no danger." With Danenhower "muzzled" the gravest threat could only come from the family of Jerome Collins, and it was during Melville's second week in the witness chair, while he was explaining the reasons for the delay at Zemovialach, that the brothers of the dead meteorologist came to Washington.

Certain that the Navy Department had no intention of probing their brother's arrest, the Collinses had again appealed to their congressman. As a result, Secretary Chandler invited them to the department where, in the office of the judge-advocate of the navy, Master Lemly gave them their brother's diary and other effects and agreed to ask certain questions they wanted put to witnesses, cautioning however that he would at the same time object to any he considered irrelevant or improper, such as calling for hearsay evidence. He also warned the Collinses that if they insisted on bringing out the truth about their brother's arrest, it could backfire by doing harm to his memory. As Lemly described this interview, "Before going into petty quarrels which we were not required to do under the precept, I would tell [Doctor Collins] that there were certain reports against his brother [charging] very serious offenses, and things will be looked at by this court from a naval standpoint."

Lemly was proposing a deal. De Long's charges of insolence and insubordination would remain concealed if Daniel and Bernard Collins returned to Minneapolis and Brooklyn and said no more about their brother's suspension. When they refused, Lemly told them that they had better be represented before the board by counsel, "that I could not very well fight for both sides." The brothers did not hire counsel and Lemly did as he had said he must, reading off their questions and repeatedly objecting, the court being each time cleared and reassembled to hear the objection invariably sustained.

The gist of Melville's answers, such as they were, was that Jerome Collins had invited disciplinary action through his crass disobedience, that his own relations with the meteorologist had been cordial except for when he sometimes got his back up by bellowing Irish songs.

Melville returned to Philadelphia, where he was assigned duty at the navy yard. His wife meanwhile was judged "unfit for treatment as insane," given ninety dollars and allowed to leave the asylum. Divorce and a squalid battle for custody of the girls were in store for the Melvilles, but nothing would come of an attorney's threat to bring suit against the chief engineer and the doctors for having unlawfully placed Henrietta in a madhouse.

Raymond Newcomb, like Danenhower, had also begun lecturing, his talks illustrated with forty stereoptican slides, many based on the naturalist's own sketches. He told his mentor, Doctor Baird of the Smithsonian Institution, that learned graybeards looked upon him now "as a big name . . . but, my dear Professor, I am only a boy yet and need more guidance." He may have received guidance of some sort, for the performance he gave before the naval court was innocence personified as he denied knowledge of the slightest difference between the captain and Jerome Collins. And while further questions from the Collinses' list would have led to disclosure of his own treatment at the hands of the officers, he was relieved of the obligation to answer them by Judge-Advocate Lemly, who asked and objected in the same breath, each objection sustained.

The facts about Collins's arrest remained unsifted. Charlie Tang Sing professed ignorance on the matter, but surprised the court by portraying himself a victim of injustice. When Ah Sing was sent back to San Francisco as useless, Tang Sing had assumed the duties of both cabin boy and steward on the captain's promise of double pay. Tang Sing had received only a steward's salary and was still waiting for all that accumulated back pay. Nindemann followed Tang Sing with a graphic account of the separation of the boats and the ordeal in the delta, recalling nothing of any trouble between De Long and Jerome Collins. Noros was equally uninformative on this point, but startled everybody with the revelation that John P. Jackson had opened the hilltop tomb in Siberia and allowed an artist to sketch the bodies.

A distressed Emma De Long wrote Bennett: "All the annoyance to you . . . and intense suffering to me has come through your own people, Mr. Jackson and the Collinses." It was bad enough that the newsman had disobeyed Bennett's injunction against airing "soiled linen" and used the *Herald* "deliberately to defeat your own purposes." Breaking open the mausoleum transcended everything. "This last desecration seems more than I can bear." But then she was shocked anew, upon learning that the dead had been disturbed yet again, and at the quiet instigation of Lieutenant Danenhower. Shortly after his return to the United States he had, at the Collinses' request, sent a cable to Count Emil Ahfeldt, a Danish telegraph officer in Irkutsk acting as agent for *Jeannette* survivors and search parties, giving authority for the body of Jerome Collins to be removed from the tomb for transport home. Ahfeldt was surprised at the absence of reference to the secretary of the navy as contained in other communications which had passed through his hands but dutifully forwarded the letter to Lieutenant Giles Harber. Danenhower had said nothing of his action to the secretary, whose uncharacteristically lame response when Emma angrily broached the subject was that the lieutenant had meant well and what he had done "does not really seem censurable."

Under Harber's orders, Ensign Henry Hunt and a party had brought Collins's body out of the delta, hauling it by sled to Yakutsk. In the meantime Harber had received the secretary's instructions to bring all the bodies home. Soon the mausoleum Melville had designed and built stood empty and abandoned. The *Jeannette*'s found dead were again united, gathered at Yakutsk, there to remain longer than anyone foresaw, while Secretary Chandler grappled with problems for which nothing in his long and varied political career could possibly have prepared him. Pacifying the commander's widow was itself a demanding task. The Bureau of Navigation had formally designated the islands De Long had discovered so that "his name, as an American naval officer, is inscribed in higher Siberian Arctic latitudes than that of any other explorer." But this signal honor did nothing to deter Emma from threatening to make her general dissatisfaction known even at the White House.

After the first "desecration" Secretary Chandler had told James Gordon Bennett that he disapproved of Jackson's "needless act." His letter also relayed the good news that the *Jeannette* inquiry was winding up "without development of any facts discreditable to any, living or dead." Chandler wanted the *Herald*'s undiminished support for his warship program, which meant avoiding any naval scandal that could implicate the press baron. The secretary was compelled to a most discreet and precarious management. A mutuality of interests had bound Bennett, the embittered widow, the *Jeannette* survivors, and Chandler himself into a fragile alliance, whose severest test now loomed with the reappearance under oath of its most unstable element.

There was no telling what Danenhower might decide to say, not only in response to the Collinses' questions concerning their late brother. He might talk of the delay at Zemovialach, and in this regard Melville, perhaps anticipating the worst and anxious to head it off, complained to the secretary that Danenhower was "not keeping his compact." Acknowledging as much, Chandler advised the chief engineer not to worry, that his interests would be safeguarded. But Danenhower might even enlarge on his own affair, something the court had so far gingerly skirted. Resentful of what the world already knew of his inglorious unemployment while in the pack and during the retreat, he might seek to depict himself as wrongfully humiliated, heedless of the damage such testimony would inflict on De Long's reputation.

These possibilities weighed heavily on the commander's widow. Reflecting his publisher's concern, the editor of the *New York Herald* had confidentially advised her that "it would be unwise to lift the curtain. I am not so sure who would be injured most by an exposé . . . the one who would be charged or the one who would make the charge. It would seem like a desperate resort." But Emma felt constrained to send Secretary Chandler a warning. Should Danenhower go too far "his unfitness for duty will have to be proven at any costs . . . and many unpleasant matters will have to be opened up. I think we have been generous enough . . . You will not, I hope, allow him to pose as a hero before the public. . . . If you have any friendship for Mr. Melville and myself you will watch our interests and [if need be] not hesitate to produce the charges against Lieutenant Danenhower." Concurrent advice which Melville sent Emma makes similar unmistakable reference to suppressed material. "If you want to defend De Long in keeping Danenhower off duty, call for De Long's written charges against him. Move cautiously on this point, if you move at all, as it is supposed to be a secret."

Danenhower testified the first week in January. He seems indeed to have flirted with peril. Yes, there was trouble between the captain and Jerome Collins, repeated clashes leading to the latter's arrest and suspension. No, he would not have allowed Kusmah to leave Zemovialach for Bulun alone. Had he been in Melville's place he would have accompanied the exile or sent someone with him. It was probably at this juncture that Judge Advocate Lemly, who had promised Emma that he would cross-examine the lieutenant, decided otherwise. As he afterwards indicated to her, with someone like Danenhower it was as risky to ask too many questions as too few, unwise to raise issues merely to fight them, and he hoped she was "satisfied with the course I have taken. Confidentially, I think [Danenhower] a dangerous witness, a torch all ready to be lighted."

The naval court adjourned for deliberation. (In a different judicial setting, a Delaware judge granted Melville's wife custody of their two smaller children, the third would go to boarding school, with the chief engineer paying the bills.) In the middle of February, Secretary Chandler approved the court's findings. Everything possible was done to strengthen the *Jeannette* for Arctic service, her condition on departure satisfactory to all concerned except that she was "unavoidably deeply loaded, a defect which corrected itself by the consumption of coal, provisions and stores." The lateness of the season, the vessel's want of speed, the delay occasioned by her ordered search for the *Vega*, "placed the commander at a great disadvantage on his meeting with the pack ice." He had either to retreat, sacrificing all chance of northward exploration until the following summer, or force a passage to Wrangel Land, "then erroneously supposed to be a large continent." No one was to blame for the ship's loss. The retreat was conducted manfully. Everything possible was done by the survivors for the relief of the missing.

The Collins brothers protested that five survivors were yet to be heard from. They were still in Siberia, attached to Lieutenant Harber's search party. (Aniguin, the *Jeannette*'s surviving hunter, had contracted a disease in Irkutsk and died.) When they returned in April, Chandler ordered the court reconvened, the Collinses' questions again read off, with the same simultaneous objections. The witnesses were still under naval jurisdiction, a point of some significance later on. Fireman Bartlett in fact had come home technically under arrest for disrespect, following a run-in he had had with Ensign Hunt in Irkutsk. This charge against Bartlett was quietly dropped. Chief Engineer Melville, by his own admission, "fastened on" the fireman as soon as he arrived in Washington, staying with him until he left town. Before the court, Bartlett denied any knowledge of unpleasantness between Collins and De Long or of papers taken off the meteorologist's body and allegedly stolen or destroyed. The fireman, Leach, Lauterbach, Raymond Newcomb, freed of "intimidation," were all soon telling a different story, in collusion with the two Collinses who attacked the court of inquiry as a whitewash and renewed their demands for Congress to investigate. Chandler might have realized that he was not finished with the controversy even as he declared that nothing had transpired to alter the court's February findings and that the only duty left the Navy Department was the melancholy one of bringing home the remains of the dead.

As Chandler had already discovered, this was a most vexatious undertaking. The caskets from America had reached the Russian railhead at Orenburg. The bodies were still at Yakutsk, more than four thousand miles distant. Amid much confusion as messages criss-crossed between Washington, St. Petersburg, and remote Siberia, no one could decide whether to haul the ten caskets (each weighing eight hundred pounds) by sled to Yakutsk or to transport the bodies in their frozen state all the way to the railhead. And the Russian authorities, while willing to help seek the living, were distinctly uncooperative about moving the dead. There was enough political unrest in the Tsarist empire without a revolt by Siberian natives fearful that the passage of the bodies through their settlements would bring punishment from the gods in the form of famine and pestilence. On 13 February 1883 an exasperated Minister Hunt wrote from St. Petersburg, "The distances are so great, the communications so uncertain, the accounts of means of transportation so unreliable, that I am embarrassed as to which course is wisest."

By spring the bodies were still at Yakutsk. They would have to remain there, in makeshift coffins, until the following winter. Lieutenant Harber had emerged from the Lena delta after an unsuccessful search for Chipp to learn that he must see to the preservation of the dead and stay with them at Yakutsk until the return of the sledding season.

Emma De Long's sanitized version of her husband's journals was published in the fall. She omitted all reference to his troubles with Collins, Danenhower, and the others. An appendix in the book described Melville's plans for a ship to conquer the Arctic, a design he claimed to have discussed with De Long while in the pack and which had the late commander's enthusiastic endorsement. Soon the engineer's and Danenhower's separate accounts of the expedition were also before the public, each full of fascinating detail, predictably self-serving, betraying only here and there, perhaps to be read between the lines, something of the jealousy that continued to smolder between the two men.

At about this time, another American expedition was in trouble. Greely and twenty-five men were stranded north of Greenland. Melville volunteered to lead an immediate sled party to Greely's relief, but a board rejected his proposal as impracticable. Notwithstanding repeated assurances that his reputation at the Navy Department was secure, Melville felt his career very much on the line. Fretting in a routine post at the Philadelphia navy yard, beset by family problems, still privately seething against Danenhower, the chief engineer knew that his battle to defend himself against charges of "murder," his own term, was by no means over.

*   *   *

In late November all Yakutsk had turned out in farewell to the *Jeannette*'s dead. The funeral cortege consisted of seven large sleds, five of them each carrying two coffins, drawn by twenty-one horses. A Russian military escort fired a salute as it left the town borders. It covered the twenty-five-hundred-mile journey to Irkutsk in nineteen days and gathered more wreaths and honors, while printed copies of an epic poem recounting the story of the *Jeannette* were distributed among the crowds on the streets by members of the East Siberia Geographic Society. Under Lieutenant Harber's firm control the cortege of sleds crossed the steppes to Tomsk, another eight hundred miles, arriving 1 January 1884. Despite heavy snow, crowds thronged the streets, a Cossack band played, and at a special reception the mayor recited a history of the expedition. At every stop across Siberia the American cortege was received with military honors. Local inhabitants flocked to the caskets with more and more wreaths, so that by the time Giles Harber's strange command had reached the Orenburg railhead he had to arrange for special crates to accommodate the wealth of floral tributes.

Transferred to the waiting metal caskets, the dead were entrained for Moscow, a distance of nine hundred miles. The journey was accomplished in a week, and a cross-section of Russia's future capital ranging from scientists and soldiers to Moscow University students turned out to pay their respects to the dead Americans. The European phase of the journey via Berlin to Hamburg measured thirteen hundred ninety miles. Sixty-three days after leaving Yakutsk the *Jeannette*'s dead were ceremoniously mourned on the wharf of the Hamburg–America Steam Packet Company, then placed on board the steamer *Frisia*. She arrived off Hoboken, New Jersey, on 20 February, to complete an unprecedented funeral journey in excess of twelve thousand miles and also to bring to a close a unique personal odyssey, of two years' duration, in the career of Lieutenant Giles Harber.

Again the *New York Herald* ran black-bordered columns. The dead were borne by tug to a metropolis draped in mourning. Flags hoisted to honor the birthday of De Long's boyhood hero flew at half-staff. Church bells tolled continuously. The procession formed at the Battery with bluejackets flanking each of the ten caskets. Carriages followed with survivors and the bereaved. The cortege crossed the new Brooklyn Bridge, where police applied all their skills in crowd control to prevent a repetition of last year's Decoration Day disaster when twelve died in a panic on the span. At the Brooklyn Navy Yard, where the bodies would lie in state, the Marine Band interspersed its solemn dirges with renditions of the Russian anthem in recognition of honors accorded the dead and the assistance furnished searchers and survivors by the tsar's government and people. On each casket rested a wreath in the shape of an anchor, sent by James Gordon Bennett, who attended none of the obsequies. Jerome Collins's brothers took away his casket. It would travel (with that of their mother) once more across the ocean for final interment in a cemetery outside Cork. Doctor Ambler was buried in his native Virginia and Seaman Boyd in Philadelphia. The bodies of the remaining seamen were unclaimed and an agreement among the secretary of the navy, the widow, and cemetery officials approved their interment with their captain.

Sleet changed to a driving snow on Saturday morning, 23 February, when the bodies of Lieutenant De Long and six shipmates, after a service at the Church of the Holy Trinity, were taken by carriage to Woodlawn Cemetery in the Bronx. They were lowered to rest on a hillside. Chief Engineer Melville threw the first spadeful of earth into De Long's grave, Lieutenant Danen-hower, Seamen Nindemann and Noros, and the steward Tang Sing performing the same ritual at the graves of Kaak, Lee, Iversen, Dressler, Görtz and Ah Sam.

In those same wintry days, Daniel Collins had obtained depositions from ex-Fireman Bartlett and others to the effect that witnesses before the naval court had been suborned or intimidated, facts distorted or suppressed. The week after the burials at Woodlawn, the persistent M.D. from Minneapolis alleged in a petition to Congress that his late brother was mistreated and humiliated, that the meteorologist and others might have been saved had

Melville done his duty, and that before the naval court of inquiry "all possibility of the truth coming out was destroyed." On 3 March the House of Representatives, acting on Collins's petition, resolved that the Committee on Naval Affairs be directed to investigate.

With the House about to debate naval appropriations, Secretary Chandler was understandably alarmed. He had no doubt of the doctor's main intention, namely, to wring from Lieutenant Danenhower verification of the things he had presumably told him in the Fifth Avenue Hotel and was reported to have told the newsman Jackson in Siberia. Chandler also knew how eagerly Collins's indictments of the *Jeannette*'s officers, living or dead, were welcomed by antinavy segments of the press, especially those newspapers whose circulations had suffered as a result of that thirst for scoops which the *Jeannette* misadventure, in their view, so grossly typified. In a letter to the chairman of the Naval Affairs Committee, Chandler attacked the Collinses' efforts to obtain another investigation as "a second pitiless sacrilege to again tear open the graves of the dead for the purpose of indecently calling attention to what the court of inquiry correctly termed 'trivial difficulties' common to life on any ship."

At the same time, Chandler moved to secure a traditional base of support, James Gordon Bennett's *Herald*. Citing the president's message to Congress on the need for a stronger fleet he told the publisher that it would be "in the country's interest if you and the *Herald* would favor said unbroken progress in the reconstruction of the American navy. Will you give your personal direction?" As a politician, Chandler had never been among Bennett's favorites, but he responded as hoped, replying that it was "a pleasure and a duty to support" the secretary's program and that he had issued instructions. Chandler acknowledged Bennett's "prompt and patriotic action" with thanks. On 2 April the *New York Herald* declared that "this country needs at least a dozen actual modern war vessels." None should hesitate in approving the expenditures required to "put a new navy under way." An editorial the following week more boldly stating the need for increased naval strength was headlined: "Our Defenseless Position." And by then the congressional hearing on the *Jeannette* expedition had begun, with careers, reputations, and just possibly the very prospects for America's entry into the twentieth century as a first-rate naval power riding on the outcome.

CHAPTER TWENTY-TWO

SAFETY VALVES OF SCANDAL

There is a great deal we both might say that has not been said. . . .
I know the true history of the Expedition will never be written.
George Melville to Emma De Long, 10 August 1883

THE NAVAL AFFAIRS Committee Room was on the third floor of the House wing of the Capitol. Through its main window, facing west, could be seen the new Washington Monument, bleached in spring sunshine and complete but for capstone. Also visible across the tree-tangled Mall, which was not yet the open plaza L'Enfant had envisioned, the red turrets and spires of the Smithsonian Institution might have served as a reminder of the goals the closing century's scientists and explorers pursued with such dedication and sacrifice. But in the committee room complex emotions simmered around the burnished mahogany table and too often the vaulted ceiling with its heavy gaslight chandelier echoed hostile tones from the floor beneath.

All three men forming the subcommittee to "investigate the facts connected with the expedition and the alleged unofficerlike and inhumane conduct therein" were staunch pro-navy legislators. Republican Charles A. Boutelle of Maine was a former naval officer and an active champion of Secretary Chandler's efforts to strengthen the fleet. William McAdoo was a New Jersey Democrat who had pleaded eloquently in favor of a naval build-up (he was a future assistant secretary of the navy). And subcommittee chairman Hugh Buchanan, a Democrat from Georgia, had fought for the Confederacy but now loyally espoused national union and acknowledged naval power as essential to its preservation. When it was learned that the Collinses would employ legal counsel, the subcommittee had held a pre-hearing consultation with Chandler at the Navy Department, Emma De Long also present, and the feeling was that the Navy's side should do the same. The choice was William H. Arnoux, a judge of the Supreme Court of New York, and the decision to hire his services was probably hasty, the terms of agreement ambiguous, for long after the event he was still dunning the government for compensation due.

The Collinses had hired George Milton Curtis, Jr., a veteran New York attorney whose earlier political career had almost foundered in the wake of the Tweed Ring scandals but who had achieved more recent fame as a brilliant criminal lawyer specializing in murder cases. Some that he had fought far from his Flatbush office had taken him into territory where his own neck might have been as close to the noose as that of the wretch he defended. Curtis's most recent success was on behalf of a Union cavalry colonel accused of assassination, and that in a still fiercely insurrectionist corner of Kentucky with popular sympathy wholly for the victim, no less than the state's chief justice. More than just the latest of the Brooklyn lawyer's triumphs—he never lost a murder case—that one marked the first time an American court had acquitted a confessed killer on grounds of insanity.

The hearings on the *Jeannette* began in early April and lasted more than a month. Curtis was physically impressive, robust and leonine. For the insinuating oratory with which he had melted the souls of pitiless juries or crumbled the resistance of unfriendly witnesses, he was accustomed to larger audiences. Besides himself, the only occupants of the naval affairs room were the subcommittee, a stenographer, the other side's attorney, and the day's deponents. Also the widow. Emma De Long had determined to attend each day's session. She was, in any event, subpoenaed by the Collinses and directed to bring her late husband's journals. Seated in her reserved chair, handsome in mourning weeds, she must have soundlessly dominated the proceedings; when Curtis expressed an anxiety to have original materials at hand instead of Navy Department copies, he declared it "a very delicate thing, every time we want to examine the [commander's] journal to be compelled to go to Mrs. De Long."

Once the preliminary arguments were disposed of, Doctor Daniel Collins was allowed to read a statement, mostly a recapitulation of the charges he had well aired to the press. Its only surprise was the letter of anguish which Jerome Collins had written while on the trapped ship, a rough draft having been found on the meteorologist's body. The doctor concluded his statement by recounting the meeting with Danenhower in the Fifth Avenue Hotel and it was this point on which Judge Arnoux seized in an early attempt to confuse the doctor and thus belittle his accusations. Had Danenhower said Collins had led a hell of a life or been in hell? Had the lieutenant been sitting or lying on the lounge? Did he say the meteorologist was under arrest? Could the witness so swear? And there was Newcomb, who had allegedly told Doctor Collins that other members of the expedition besides his brother were treated with every outrage. Did the naturalist say "outrage"?

Collins hedged. "Well, every indignity or—"

"I asked you that word. Do you swear he said outrage?"

"I swear that he used the word outrage with the meaning of indignity."

"I did not ask what the meaning was. Did he use that word?"

"To the best of my recollection."

"Who told you that the court of inquiry ruled out nearly every question that would bring out the true history of the expedition?"

"I judged so from the report. And Mr. Lemly's statement that he would not ask any question reflecting on a dead man."

"Does that prove to you that he ruled out nearly every question that would bring out that true history?"

"I think it is pretty conclusive."

"You think so? But I ask not for your opinion but the fact. Was that what you based your opinion on?"

"Partly," Collins answered, a feeble response, but Arnoux could have achieved little more in this direction and after getting him to read from his late brother's notebook he let the doctor go. Fireman Bartlett was the next witness. Freed from official jurisdiction which allegedly had curbed his tongue before the naval panel, and led now by George Curtis, he had little good to say of his superiors. "They would congregate on the sunny side of a lump of ice and sit and warm themselves and wait for the people to come up with the boats." He told of jealousy between Danenhower and Melville, of the availability of dogs at Zemovialach. And if the whaleboat party had left Zemovialach after, say, sixteen days and started a search north from Bulun, the chances were high that they would have fallen in with Noros and Nindemann who could have directed them to the captain's party.

Raymond Newcomb recalled "a spirit of turmoil" that developed after the ship became imprisoned. "Sociability rather suddenly died, and I don't think it ever revived. Conversation withered like a plant for want of nourishment." And who was to blame? "Well," replied the young naturalist, "you might consider De Long the pot that held the plant."

But Curtis grew nettled when Newcomb's testimony appeared to slight the memory of Jerome Collins. It had gratified the lawyer to hear Newcomb describe Collins as kindly, eager to cheer, composing Christmas carols for the crew. But Collins also sang, "had a certain way of singing or quoting *Pinafore* until I got tired of it. And I would say 'You will give me an earache.' "

And what about Melville's singing of Irish songs to enrage Collins? Had not they caused the witness's ears to ache?

"I never had to go to a doctor, sir."

"That was a little metaphor on your part?"

"A figure of speech."

"Your imagination is vivid, is it not?"

"That is a question."

"When Collins was singing *Pinafore*, was he not trying to keep up a feeling of hope and confidence?"

"You might generally say so."

Congressman McAdoo effectively if unintentionally ended this diversion into musical matters by interjecting, "Did he ever sing *Sweet Violets* or any of those new airs?"

Nindemann followed, to agree with George Curtis that priority in loading the sleds should have gone to compasses, tools, and provisions, instead of the ship's journals, logbooks, and expedition records, which the lawyer called "literary freight." Nindemann also stated that earlier action on Melville's part after the whaleboat crew arrived at Zemovialach would probably have saved the commander's life. Noros, the next witness, echoed these serious assertions, but Judge Arnoux redressed the balance somewhat by briskly eliciting Noros's agreement that those books were indeed the more valuable, that nautical instruments vital on shipboard became excess baggage when ashore.

To properly discharge his assignment, which was to clear Jerome Collins's name of any taint of wrongdoing and establish that he had been persecuted, George Curtis intended to make Lieutenant Danenhower stand by what he had reportedly told John Jackson in Irkutsk. The late meteorologist's brothers had engaged Curtis in the belief that if a conspiracy of concealment had indeed been hatched at the Navy Department, Curtis was the man to pierce it even if, in the process, he had to portray the revered and lamented commander as a stern disciplinarian transformed by a series of tragic misfortunes into a crazed and dangerous martinet. But it was during his examination of Danenhower, though often caustic and penetrating, that the veteran criminal lawyer felt compelled for one reason or another to leave certain paths unexplored.

But Curtis's patience was sorely tried, or so he protested, right from the start, by Danenhower's tendency to deliver speeches instead of simple responses. And when the subcommittee ruled that the witness could accompany his answers with explanatory matter Curtis told him that although "the chairman has given you large liberties, I would prefer that you would not put arguments or statements. I am asking you simple questions susceptible of simple answers."

"And leaving the thing doubtful," Danenhower retorted. "This is not a court of law."

In short order Curtis placed his opinion of Danenhower on the record as a hostile witness. He framed his next questions in a manner to suggest that the lieutenant had engaged in an improper collusion with other witnesses, the commander's widow, and Judge Arnoux. Then he got down to the business of comparing Danenhower's recent utterances and writings with what he was reported to have told Jackson in Siberia when his experiences north of the Arctic Circle were still fresh in his memory. Were not those stories he had given the newspaperman true?

"True, but my feelings then were quite different. My mind was full. My head was full. I was in a spirit of resentment. Little things that occurred were magnified in my mind. Now I can see the better elements in men's character."

"That is hardly an answer to my question."

"I have not finished yet. I am making a statement to the committee."

The chairman admonished him to answer directly, but only after an irate Curtis had threatened to discontinue, blustering, "It is impossible to examine him." Thereafter the lawyer pressed harder, drawing Danenhower's admission that he knew Jackson was under his publisher's orders to keep a lid on unsavory facts. Jackson had asked him to similarly impress the members of the whaleboat party with the need to watch their tongues and the lieutenant had complied. Curtis next announced that he would read from the published interviews with Jackson. "I respectfully ask you to listen," he told Danenhower, "and as the mistakes occur you indicate them."

Throughout this uncomfortable period Danenhower kept his demeanor. Seldom was he at a loss for words. The fight he had sworn to resume against De Long before the commander's fate was known shrank in his latest version to merely a confession of pique. Throttling Newcomb and hurling him to the bottom of the whaleboat? Justified at the time and for which he had since been forgiven, indeed thanked. His reported comments on Melville's failure to mount a prompt search for the missing? Misquotations. Did he not tell Jackson that De Long had erred in ordering a course from Semenovskiy Island to the Lena delta instead of striking due south for the mouth of the Yana?

"I never made such a statement. I talked to Jackson as if I had been a brother. I cannot swear today what I told him and what I did not tell him."

Congressman McAdoo came to Danenhower's relief by changing the subject. "Let me ask you. There is always more or less strife in the Navy between the staff and the line, is there not?"

"Between some. Melville and I never had any."

"I mean as a general thing."

"Yes, sir, there is what is known as a staff and line fight. Just like a competition between two lawyers."

Curtis had only limited success in trying to portray De Long's decision to abandon the second whaleboat instead of the second cutter as a blunder but then tried to indict the late commander for also leaving instruments on the sinking ship. He asked Danenhower if they had a *Bowditch Navigator* with them during the retreat.

"No, sir, it would have been useless without the instruments."

"But if you had had the instruments it would not have been useless, would it?

"If we had had a sextant we could have determined the latitude, even if we did not have the longitude, and, of course, if we had a chronometer that was regulated . . . we could have determined the longitude. But in fitting out from the ship evidently the captain expected to keep all three boats together, and that one set of nautical instruments would be sufficient for the whole party."

"But if you had had the instruments, including a *Bowditch Navigator*, would you not have been able to ascertain your position pretty correctly?"

"Yes, we could. In the boat we could have determined the position."

Then Danenhower took fire from both sides. That Curtis sniped at him was to be expected. But Judge Arnoux, fulfilling his assignment to protect De Long's reputation, had of necessity to threaten Danenhower's in order to show that the captain was justified in keeping him off duty. The lieutenant struggled to hold his ground. He had glibly attributed his latest revision of what he was supposed to have said at Irkutsk to altered perspectives. But one of those controversial Siberian statements he had not altered, namely, that De Long's keeping him off duty during the retreat had been unjust and jeopardized the expedition. He declared with emphasis that he had resented De Long's calling him an impediment. But then, doubtless to his surprise and dismay, Congressman Boutelle proceeded to read extracts from the *Jeannette*'s medical log which, deemed irrelevant, had not been introduced before the naval board of inquiry. Fortunately for Danenhower the selections dealt mostly with the disabling symptoms of his affliction. Nothing was said of Ambler's diagnosis nor of the surgeon's (and De Long's) shocked discovery that until his left eye broke down the *Jeannette*'s navigation officer had kept his medical condition a secret. All the same, it was probably again to Danenhower's relief when his testimony was suspended so that George Melville could get his over and done with before sailing on the *Thetis*, one of three vessels ordered to the rescue of Captain Greely's party, by then facing death at Cape Sabine.

QUESTIONED BY JUDGE Arnoux, the chief engineer described De Long as a fair and equable man who at no time inflicted indignity upon any of his subordinates, an officer who ran his ship by the rules and for whom the health of his people was practically an obsession. With a straight face that must have demanded inner effort, Melville also praised Danenhower, as efficient, dutiful, manly in every respect. With zest and even geniality he heaped abuse on the name of Jerome Collins. As a scientist Collins was a duffer, bone lazy, so contemptible a landlubber as to make no allowance for the roll of the ship, in consequence losing overboard one expensive instrument after another. Almost in apology for having so begrimed the dead man's memory Melville chided the subcommittee with, "It seems a shame to talk about all sorts of little petty foolish things, but that is what you all want to know about." As for the delay at Zemovialach, all but the whaleboat crew were presumed dead. "There was no question of going to hunt De Long or Chipp, the question was about saving our own lives."

Before the engineer left the hearing room Curtis had blunted his scornful appraisal of Jerome Collins by forcing him to admit that he was the only living witness of several instances he had alleged as showing up the meteorologist's incompetence. For what it was worth, the lawyer also nudged Melville into confessing that he had carried poison as a precaution against possible cannibalism, though not, the engineer insisted, out of a rank-conscious apprehension that officers might be eaten by the men. But that was about as far as George Curtis could go. Melville's latest Arctic assignment ruled out lengthy grilling. Curtis would have to make do with Danenhower.

The lieutenant resumed testimony on the last day of April and Curtis took him firmly over the interview with the Collinses at the Fifth Avenue Hotel. On that occasion, while still under the effects of his Arctic ordeal, was he mentally competent?

"I believe I was, fully."

"Did the Collinses speak of trouble between De Long and their brother?"

"I suppose they must have."

"Did they or not?"

Danenhower registered uncertainty. He recalled that the subject arose because "my brother-in-law came in and said he had seen—"

"Never mind that. Did you or not say that Mr. Collins on that ship had led a hell of a life?"

"I believe I did not but I cannot swear. I exaggerated perhaps, used metaphors."

"Now, lieutenant, are you a practical photographer?"

"I was an amateur, but I have forgotten it."

"My dear lieutenant, that is not the question I have asked you. Tell me on how many occasions, to your present knowledge, Mr. Collins failed when he attempted to take a photograph?"

"All I know is that Collins could not develop a plate."

"No, no. I don't want your general opinion, your observations, your judgement. When was the first time?"

"I cannot remember."

"Who can testify about it besides yourself? Is there a living being can do it?"

"I do not know."

"Have you any other information to justify your statement that Mr. Collins was incompetent as a photographer?"

"Mr. Collins showed complete ignorance on the subject."

"I don't want your judgement, your conclusion, your argument. I want fact."

"The fact is that Collins demonstrated to me fully that he knew nothing of the subject."

Curtis took a different tack, one he knew the lieutenant must have dreaded. His physical disabilities were such that for much of the retreat he could do no active duty, "as a matter of fact, you were carried along by other men, were you not?"

"I was never carried an inch."

"You did no work?"

"I did no work and I was never carried an inch, and I made up my mind if it came to that, I would step overboard and I believe I would have done it."

Curtis snapped it up at once. "Overboard?"

"Through the ice."

"Not over the ship's side? Is not that a favorite metaphor of yours?"

"It is with every seafaring man." Collins's trouble had grown from his sullen refusal to ask De Long's permission to go over the ship's side, on to the ice, and it was in this sense that he, Danenhower, has used those words at the Fifth Avenue Hotel. "It is very natural that Doctor Collins and his brother, if they did not take my words down verbatim, should have made some mistake. I assert that that is the only way I used the words. I had no idea of committing suicide on board the ship." Curtis listened, allowed him to run on. "I had a perfect hell on earth owing to the suffering I endured but I never had the slightest intention of stepping over the ship's side there . . . of committing suicide."

"Did I ask you about committing suicide?"

"I have made this statement to the committee."

"I ask you to answer my question."

Danenhower's equanimity had vanished. "I consider that I am nagged here today."

"Nagged? In what way?"

"When I tell you I do not recollect a thing you try to push me in all sorts of ways."

"I have simply asked you questions that any honest man could answer."

"I take exception to that, sir!"

SCATHING THOUGH GEORGE Curtis had sometimes been in his handling of Lieutenant Danenhower, the ace criminal lawyer was careful not to betray the officer's secret. He must have known of it. On 2 May he offered in evidence Doctor Ambler's private diary, actually the Navy Department's copy, the original having gone to Ambler's family. He read it aloud in the committee room, but at the entry dated 6 July 1881 he omitted a dozen words that might have served as a lever to prise an amalgam of guilt into the daylight. The entry contained an impatient reference to "our two friends of the line" on Ambler's sick list. They were Chipp and Danenhower, and without specifically naming them that day, the doctor had written that one had come out on the *Jeannette* "knowing that he was diseased and that he was liable to be laid up and concealed it as long as possible." In the expurgated form as read by Curtis—"knowing that he was liable to be laid up"— the passage sounded relatively harmless and could have applied equally to the lost Lieutenant Chipp. (The department's inked copy is faithful to the penciled original but traces of an attempted erasure can be seen at the twelve words left out by George Curtis.)

The lawyer's self-restraint in matters of "extreme delicacy" was due in part to the disturbing presence of Emma De Long, who herself took the witness chair near the close of the hearings to give Judge Arnoux her views on "the complete preparations of the voyage." Curtis's objection that "I hardly think the lady is competent to express an opinion" went unheeded. Arnoux led her to express complete satisfaction with the ship's outfitting, discount instances of bad provisions as the sort of thing that might happen in any household, and praise all concerned in the efforts to save her husband's life. Although the reporter Jackson had crossed the ocean to repeat his own conclusions before the committee, detail the circumstances of the Irkutsk interviews, and defend himself against charges of ghoulishness, at no time was his publisher-employer, the expedition's promoter, called to testify. But Emma De Long quoted Bennett to the effect that he did not blame the commander for putting people under arrest. "I wished this expedition to be a military one," Bennett had told her, "and I recognize that it is necessary to have a different discipline in the Arctic regions than what a man might have in open water."

Before delivering their closing remarks, Curtis and Judge Arnoux each read excerpts from De Long's journals, carefully chosen to score points. Afterwards, in his summation, Arnoux extolled the virtues of De Long and Melville, said little of Danenhower, and portrayed Collins in mildly pitying tones. The meteorologist was "a genial companion until his brain became abnormal in the Arctic cold," turning him into "a voluntary sloth on board." Those who had testified mischievously were unworthy of regard, Newcomb immature, Bartlett a drunk and perjurer, Nindemann not to be trusted since admitting in the witness chair that he did not believe in a Supreme Being, that "Nature is my god."

Arnoux's goal throughout the investigation had been generally clear. Conflicting influences, however, had placed Curtis in an unusual quandary.

The *Jeannette* may have been the ace criminal lawyer's toughest case. For the bureaucratic prestige, professional careers, and private fortunes quite evidently at stake he probably cared not a whit. But other considerations had gathered. Curtis had fought in Civil War front lines with the Third Battalion, Massachusetts Rifles, was a Freemason, a member of the Lafayette Post of the Grand Army of the Republic. Given such patriotic credentials he would not have relished even the appearance of dragging the navy's name in the mud, especially with the naval appropriations bill before Congress. And conventional codes of decency appear to have operated upon him, a chivalrous regard for female sensibilities preventing him from steering witnesses too far along forbidden paths. Yet he could never lose sight of his duty to his clients, the Collinses. The lawyer's dilemma is detectable in his closing address, and equally implied is the only course he felt left to him. To the extent that he knew of or suspected a compact of secrecy on the other side George Curtis found himself, in the end, with no alternative but to join it.

The committee's purpose, as Curtis saw it, was to "draw the line between the arbitrary caprice of Navy officers and the rights of American citizens." But he had only sympathy for the lost commander. Petermann's charts and geography were all wrong. De Long could not be blamed for relying on imperfect information. Nor yet condemned for his harsh treatment of Jerome Collins. A stubborn man he no doubt was, a martinet if not petty tyrant, but "I believe his understanding was disordered by his calamities." Of course, what the expedition's promoter now thought of its commanding officer was unknown. Mrs. De Long had testified that he had approved of her husband's conduct, but "can it be supposed for one moment that he could heartlessly add to her grief by revealing the opposite sentiment?" It was "very significant" that the committee had received no direct word from Mr. Bennett. And Jerome Collins, who went to the Arctic full of hope and ambition? That poignant letter of his was "the last wail of a broken heart" and had Curtis been in the meteorologist's shoes, "So help me God, I would rather Lieutenant De Long had taken a rifle and put a bullet through me."

Curtis had no compassion to spare for Melville or Danenhower. The chief engineer had not done his best to search for De Long. As for the navigation officer, "You have only to look in Doctor Ambler's journal to see that Danenhower should have been more severely punished than poor Collins." Curtis did not amplify. Instead, in a final burst of self-defense before the committee he made cryptic allusion to suppressed facts. There were "influences at work against me, against my client, natural influences created by the spectacle, most pathetic, of beauty in distress." But he had been careful to avoid producing unnecessary grief. "Although I have personally been aspersed throughout by the venal portion of the press as one desirous of creating a scandal, unearthing the dead, the truth of the matter is that I have sat on more safety-valves of scandal in this investigation than the committee dreamed of." He had done so with one view alone, to keep out of sight "extraneous matter" which, if made public, "might injure and wound the innocent. And I thank God that my conscience in regard to that matter is clear."

The following year, on 17 February, the congressional investigating subcommittee issued its report. De Long had done right in entering the lead while the sea froze about him. "It is useless to send a ship to the Arctic for the purposes of discovery unless it is put in the ice." All hands deserved the generous praise of their country. The ship was sound and properly provisioned. Collins was obliged to enlist as seaman by virtue of an Act of Congress, and sensitive by nature, unaccustomed to naval discipline, he took objection to acts and words he would otherwise not have noticed. His arrest and continued suspension were in the interests of the expedition's general health and welfare. On the retreat De Long did all to be expected of an intelligent, brave, and kind officer. Had Melville learned in time what he afterwards discovered of De Long's arrival in the Lena delta he could and would have rescued him. The naval court of inquiry was properly conducted, no witnesses intimidated, "and no important and valuable testimony was suppressed."

That was the last official denouement to the *Jeannette* affair. It was published a month before William Chandler relinquished the office of secretary of the navy. He might have done so secure in the belief that the controversy over the expedition, like that simultaneously touched off by his flagrant award of shipyard contracts to low-bid favorites, would pose no further threat to the construction plans he had set in motion heralding a new era of steel for the U.S. Navy.

CHAPTER TWENTY-THREE

SACRIFICE NOBLER THAN EASE

*All enterprise will stop if we were never to act without being able
to point to a decidedly successful result of our undertaking.*

Sir George Nares, Captain, R.N., at Annapolis, 1885

IN THE WANING nineteenth century the Arctic Question, still unsolved, lost
some of its allure. This was in part due to a revival of interest, chiefly European, in the unexplored Antarctic regions. But there had also begun, certainly in the United States, a decline in popular romanticism of the subject.
The *Jeannette* tragedy, followed by the loss of three-quarters of Lieutenant
Greely's party in Smith Sound, had dampened national zeal for a "polar dash."
American activity did not altogether cease. Lieutenant Robert E. Peary, who
had joined the U.S. Navy in the same month when De Long pitched his last
camp, made his maiden voyage north of the Arctic Circle only five years
later. But the Arctic initiative was then held firmly by Norway's Doctor
Fridtjof Nansen and would remain his until Peary's emergence in the dawn-
ing 1900s.

Chief Engineer George Melville, who was among the first to reach the
Greely survivors, saw his own dreams of leading a polar expedition evaporate

in the new mood of indifference or more realistic assessment but could hardly have anticipated defending the cause of Arctic exploration in a direct confrontation with Lieutenant John Danenhower.

It took place 9 October 1885 under the auspices of the United States Naval Institute on the grounds of the Naval Academy, where the lieutenant was then stationed. The occasion was an international symposium on the Arctic, with Clements Markham of the Royal Geographical Society in the chair and his compatriot, Captain George Nares, R.N., also Lieutenant Adolphus Greely, U.S. Army, among the guests. That such a distinguished assembly hung raptly on Danenhower's words was enough to have made George Melville writhe, but the paper the lieutenant had composed on the voyage of the *Jeannette* and its proper place in the annals of polar exploration was eloquent and exhaustively detailed. As Danenhower portrayed it, the expedition's main accomplishment was to disprove August Petermann's theories. Wrangel was no continent, no great warm current existed in those latitudes, no open polar sea. Was it, then, Danenhower asked, worth all the investment in money and lives merely to correct the caprices of stay-at-home geographers and map-makers? "I unhesitatingly record myself as opposed to further exploration of the central polar basin. . . . It is time to call a halt."

Markham politely demurred, called the *Jeannette* expedition "a noble work, so far as it went." Melville was more vehemently aroused. He decried Danenhower's views as springing from an assumption that men ventured north only in hopes of monetary gain. "If men must die," declared the chief engineer, "why not in honorable pursuit of knowledge? Far be it . . . that our ideas of manhood should be dwarfed to the size of a golden dollar. Woe, woe, to America when the young blood of our nation has no sacrifice to make for science."

Danenhower was back on his feet. Prudence, not considerations of commercial profit, had inspired his plea for a moratorium on polar expeditions, and while "lurid rhetoric and sentimental phrases" might appeal to "romantic and adventurous spirits . . . they are not arguments and they have no weight with thinking men. There are better directions [than Arctic exploration] for the display of true manhood and heroism in the everyday life of our great cities."

Such expressions were not typically forthcoming from most men in uniform, much less Arctic explorers, and they invite speculation as to the course of John Danenhower's career had it not ended so abruptly. Although the victim of physical and mental disorder, at his best he displayed proficiency and calm intelligence, showed generosity and concern for lower ranks, and was undoubtedly courageous. It was courage, of a self-sacrificial nature, that on 20 April 1887 he seems finally to have summoned.

He had felt the old horror creeping back on him soon after taking command of the practice ship *Constellation*—the headaches, the fits of depression. Clearing Annapolis harbor on a trip to Norfolk the *Constellation* struck bottom. On arrival in Hampton Roads she grounded firmly in the channel off Craney Island. Manifestly agitated despite reassurances from colleagues that running one's ship aground in that vicinity was a not uncommon occurrence, Danenhower handed command over to an ensign and returned to Annapolis in the gig. His wife and their two infant children were with her family in upstate New York. Next morning after breakfast, alone in his quarters on the fourth floor of 12 Goldsborough Row, he spread a gumcoat to protect the carpet and tied a farewell note to the lapel of his tunic. Then Lieutenant Danenhower pressed the muzzle of a fully loaded .32 caliber Smith and Wesson revolver to his temple and pulled the trigger.

That same year in which Lieutenant Danenhower committed suicide, President Grover Cleveland appointed George Melville over forty-four senior officers to head the Navy Department's Bureau of Steam Engineering. Melville held the position for sixteen of the navy's most innovative years and was himself largely responsible for the revolutionary features that enabled the service to enter the twentieth century enjoying technical if not numerical parity with the best of Europe's navies. He was by then rear admiral, engineer-in-chief of the navy, a world-famous authority on steam propulsion and a powerful advocate of multi-tonnage battleships. (He did not, however, think submarines had much of a future.) Perhaps Melville was never fully satisfied of vindication in the *Jeannette* affair. When Peary sought his advice on whether to attach a newspaperman to an expedition he was working up, the chief engineer urged emphatically that he do so. "You will find it a decided advantage to have the *Herald* back of you. You can never tell what may turn up. After I had done all that men could do [in the search for De Long's party] I little thought that when I got home I should be put on the defensive for not going after them sooner."

Melville became a principal source for the theory that Nansen's achievements in the North were made possible by the *Jeannette*'s experience. When Nansen visited the United States in 1897 and spoke at a Washington reception, Melville reminded him that he had "simply finished our drift and [taken] hold where De Long let go." Melville had promised Emma De Long that he would thus address the Norwegian, assuring her that "I will see that our expedition gets full credit." He kept his word.

Strikingly built, with bald dome and white flowing mane, Melville is said to have sat for a German painter who wished to capture the spirit of American manhood on canvas. Melville himself saw to other personal imagery, paid $10,000 for a bronze statue of his likeness which he wanted prominently displayed, the single word "Melville" carved on its pedestal, as a gift for Philadelphia. (With a more informative plaque attached, it stands today in the city's naval district.) The Siberian sepulchre Melville built inspired the design of a monument to De Long in a hillside cemetery overlooking the Severn River and the Naval Academy at Annapolis. For his own final resting place he had a sarcophagus installed at Arlington National Cemetery, but when he died in 1912, two years after his second wife, Melville was buried in Philadelphia.

That original cairn tomb in Siberia is as remote and inaccessible today as when Melville had it erected. Its site is in one of the areas ruled off-limits to foreign travelers, no doubt for Soviet security reasons yet equally likely because tourist facilities in certain corners of Yakutia province are simply nonexistent. A Siberian journalist named Leonid Shinkarev who flew to the Lena delta in 1973 described the region as a superb natural laboratory and wrote of some future day when "the area now barren and uninhabited will become a bustling and highly profitable center of Arctic tourism . . . a Soviet Arctic National Park." While this still seems unlikely, modernism has made inroads. Cape Bykovskiy is the site of a major fish cannery, and what remains of Zemovialach, the scene of Melville's controversial halt, is overshadowed by the loading cranes at the port of Tiksi and the hulls of ocean-going freighters. Icebreakers plough across the Bay of Buorkhoya. At the head of the delta itself a polar station occupies the island rock Stolboi.

But Melville's cairn mausoleum has not entirely vanished. The hill on which it stands, Kuyel-Haya Cliff, is still known to local huntsmen and Soviet visitors of one kind or another as the American Mountain. Shinkarev climbed to the crest and found the upright of the cross, the names of the *Jeannette*'s dead still decipherable, the stones about the empty tomb overgrown with moss. Wrote Shinkarev: "All about, there are gun cartridges lying on the ground, and reindeer tracks; down below spreads the wide expanse of the Lena with the tundra stretching beyond it and beyond that, distant mountains on the horizon. Never before in my life had I been more acutely conscious of the boundlessness of space, of its immensity and infinity."

BY ACT OF Congress the U.S. government awarded various sums to the *Jeannette* survivors and the kin, where known, of those lost. Gold and silver medals were struck. More medals, swords, money, also supplies, were sent to Siberia, in charge of Lieutenant William Schuetze, and distributed among the interpreters, agents, exiles, *ispravniks*, and sundry Yakuts who had given aid to the men of the *Jeannette*. It was reported that at the tsar's command certain exiles might be rewarded with amnesty or reduced sentences. In due course the Navy Department, which he once bitterly protested "had cast us adrift," honored De Long in the traditional form, naming first a torpedo-boat after him, in 1900, and eighteen years later a destroyer. The first *Melville*, after the chief engineer, was a destroyer-tender that served in two world wars, and a second, launched in 1968, was a scientific research vessel chartered to the Scripps Institute of Oceanography. The honor to Melville was in recognition of his accomplishments in warship design and construction and unrelated to his service as the *Jeannette*'s engineering officer.

William Nindemann, who had gone back to the Arctic (his third such venture) as a member of the Greely relief expedition, later found employment with the Holland Submarine Boat Company and took submarines to Japan for that firm during the Russo-Japanese War. He died in 1913, reportedly of a broken heart following his son's death in an accidental drowning. Louis Noros spent the last thirty years of his life as a Fall River, Massachusetts, letter-carrier and died in 1927. Raymond Newcomb's career as an active naturalist was short-lived. Three years after his return from Siberia he no longer lectured on the *Jeannette* expedition but became clerk of the city board of health in Salem, a post he held more than twenty-five years. He died in 1918. The last survivor of the *Jeannette* was Herbert Leach, who joined De Long's widow at the 1928 dedication of a white granite statue of the commander at Woodlawn Cemetery. Leach died five years later.

In 1938, the year Emma De Long completed her memoir, *Explorer's Wife*, a biologist of the Soviet Arctic Institute sifted through the remains of a cairn on Henrietta Island and discovered the copper cylinder Melville had deposited there fifty-seven years earlier. The cylinder was intact except for the toothmarks of polar bears but water had got in, to pulp and saturate the contents, and after Russian experts in the preservation and restoration of documents had tried unsuccessfully to piece together the fragments, the relic was presented to the U.S. government.

Emma De Long died in 1940 in her ninety-first year. She had spent her last summers living alone but industriously on a New Jersey farm, and receiving visitors, with whom she was always ready to talk of the *Jeannette*, the commander, the expedition. To a journalist who called upon her she said, "I don't think my husband died in vain, do you?" She had of course long adjusted her opinion of the expedition's gains in terms of scientific knowledge. Charles Chipp's 262 notes on the aurora borealis, the discovery of three small islands, the refutation of Petermann's theories, Raymond Newcomb's three rare Ross gulls, even the probable guidance which the *Jeannette*'s helpless drift afforded Fridtjof Nansen in the *Fram*—it did not seem very much secured, considering the original goals and the ultimate cost. But she had raised the question, and answered it to her own satisfaction, even before her husband had been brought home from Siberia. "Is it said that too high a price in the lives of men was paid for this knowledge? Not by such cold calculation is human endeavor measured. Sacrifice is nobler than ease, unselfish life is consummated in lonely death, and the world is richer by the gift of suffering."

Brave words these, perhaps easily dismissed as self-delusion, false comfort, blind faith. But when we have to ask ourselves if people have died in vain, in the exploration of space as well as on polar expeditions, to rationalize in this manner may be the only sane recourse.

REFERENCES

The largest collection of primary material pertaining to the *Jeannette* expedition is in the National Archives, Washington D.C., Office of Naval Records and Library, Naval Records Collection, Record Group 45. This record group contains correspondence on the expedition's fitting out, the loss of the *Jeannette*, the search for survivors, and the return of the dead; the *Jeannette*'s logbook; Lieutenant Commander De Long's letterbooks and true copies of his private journals (the originals are in the Naval Academy Museum, Annapolis); the *Jeannette*'s medical journal; and a copy of the private diary kept by the ship's surgeon. Related letters and other memoranda, such as documents tracing the previous careers of the *Jeannette*'s officers, are also included. Unless otherwise stated, all items cited in the following sources can be found in this National Archives record group.

CHAPTER ONE   *A Curious Departure*

For descriptions of the *Jeannette* and her company upon departure from San Francisco harbor, see the *San Francisco Chronicle* and the *New York Herald*, 7–9 July 1879. High hopes for the expedition's accomplishments and the possible solution of "great problems important to humanity" were expressed in the *Watertown Times*, 7 July 1879 and reported in the *New York Herald* two days later. For details on the expedition's promoter, see Richard O'Connor, *The Scandalous Mr. Bennett* (New York: Doubleday & Co., Inc., 1962). Also see *Dictionary of American Biography* (New York: Charles Scribner's Sons, 1929), vol. 2, pp. 199–202. The manifest snub by naval vessels in San Francisco harbor is described by the snubbed commander, with reference to the Navy Department's refusal to grant ım an escort vessel, in De Long to Bennett, 17 July 1879, and De Long, *Journal*, 8 July 1879. That the Secretary of the Navy had invested the lieutenant with an admiral's authority is stated in De Long to Bennett, 20 February 1879. Artist William Bradford's description of the De Longs' parting at the Golden Gate, first published in the *Boston Herald*, is reprinted in Emma De Long, *Explorer's Wife* (New York: Dodd Meade Co., 1938), pp. 162–63. De Long's own emotional impressions are in a letter to his wife, 15 July 1879, reprinted in De Long, *Explorer's Wife*, pp. 172–73.

CHAPTER TWO *George and Emma*

For background and anecdotes on De Long's early life, see *Dictionary of American Biography*, vol. 3, pp. 227–28 and Thomas A. Delong, *The DeLongs of New York and Brooklyn* (Southport, Conn.: Sasco Publications, 1972). Orders, ship assignments, commissions, and other documentation relating to De Long's early naval career are gathered in ZB Collection, Operational Archives, Naval History Division, Washington D.C. For Emma's girlhood, De Long's courtship and love letters, the "test period" her family imposed on the pair, and their marriage at Le Havre, see De Long, *Explorer's Wife*, pp. 11–49, also De Long to Emma Wotton, 21 October 1868, 13 February, 6 April 1869, De Long Family Papers. De Long is portrayed as having virtually forced his way into the Naval Academy, "a midshipman who dispenses with red tape," in *The Voyage of the Jeannette, Ship and Ice Journals of Lieutenant Commander De Long*, ed. by Emma De Long (Boston: Houghton, Mifflin and Co., 1883), pp. 6–9. The impression of De Long as having developed a penchant for ruffling the feathers of his superiors is further conveyed by correspondence in the ZB Collection, especially Lieutenant Daniel L. Braine to De Long, 18 October 1872, and De Long, *Explorer's Wife*, pp. 4–10. Also see De Long to Commodore Daniel Ammen, 3 January 1874. For De Long's return from South American waters in charge of a prisoner, see Rear Admiral Joseph Lanham to De Long, 20 November 1870, and De Long to Secretary Robeson, 15 January 1871. De Long's dissatisfaction with service life in the West Indies colors his letters to Emma, in De Long, *Explorer's Wife*, pp. 61–66, and in 2, 3 June 1872, De Long Family Papers. For the controversy over his status on the *Juniata*, see De Long to Offley, Navy Department, 5 June, W. P. Moran, Navy Department to De Long, 6 June 1873 (which also contains the reference to the Navy Department's treatment of the *Polaris* expedition as "a mum affair"), De Long to Rear Admiral Daniel Ammen, 3 January, Ammen to De Long, 2, 7 January, Moran to De Long, 11 January 1874, ZB Collection. The cruise of the *Juniata* and voyage of the *Little Juniata* are described in the *New York Herald*, 11, 12 September 1873, De Long, *Explorer's Wife*, pp. 70–83, and *Annual Report of the Secretary of the Navy*, 1873, pp. 200, 223–31. De Long's wish to be "where the Navy Department would not bother me" is in De Long, *Explorer's Wife*, pp. 85. The *New York Times*, 12 September 1873, published August Petermann's letter to Robeson, with further comment from the sage of Gotha in the next day's issue. The request for Arctic command is De Long to Robeson, 12 October 1873 and the Bureau of Navigation's response Ammen to De Long, 3 November 1873.

CHAPTER THREE   *The Petermann Factor*

For De Long's letters to Emma during the first weeks outward bound see De Long, *Explorer's Wife*, pp. 173, 177. Reproaching the publisher for his failure to attend the departure is in De Long to Bennett, 17 July 1879. The pivotal meeting at Grinnell's home is discussed in De Long (ed.), *Voyage*, vol. 1, pp. 42–43, and in J. E. Nourse, *American Explorations in the Ice Zones* (Boston: D. Lothrop & Co., 1884), pp. 364–65, and De Long's invitation to it, Robert Grinnell to De Long, 31 October 1873, is in ZB Collection. For the grounding of the *Brooklyn*, see Court Martial Proceedings, the *Brooklyn*, 3 November 1874, Records of the Judge Advocate General (Navy), Record Group 125, National Archives; also Secretary Robeson to De Long, 12 November 1874, and Captain William T. Truxtun to De Long, 20 January 1875, ZB Collection. Allen Young, *Two Voyages of the Pandora* (London: E. Stanford, 1879), recounts the *Jeannette*'s first Arctic experience. Information on De Long's search for a ship is in De Long, *Explorer's Wife*, pp. 108–116 and letters or telegrams, J. G. Stephens to De Long, 8, 10, 12, 13, 24 January 1877; also Bennett (New York) to De Long (London), 12, 14 January 1877, and Young to Stephens, 16 January 1877. For Bennett's duel, see *New York Times*, 4–24 January 1877. Nordenskjöld's rejection of the *Pandora* is in George Kish, *Northeast Passage: Adolf Erik Nordenskjöld and His Times* (Amsterdam, Holland: Nico Israel, 1973), p. 146. For the purchase of the *Pandora*, see Bennett to De Long, 13 January 1878 and Thos. L. Connery to De Long, 17, 18 January 1878, which also reflect Bennett's interest in De Long's choice of the Pacific route to the Pole as outlined in De Long to Bennett, 25 January 1878, reprinted in Nourse, *American Explorations*, p. 365. Howgate's project is discussed in the *New York Times*, 11 July 1877; also American Geographical Society, *Journal*, vol. 10, 1878, pp. 276–98. Bennett's meeting with Professor Petermann is in Bennett to De Long, March 1877, reprinted in De Long, *Explorer's Wife*, p. 116. Trouble on the *St. Marys* involving De Long is the subject of Simeon Brownell to De Long, 7 September 1877, M.D. Hubbard to De Long, 31 December 1877, and De Long to Hubbard, 6 January 1878. For Chipp's keenness to join the expedition see Chipp to De Long, 9 January, 21 June 1877, and for Master Danenhower's involvement, with Bennett's intervention and Ulysses S. Grant's recommendation, see Grant to Bennett, 20 April 1878 and Danenhower to Young, John Russell Young MSS, Library of Congress; also Danenhower to De Long, 23 May, 13 June 1878, and De Long to Danenhower, 2 June 1878, reprinted in *Proceedings of a Court of Inquiry into the Loss of the Exploring Steamer Jeannette in Arctic Seas*, House Exec. Doc. 108, 47th Cong., 2d Sess., Ser. 2113, hereinafter cited *Naval Inquiry*. For early inklings of Danenhower's mental trouble see De Long, *Explorer's Wife*, p. 150 and De Long to Bennett, 15 May 1878.

The launch of the *Jeannette* is described in De Long, *Explorer's Wife*, pp. 123–25, and the *New York Herald*, 5 July 1878. That Bennett considered premature landfall on a maiden voyage "a bad omen" is in Bennett to De Long, 28 May 1878. For Silas Bent's theories on thermometric gateways, see "The Eastern Portal to the Pole," *Putnam's Magazine*, April 1870, pp. 437–45. Clements R. Markham's attacks on Petermann are in *Nature*, 30 November 1871, 12, 22 November 1874; also see Markham's unpublished memoir, pp. 375–77, Royal Geographical Society, London, and the Society's *Proceedings*, vol. 21, 1876–77, pp. 536–55. That De Long thought whaling skippers favored the Pacific route is in De Long, *Explorer's Wife*, pp. 114–15. Petermann's last interview is in the *New York Herald*, 15 July 1878 and his death reported in the *Times*, London, and the *New York Herald*, 28 September 1878.

CHAPTER FOUR *Fitting Out*

The arrangements to launch a private enterprise under naval colors are detailed in Thos. Connery to Secretary Thompson, 28 December 1878, and on the same subject see Thompson to W. C. Whithhorne, House Naval Affairs (undated), Thompson MSS, Lilly Library, University of Indiana. For De Long's opening barrage upon the naval bureaucracy see De Long to Bennett, 24 January 1879, De Long to Bennett, 12, 25 March, 14 April 1879, and De Long, *Explorer's Wife*, pp. 144–45. Bennett viewed the naval board's estimates as "preposterous" in Bennett to De Long, 4 February 1879, the Secretary promptly approved De Long's figures in Thompson to Bennett, 21 February 1879, and Bennett to De Long, 24 March 1879, conveyed the publisher's congratulations on "getting everything your own way in Washington." De Long to Bennett, 20 February 1879 touched on the possibility of taking balloons, De Long to Bennett, 4 April discussed pemmican, 7 April "prodding" the bureaucrats and 10, 15 May 1879 pressuring the Secretary. Danenhower to De Long, 2, 3, 4 April 1879 discussed ship's boilers and other technical matters; also see W. H. Shock to Edmund Colhoun, 9 April, De Long to Danenhower, 11, 20 April, Danenhower to De Long, 23 April and De Long to Chipp, 9 May 1879. Additional information on the *Jeannette*'s overhaul and fitting out is in the *San Francisco Examiner*, 9 July 1879 and Nourse, *American Explorations*, pp. 369–72. The Secretary's less than outright promise to provide an escort ship is in Thompson to Bennett, 21 February 1879, with Chamberlain to De Long, 10 March and De Long to Chipp, 2 May 1879, reflecting an assumption of an unconditional pledge to do so. Biographical material on Surgeon Ambler is in *Dictionary of American Biography*, vol. 1, pp. 240–41. For Bennett's plan to have the *Jeannette* search for the *Vega*, see Bennett to Thompson, 4 February, Thompson to Bennett, 21 February 1879, the *New York Herald*, 6 February 1879, and *Proceedings*, Royal Geographical Society, March 1879, p. 208. Also see A. E. Nordenskjöld, *Voyage of the Vega Around Asia and Europe* (New York: Macmillan and Co., 1881). For De Long's initial dismay on hearing that Bennett could not attend the departure, see De Long to Bennett, 15 May 1879, which also attests to his bitter reaction to word from the Navy Department that no escort vessel could be provided. The Danenhower crisis is thoroughly documented in De Long to Whiting, 18 May 1879, Medical Journal of USS *Portsmouth*, 1873–75 (entries 11, 26 August, 9, 11 September 1874) and Medical Journals of Shore Stations, Mare Island Navy Yard, both series in Records of the Bureau of Medicine and Surgery, RG 52, National Archives. Also see De Long to Doctor E. Bates, 11, 18 May, Bates to De Long, 20 May, W. Danenhower to De Long, 12, 16 May, De Long to W. Danenhower, 18 May, De Long to Bennett, 8, 15 May, Whiting to De Long, 23 May, and, Bennett to De Long, 5 June 1879.

CHAPTER FIVE   *"Everything but Skates"*

Raymond Newcomb's enlistment and projected role in the expedition are described in Spencer Baird to De Long, 10 May, Baird to Newcomb, 10 May, and Baird to De Long, 29 May 1879, Baird MSS, Smithsonian Archives, Washington D.C. Also see Baird to De Long, 17, 29 May 1879. For the plan for "lighting the North Pole" see Collins to Edison, 2, 7, 9 May, De Long to Edison, 21 April, Thos. A. Edison Library, Edison National Historical Site, West Orange, N.J., and Francis R. Upton to his father, 24

May 1879, American Historical Museum Library, National Museum of History, Smithsonian Institution. Also see Collins to De Long, 5, 14 May, and De Long to Bennett, 15 May 1879. Irritation with the press is registered in De Long to Connery, 26 July 1879. The *Vallejo Chronicle*, 27 June 1879, attacked the expedition. For the refusal to assign De Long an escort ship see Secretary Thompson to De Long, 27 June, De Long to Connery, 30 June, Nordhoff to Thompson, 28 June 1879; also Thompson to President Hayes, 29 June 1879, Rutherford B. Hayes Library, Fremont, Ohio. The Secretary's sailing orders to De Long, including instructions to seek Nordenskjöld, are Thompson to De Long, 18 June 1879, in Richard Thompson MSS, Lilly Library, University of Indiana, Bloomington. For De Long's last-minute efforts to have Bennett on hand for the send-off and his final stunning defeat, see telegrams Bennett to De Long, 5, 6 June, De Long to Bennett, 5 June, Connery to De Long, 27 May, 9 June, and Whiting to De Long, 19 June 1879. Also see De Long to Bennett, 17 July 1879, which contains De Long's vow to "keep at it as long as the *Jeannette* floats." The Mare Island board of inspection's report on the *Jeannette*'s condition is in *Naval Inquiry*, p. 290.

CHAPTER SIX *Through Bering Strait*

Unless otherwise stated, the quotations in this and subsequent chapters are from De Long's private journals, originals in the Naval Academy Museum, Annapolis. They include significant passages omitted from the published *Voyage*, the journals as edited by his wife. For the ship's reinforcement against ice, see board of inspection report and Engineer Much deposition, *Naval Inquiry*, pp. 290, 310–13; also see *Dictionary of American Fighting Ships*, Navy Dept., 1870, pp. 509–10. For De Long's search for Nordenskjöld, immediate and long-range plans, and the sense of a golden opportunity unhappily lost, see his reports to the Secretary of the Navy from Unalaska and St. Lawrence Bay, 4, 26 August 1879, reprinted in *Naval Inquiry*, pp. 297–98. Also see De Long to Bennett, 26 August 1879 and De Long, *Journal*, July–August, 1879. De Long's thumbnail sketches of his officers and others, including the maladroit Ah Sing and the painfully punning Collins, also personal observations on problems of command, are in his farewell letters to Emma, reprinted in De Long, *Explorer's Wife*, pp. 174–77, 181–83. That De Long was at first "very much pleased" with Collins is in De Long to Bennett, 25 March 1879. For biographical data on Collins, see the *New York Herald*, 9 July 1879, and *Journal of the Cork Historical and Archeological Society*, vol. 24, no. 119, pp. 133–45. His tortured letter about feeling "trapped" on the eve of sailing is in *Proceedings of an Inves-*

tigation into the Jeannette by the Naval Affairs Subcommittee, 48th Cong., 1st Sess., House Misc. Doc. 66, pp. 14–15, 153–54, hereinafter cited *Congressional Investigation*. De Long's interview which so incensed the meteorologist is in the *Washington Post*, 28 February 1879. The commander's doubts about Danenhower are in De Long to Emma De Long, 13 July, 9 August 1879, De Long Family Papers.

CHAPTER SEVEN *Cul-de-sac*

For the whaling captain's last glimpse of the *Jeannette*, see Charles W. Brook's address "The *Jeannette* Arctic Expedition and the Missing Whalers," in California Academy of Sciences, *Proceedings*, 6 December 1880. The Kuro Siwo study was headed by Professor William H. Dall and is discussed in *Annual Report of the Superintendant of the United States Coast and Geodetic Survey*, vol. 15, 1883, pp. 101–32. Also see Nourse, *American Explorations*, pp. 367–69. For Nindemann on De Long's determination to reach Wrangel Land, see his testimony, *Congressional Investigation*, pp. 106–8. De Long's detailed review upon which, with his journal, my narrative of the *Jeannette*'s voyage and entrapment is substantially based, is *Rough Draft of Lieutenant Commander George W. De Long's Report to the Hon. Secretary of the Navy, August 26, 1879–December 31, 1880*, published as an appendix to *Naval Inquiry*, pp. 325–60.

CHAPTER EIGHT *No Place for a Ship*

For Collins's alleged incompetence in the photography department, see Danenhower's and Melville's testimonies, *Congressional Investigation* pp. 412–415, 446–51, 514–52, 590–96. Collins's humiliating inference from the "withdrawal of instruments" is in his letter to De Long, *Congressional Investigation*, pp. 1004–5. For the first ice onslaughts, see *Rough Draft*, in addition to De Long, *Journal*, entries 6–24 November 1879.

CHAPTER NINE *Danenhower's Secret*

For the clash with Collins, see De Long's official reports 2, 4 December 1880 and 20 March 1881, printed in *Naval Inquiry*, pp. 322–23. Surgeon Ambler's first reference to Danenhower's eye trouble is 23 December 1879, with "a history of his case" noted 31

December 1879, in *Medical Journal of the Jeannette*. Ambler's method of treatment and the course of the patient's condition are recorded thereafter almost daily. The medical journal is among Records of the Bureau of Medicine and Surgery, RG 52 National Archives, as is a copy of the notebook diary Ambler kept after the *Jeannette* sank. The original is at the Virginia Historical Society, Richmond, and for an edited version, see *U.S. Naval Medical Bulletin*, vol. XI, no. 2, April 1917, with its accompanying observation from J. D. Gatewood, Medical Director, U.S. Navy, that "the nature of Danenhower's case will be apparent to any medical man."

CHAPTER TEN   *Against the Sea*

For the fight to save the ship, see De Long, *Rough Draft*, pp. 338–46, De Long, *Journal*, entries January–February 1880, and ship's medical journal for the progress of Danenhower's affliction. Also see Melville's testimony, *Naval Inquiry*, pp. 75–165, and George W. Melville, *In The Lena Delta* (Boston: Houghton Mifflin Co., 1892), pp. 12–15.

CHAPTER ELEVEN   *Another Long Night*

For the rumored mutiny, see De Long, *Journal*, 4 June 1880. The commander's despair is particularly evident in entries 14, 16, 20 June, 1, 7, 18, 19, 26 July, 17, 31 August, 6 October 1880. The second Collins incident, including his suspension from duty, is related in De Long's memorandum and report, 20 March 1881, *Naval Inquiry*, pp. 320–27; also see *Congressional Investigation*, pp. 152–54 and 382–88 for Danenhower's account of it. Collins's letter appears in *Naval Inquiry*, pp. 318–19, and *Congressional Investigation*, pp. 1004–5.

CHAPTER TWELVE   *Relief Plans*

For comments on the *Jeannette*'s whereabouts or possible fate, see the *New York Herald*, 24 October, 7–9 November 1880, 27–30 January, 21–23 March 1881. Also see Charles Wolcott Brooks, Paper read before California Academy of Sciences, San Francisco, 6 December 1880. For proceedings and recommendations of the *Jeannette* Relief Board, see *Annual Report of the Secretary of the Navy*, 1880, pp. 29–30 and 1881, pp. 6–10, 755–

817, and the *New York Herald*, 21, 29 March 1881. Judge Charles P. Daly's letter to President Hayes calling for a relief expedition is in the *New York Herald*, 26 January 1881. Henrietta Melville's letters to Emma De Long, 9, 24 August 1880, 26, 29 January 1881, are in the De Long papers, Polar Gift Collection, RG 40, National Archives.

CHAPTER THIRTEEN *The Last of the* Jeannette

For Melville's trip to Henrietta Island, see his report, *Naval Inquiry*, pp. 360–63. The attack of food poisoning is detailed in ship's medical journal, 1–10 June 1881. Danen-hower almost seeing the island "through the ship's side" is in John Wilson Danenhower, *Lieutenant Danenhower's Narrative of the Jeannette* (Boston: J. R. Osgood & Co., 1882), p. 33. De Long, *Journal*, 9–11 June, ship's medical journal, 11 June 1881, and Danen-hower, *Narrative*, pp. 40–42, describe the icepack's coup de grace.

CHAPTER FOURTEEN *Retreat*

Danenhower's testimony, *Naval Inquiry*, pp. 31–41, excerpts from Collins's private diary, *Congressional Investigation*, pp. 178–82, and Melville, *Lena Delta*, pp. 40–62 augment De Long, *Journal* entries 11–30 June 1881, in portraying the first days on the ice. Also see the private journal of James Markham Ambler, M.D., Virginia Historical Society, Rich-mond, copy in Records of the Bureau of Medicine and Surgery, RG 52, National Ar-chives. For De Long ordering Danenhower off the work force, see De Long, *Journal*, 23 June 1881, and Danenhower interview in *New York Herald*, 5 May 1882. For similar action against Collins, see De Long, *Journal* and Collins's diary, 5 July 1881.

CHAPTER FIFTEEN *Bennett Island*

For the Seaman Starr incident, see De Long, *Journal* and Ambler, *Diary*, 13 July 1881, and Newcomb's "arrest" in De Long, *Journal*, 21 July 1881, also *Congressional Investi-gation*, p. 857. Danenhower blamed De Long for slowing the party in *New York Herald*, 5 May 1882, with the commander's case forcefully stated in De Long, *Journal*, 8, 21 August and Ambler, *Diary*, 14, 21 August 1881. For the landing on Bennett Island, see Ambler, *Diary*, 25–31 July 1881, and Raymond L. Newcomb, *Our Lost Explorers*

(Hartford, Conn.: American Publishing Co., 1882); also *Congressional Investigation*, p. 205. De Long's 5 August 1881 letter giving Melville command of the whaleboat is in *Naval Inquiry*, p. 295, with Danenhower's assertion that this was "unlawful" in Danenhower, *Narrative*, p. 93.

CHAPTER SIXTEEN   *The Boat Dash*

For the storm and separation in the Laptev Sea, and loss of the second cutter, see De Long, *Journal*, as 12–18 September 1881, Ambler, *Diary*, 18 September 1881, and Melville, *Lena Delta*, pp. 62–76. Danenhower's account is in Danenhower, *Narrative*, pp. 64–73. Also see Newcomb, *Our Lost Explorers*, pp. 207–44, and survivors' testimonies in *Naval Inquiry*, pp. 75–165, 225–56. See *Congressional Investigation*, p. 430, for Danenhower's threat to kill Newcomb. De Long's chart was copied from a map which appeared in *Geographische Mitteilungen*, 1878.

CHAPTER SEVENTEEN   *A Fatal Delay*

For a probably reliable estimate of mileage distances and climatic conditions in the Lena delta, see *Lieutenant Giles Harber's Report on the Search for the Missing Persons of the Jeannette Expedition*, 48th Congress, 1st Session, House Exec. Doc. 163, pp. 58–65. Melville slights Danenhower's abortive search and explains the delay at Zemiovalach in Melville, *Lena Delta*, pp. 110–41, *Naval Inquiry*, pp. 125–30, and *Congressional Investigation*, pp. 460–67.

CHAPTER EIGHTEEN   *Death in the Delta*

For the final days of De Long's party, see his and Surgeon Ambler's journals, September–October 1881, and Nindemann's testimony, *Naval Inquiry*, pp. 176–211. Ambler's last letter was reprinted in *U.S. Naval Medical Bulletin*, vol. XI, no. 2, April 1917. Also see "Tragedy at Lena Delta," *U.S. Navy Medicine*, March–April 1984, pp. 16–24. Articles found with the dead, and other relics including the blue silk pennant, Erikson's bible, weapons and instruments and Newcomb's Ross gulls, may be seen at the Naval Academy Museum, Annapolis, the Smithsonian Institution History Department, Naval Section,

Washington D.C., and the U.S. Navy Memorial Museum, Navy Yard, Washington D.C. Also see Smithsonian Institution, *Annual Report*, 1882, p. 14.

CHAPTER NINETEEN   *Melville's Search*

For the search expeditions, discovery of the dead, and construction of the hilltop tomb, see Melville, *Lena Delta*, pp. 328–45, and his official report, 17 October 1882, in *Secretary of the Navy's Annual Report*, 1882, vol. 1, pp. 57–73; also Gilder's dispatch and interview with Melville, *New York Herald*, 12 April, 20 June 1882. Melville's first messages reporting the *Jeannette*'s loss were published in the *New York Herald*, 21–23 December 1882 as was Secretary Hunt's telegraphed order to the surviving officers to "omit no effort." The *New York Times*, 25 March 1882, published Melville's directives to the Bulun and Verkhoyansk *ispravniks*, copies furnished by the Navy Department, and for the glimpse of Henrietta Melville see the *Philadelphia Times*, 26 December 1881. For George Kennan's criticism, see the *New York Herald*, 18 January 1882. Secretary Hunt's retraction of his search order to Danenhower and the latter's written outburst—"I begged to go in harness"—9 February 1882, are in National Archives RG 45 collection as are Bennett to Emma De Long, 20 December 1881, 19, 20 January 1882, and Emma De Long to Bennett, 29 December 1881, reflecting the news of De Long as Bennett received it and Emma's reactions. Emma's last, unreceived, letters to her husband are quoted in De Long, *Explorer's Wife*, p. 208, full copies in De Long Family Papers. Some letters that reached the Far North were recovered years later by Peary and returned to her. For press correspondent Jackson in Siberia, see his testimony, *Congressional Investigation*, pp. 770–76, and *Illustrated London News*, 13 May, 7 October 1882.

CHAPTER TWENTY   *The Survivors Come Home*

For Henrietta Melville's disclosures to the press, see the *New York Times* 15 March, the *Philadelphia Times*, 16 March, the *Brooklyn Eagle*, 10 April 1882, and Emma De Long to Bennett, 15 March 1882. Melville's harsh reaction upon learning what his wife had done is in Melville (St. Petersburg) to Emma De Long, 24 August 1882, in De Long Papers, Polar Gift Collection, RG 401, National Archives. Accompanying the headlined news that De Long was found dead, the *New York Herald*, 6 May 1882, ran the texts of the five records he had left on the retreat. George Kennan's characterizing of De Long as a victim of inimical fates is in the *Chicago Tribune*, same date. Danenhower's home-coming was reported in the *New York Herald*, 29, 30 September, Melville's in the *New York Times*, 14 September, the *Philadelphia Press*, 14, 16 September 1882. For Danen-hower and Doctor Collins at the Fifth Avenue Hotel and the physician's subsequent efforts to secure an inquiry, see Judge Advocate Lemly's and Collins's testimonies, *Congressional Investigation*, pp. 551–65. For Gilder in Siberia, see William Gilder, *Ice Pack and Tundra* (New York: Charles Scribner's Sons, 1883) and Gilder to Chandler, 3 March 1883. Leeon's "Americans again!" is in S. Leeon to Melville, 25 March 1882, George Melville Papers, Franklin D. Roosevelt Memorial Library, Hyde Park, N.Y. Jackson's reasons for breaking open the tomb are in Jackson to Bennett, 5 January 1883; also see Jackson to Chandler, 27 January 1883, Chandler, MSS, Library of Congress, Chandler to Bennett, 8 January 1883, and Noros testimony, *Naval Inquiry*, pp. 230–32. "Something hidden" is in the *New York Commercial Advertiser*, 28 July 1882. Chandler doubted the feasibility of bringing home the bodies in Chandler to Emma De Long, 26 June 1882. For Emma's insistence that the attempt be made, see Emma De Long to Chandler, 20 June, 11, 27, 31 December 1882, 7, 15 February 1883, Chandler MSS, Library of Congress. For the occurrence at Sharon Hill, see Melville to Chandler, 17 September 1882, the *Philadelphia Ledger*, 18, 19 September, the *Philadelphia Press*, 19 November 1882, and the *Philadelphia Inquirer*, 9–12, 18 January 1883.

CHAPTER TWENTY-ONE   *The Naval Inquiry*

For the Lemly-Collins exchanges and other matters bearing on the court of inquiry, see *Congressional Investigation*, pp. 551–60. Emma's request to the *Jeannette*'s original owner for a testimonial to the ship's fitness is Emma De Long to Allen Young (London), 14 October 1882. Also see Emma De Long to Chandler, same date. For Melville's private thoughts on Danenhower and indications of a "compact," see Melville to Emma De Long, 18 October, 10, 13, 20 November 1882, Polar Gift Collection, RG 401, National Archives. Assurance that De Long's memory is "in no danger" is in William G. Temple to Emma De Long, 10 November 1882. The naturalist registers modesty in Newcomb to Baird, 8 January 1883, Smithsonian Institution Archives. For Emma's distress over the "desecrations" at the hilltop tomb, see Emma De Long to Bennett (undated, prob. December 1882), Chandler to Emma De Long, 6 January and Emma De Long to Bennett, 7 February 1883. Emma warns of "unpleasant matters opened up" should Danenhower go too far in Emma De Long to Chandler, 30 March 1883, Chandler MSS, Library of Congress, and Danenhower is deemed "a dangerous witness" in Lemly to Emma De Long, 4 January 1883. Also see Thomas L. Connery to Emma De Long, 10 October 1882, De Long Family Papers. For Lieutenant Harber in Siberia, Aniguin's death, and the prolonged and difficult attempt to return the bodies, see Harber (Irkutsk) to Chandler, 23 June 1883, reprinted in Nourse, *American Explorations*, pp. 419–23; also Hunt to Chandler, 18, 26 January, 3, 15, 17 February 1883, Chandler to Hunt, 15 January, 2, 12 February 1883, and *Annual Report of the Secretary of the Navy*, 1883, p. 22 and 1884, p. 21. For the long journey home and ceremonial funeral, see the *New York Herald*, 7, 23, 24 February 1884. Collins's petition to Congress is in *Congressional Investigation*, pp. 808–10, Bartlett's prompting in Bartlett to Collins, 14 February 1884, ibid. p. 19, and Chandler's charge of a "second pitiless sacrilege," Chandler to S. S. Cox, 11 March 1884, ibid. p. 9. Chandler solicits Bennett's support for his naval program in Chandler to Bennett, 26, 27 March 1884, Chandler MSS, Library of Congress, and Bennett editorially obliges in the *New York Herald*, 2 April 1884.

CHAPTER TWENTY-TWO   *Safety Valves of Scandal*

Biographic information on George Curtis comes from *Bench and Bar of New York*, ed. by David McAdam et al. (New York: New York Historical Company, 1897) vol. 2, and Henry I. Hazelton, *The Boroughs of Brooklyn and Queens, Counties of Nassau and Suffolk* (New York: Lewis Historical Publishing Company, 1925), vol. 6, pp. 133–34. Subcommittee members Boutelle and McAdoo are cited in *Dictionary of American Biography*, vols. I & IV, and Buchanan in *Biographical Directory of the American Congress* (Washington: Government Printing Office, 1971), p. 659. On the question of employing counsel to counter the other side's action, see Remey to Emma De Long, 28 March, and Boutelle to Chandler, 31 March 1884, and for Emma De Long's preliminary consultation with the subcommittee, see Remey to Emma De Long, 19 March and McAdoo to Emma De Long, 31 March 1884. William Arnoux's obituary, *Martha's Vineyard Herald*, 25 April 1907, says he was "retained by the Navy Department to protect the name and fame of De Long against attacks." Information on House of Representatives Room 323, nowadays used for storage, is drawn from personal inspection, and documentation in the Office of Architect, U.S. Capitol. For Curtis's reading of Ambler's diary, with significant omission, see *Congressional Investigation*, pp. 671–90.

REFERENCES

CHAPTER TWENTY-THREE *Sacrifice Nobler than Ease*

The Melville–Danenhower confrontation at the polar symposium is fully reported in *The Proceedings of the United States Naval Institute*, vol. XI, no. 4, 1885, pp. 633–99. See the *Washington Evening Star* and the *New York Herald*, 21 April 1887, for Danenhower's suicide. Melville's advice to Peary is in Melville to Peary, 29 April 1891, Peary Collection, RG 401, National Archives. For Melville's later years, see "George Wallace Melville" by William L. Cathcart, *Cassier's Magazine*, vol. 24, no. 2, May 1912, and George W. Melville MSS, Library of Congress. For the Lena delta, see Leonid Shinkarev, *The Land Beyond the Mountains: Siberia and its People Today* (New York: Macmillan and Co., 1973). Nourse, *American Explorations*, p. 427, tells of Russian helpers rewarded monetarily or with promised release from exile. A detailed account of the distribution of rewards is in William Henry Schuetze, *Memoir and Letters*, privately printed, 1903, copy in Rare Books Division, Library of Congress. For ships named after De Long and Melville, see *Dictionary of American Naval Fighting Ships*, vol. II, pp. 257–58 and vol. IV, p. 314 (Navy Department, 1969). The story of the cylinder from Henrietta Island is in Academy of Sciences, USSR Laboratory for the Preservation and Restoration of Documents, *LKRD Bulletin* No. 41, and *New York Times*, 11 June 1938. The *New Brunswick Sunday Times*, New Jersey, 1 Dec. 1940, published "Memories of Mrs. De Long."